RELIGION
and the
PRESIDENCY

THE MACMILLAN COMPANY
NEW YORK · CHICAGO
DALLAS · ATLANTA · SAN FRANCISCO
LONDON · MANILA

IN CANADA
BRETT-MACMILLAN LTD.
GALT, ONTARIO

RELIGION

and the

PRESIDENCY

A Recurring American Problem

by BERTON DULCE
and EDWARD J. RICHTER

NEW YORK

THE MACMILLAN COMPANY

A Division of the Crowell-Collier Publishing Company

1962

F O R   O U R

GRANDCHILDREN

The Macmillan Company, New York
Brett-Macmillan Ltd., Galt, Ontario

Printed in the United States of America

Library of Congress catalog card number: 62-11354

INTRODUCTION

American presidential politics have always reflected changes in the nation's social identity. American society encompasses several of the world's major faiths within a common culture. It was perhaps inevitable that religious and political controversy should have become entangled almost from the beginning.

At first the religious issue was rooted in the antagonisms and conflicts of the Old World in which church was identified closely with government. Gradually the issue became stated in terms of the New World's society and principles. Once that occurred, the struggle toward resolution of the issue began in earnest. Ever since Thomas Jefferson had to endure charges of atheism, the religious issue has been prominent in approximately one of every three campaigns for the Presidency.

We have tried to capture the excitement as well as the meaning of those campaigns. Throughout the changing circumstances and guises in which the religious issue has manifested itself, Catholics, Protestants, and Jews all remained party to a larger consideration: the persistent reaffirmation of a nation's heritage in the face of continued assaults.

The uniqueness of America as the first great modern nation not ruled by an alliance of political and religious authority is rarely contemplated.

In preceding centuries, religious zeal coupled with political power had contributed heavily to the most catastrophic of Europe's misfortunes. America, in its political birth, carried religious principles into practice with vigor and decisiveness of unprecedented scope. But in the open society that characterized the new nation, religious differences took on new modes of expression and accommodation.

v

The break with the past was not immediate nor was it total. The relation between politics and religion did not disappear when presidents began to succeed kings as heads of state. Government and church, law and religion have their common origin in man's convictions regarding himself, his fellow men, and the fate of both.

In the end, a society emerged in America that sought to preserve the most treasured elements of the religious spirit while guarding itself against the worst. Religion continues to serve as an important determinant of who shall govern. It does so in the sense of being a factor in the process by which individuals are conveyed to positions of leadership within a political party. It does so in the selection of candidates on the basis of their appeal to proportions of the electorate. Studies of voting behavior in recent years have isolated religion as a major indicator in enabling observers to anticipate personal voting decisions.

In leadership too there continues to be a common chord in religious and political contexts. The boundary between the religious and the secular often becomes fuzzy indeed. When we cast our vote for a man, we are expressing or reaffirming a faith in that man. He holds out the promise of something. He is the bearer of a faith. In our vote we affirm our beliefs. The doctrine is delivered in the person. Individuals are the currency in which that doctrine is distributed. The modern president and the ancient king who sat by divine right have in common the execution of a duty, of a mission, of a purpose. There emerges a force of personality on the grand scale, something that cloaks and endows and elevates the common humanity of the man.

It is with the religious issue as a social phenomenon that we are primarily concerned. It would be a mistake for anyone to regard this book as having a sectarian viewpoint. Where religious doctrine admittedly served as the basis for political arguments, we did attempt to evaluate the political implications. We did not seek to evaluate the doctrinal bases.

As the nation's largest religious minority, Roman Catholics have historically borne the brunt of negative feeling. Thus the history of the religious issue is reviewed primarily in terms of anti-Catholicism. In the process we have sought always to present the issue in terms of its broader implications for the nation.

There are many forces at work in every presidential campaign, despite the penchant for pointing to only one or two or three major issues as having determined the outcome. The religious issue cannot be viewed solely or even primarily as a controversy over doctrine. It has never failed to reveal direct relations to other issues in a campaign—whether they be states' rights, the rights of the workingman, or internationalism. For this reason we have tried to present the conditions of the time and of the years between campaigns in some detail.

In this book, matters are dealt with which many people would prefer to forget. We have not courted controversy; neither have we shunned it. Bigotry is prominent in our story. Yet we have labeled none as bigots, and dispatched them. We have sought in every case to look behind the label at the substance of the viewpoint. We were concerned not only with how these viewpoints were received but also with why they provoked the responses they did. To do so, we felt, was much the cleaner method of keeping basic issues in perspective.

The authors have been aided in their task by many kind and perceptive persons. In our research on the 1960 campaign, valuable insights were provided by Judith Friedberg of the Citizens for Kennedy and Johnson organization and Bruce L. Felknor of the Fair Campaign Practices Committee. We are grateful to Mortimer Kass of the Anti-Defamation League of B'nai B'rith for access to materials on contemporary anti-Catholicism. For other materials and insights we are indebted to James P. Quindlen, M.D., and the Reverend William H. Mooney, and to Elizabeth Norris of the National Conference of Christians and Jews.

We especially wish to thank the staffs of the New York Public Library, particularly its American History Division; Free Library of Philadelphia and its Frankford branch; Princeton Theological Seminary Library; and St. Joseph's College Library.

CONTENTS

x   *Contents*

CHAPTER ONE

The Founding Fathers

"No religious test shall ever be required"

JUST OVER ONE HUNDRED YEARS AGO IN AMERICA, SEVEN GOV-
ernors, eight senators, and one hundred and four representatives
held office chiefly as the result of campaigns stressing anti-
Catholic sentiments.[1] Today an American of that faith occupies
the White House, entrusted with the leadership of the nation.

Founded on religious principles of freedom, this country
needed one hundred and eighty-four years, four months, and
four days to elect a "minority President." The currents at work
in 1960 bore with them the strength of distant falls rather than
sudden, fickle turmoil. The 1960 election was in a sense a reaffirmation of opportunity and an expression of the American
strength rather than a final victory. The differences that have
accompanied and generated progress are still active.

From America's earliest days Catholics as a religious minority
were involved in vigorous and persistent tests of the new society's
principles. America represented an unmatched diversity of creeds.
The struggle of Catholics to secure a place in the new land was
not a unique one. Yet gradually they came to represent the
country's largest religious minority.

The people of America, in their treatment of the religious
issue involving Catholicism, have at several stages in their history
provided a barometer of the nation's social maturity and progress.
Nowhere has this been more sharply evident than in political
campaigns. It has emerged most sharply of all in campaigns for
the Presidency. The story of what happened is the story of a

1

nation growing up. It is more than the saga of one religious group. It is the saga of the first of the modern emergent nations, and the ways in which it dealt, sometimes courageously, sometimes brutally, sometimes wisely, sometimes foolishly, with a problem that had strained and ruined nations before it since the beginning of modern nation-states themselves.

The "Catholic issue" cannot be viewed distinctly as a history of doctrine. Religious passions run deep. The issue is a history of people, singly and in groups, who have abused or given meaning to their principles. It has remained, too, at least in part, a conflict of believers versus nonbelievers.

In the early American Colonies it was the religious believer, rather than the irreligious, who was on the march. The strains of union and tension between church and state found their way into the early settlements, where the rights of the individual were carried into early civil laws, tied always to the ultimate authority of God.

As a new world was slowly taking shape on the other side of the Atlantic, a Great Rebellion had swept England in the sixteenth and seventeenth centuries, and established religious pluralism. Calvinists and Puritans alike claimed it was a nation's duty *under God* to resist a sovereign's limiting of individual liberties. Through it all, reason and the civil power stood always under the authority of God, His church, and the religious spirit.[2]

Earlier, even before the Reformation, in the tradition of a church that sought to ease the hardships of servitude among its children, while maintaining a reign over them through those who ruled, Roman Catholicism had added a new principle to the doctrine of the "divine right of Kings": *vox populi, vox Dei* (the voice of God through the voice of the people). A ruler derived his power from the Deity, but it was voiced through the will of the people; the interests of the king were declared subordinate to those of his subjects. Tyrannized or oppressed peoples were thus empowered not only to withhold obedience but also to depose the king by revolution.[3]

The colonies, then, in their coming drive for freedom, could point to varying upheavals as precedents, all tinged with spiritual ingredients. Although four of the colonies were settled primarily for religious freedom, nine others had "established" churches that ruled in concert with civil power.

But new precedents also took early root, side by side with those traditions. Roger Williams had grown up in England, spending his early years near a place where heretics were burned. As a Puritan, he arrived in Massachusetts in 1631, only to be banished for his liberal views. After selecting Providence as a site, he returned to England and won a charter for a colony where civil rule would have no authority in religious matters, and he declared that persecution had no sanction in the teachings of Jesus.[4]

In Maryland, founded by Catholics under a charter from King Charles I of England, colonists of differing creeds were free from possible penalties stemming from religious beliefs.

For the most part, religion in the colonies was an autocratic, orthodox force on men. Ministers were educated in the Old World, and prospects for the ministry had to make the round trip for education before serving a congregation. The colonists often saw in their faith an ill-equipped vehicle fit more for the patterned society of the Old World than for the rigorous life of the New.

The robust social life of the early settlers often centered in the town tavern, yet side by side there existed a continuing religious spirit.

A contemporary observer, Hector St. John Crèvecœur, in his *Letters from an American Farmer*, wrote:

What religious education will they give their children? A very imperfect one. If there happens to be in the neighborhood any place of worship, we will suppose a Quaker's meeting; rather than not show their fine clothes, they will go to it, and some of them may perhaps attach themselves to that society. Others will remain in a perfect state of indifference; the children of these zealous parents will not be able to tell what their religious principles are, and their grandchildren still less.[5]

The overriding influence in the colonies was commerce. It was close to the heart and spirit of the settler. Nearly everything he needed was imported, and the markets for his products were abroad. Commerce influenced social patterns. In New Netherlands, where the Dutch settlers allowed Catholics, Jews, Mennonites, and Quakers, the government wanted to set up the Dutch Reformed Church as the established religion. This would have allowed Mennonites and Lutherans to be active in the settlement, but not Quakers and Jews. In a strong "suggestion" to Peter Stuyvesant, the Dutch West India Company protested that these minorities be allowed to remain.

The church and state were swapping concessions, recognizing toleration and religious freedom as extremely practical in doing business. Toleration received more emphasis as a spiritual goal as religious attitudes changed with the times and the circumstances of society.

Officially established churches, the ones sanctioned by governments, were going out of existence as the colonies neared revolt. It was not merely consideration of commerce that led to the change; it was also a question of natural rights under God. The case in Virginia is significant. From complete establishment as Anglican, the colony was heading toward complete freedom of religion. In 1776 Virginia adopted a Declaration of Rights drafted by George Mason with the aid of James Madison and Thomas Jefferson. Its ringing phrases were to serve as an example for all mankind: "All men are equally entitled to the free exercise of religion, according to the dictates of their conscience."[6]

A major colony was ready publicly to acknowledge and officially to protect man's right to believe as he wished. It declared: "nor shall [he] otherwise suffer on account of his religious opinions or belief." Here was the stream of thought evident in the Declaration of Independence, born the same year, which would proclaim "all men are created equal." And from there it was just a step to the words "No religious test shall ever be required as a qualification for any office. . . ." The spirit was there. However, its implementation was a long way off.

The Virginia document reflected a deep current of feeling and much considered thought among the Founding Fathers. It read in part:

Be it enacted by the General Assembly that no man shall be compelled to frequent or support any religious worship, place or ministry whatsoever, nor shall be enforced, restrained, molested or burthened in his body or goods, nor shall otherwise suffer on account of his religious opinions or belief; but that all men shall be free to profess, and by argument to maintain, their opinion in matters of religion, and that the same shall in no wise diminish, enlarge or affect their civil capacities. . . .[7]

Yet we are free and do declare that the rights hereby asserted are of the natural rights of mankind and that if any act shall hereafter be passed to repeal the present, or to narrow its operation, such act will be an infringement of natural right. . . .[8]

Jefferson's words, on a seal affixed to his letters, were even more direct: "Rebellion to tyrants is obedience to God."* Here were words and traditions descended directly from the doctrine of the divine right of kings in medieval days, and from the Puritanical concept that the people's rights came from God. The tradition became even clearer in the Declaration of Independence:

We hold these truths to be self-evident, that all men are created equal, that they are endowed by their Creator with certain unalienable Rights . . . That to secure these rights, Governments are instituted among Men, deriving their just powers from the consent of the governed. That whenever any Form of Government becomes destructive of these ends, it is the Right of the People to alter or abolish it, and to institute new Government . . . The history of the present King of Great Britain is a history of repeated injuries and usurpations, all having in direct object the establishment of an absolute Tyranny over these States. . . .
. . . for the support of this Declaration, with a firm reliance on the protection of Divine Providence, we mutually pledge to each other our Lives, our Fortunes, and our sacred Honor.

* Reportedly from an inscription on a cannon near the remains of the seventeenth century English judge John Bradshaw, near Martha Bay, Jamaica. Found among papers of Jefferson, and in his handwriting.

Thus a higher natural law again became the guide directing the efforts of men in governing themselves. Meanwhile, colonial statutory bars against Catholics remained very much a reality, rooted in the traditions of a society that had governed England. It was partially for this reason that Catholics saw in the Revolution a means of furthering their own freedom; a break with England meant an advancement of New World pluralism. As was the case some ninety years later when Irish Catholics fought side by side with "native" Americans, fellow colonists saw little difference between themselves and their Catholic comrades in rebellion. A common cause, perhaps the most certain guarantee of toleration, was paramount.

It was important, too, that the man who was to be selected by his own fellow priests as the leader of American Catholicism was, as a signer of the Declaration, considered an equal by his fellow signers. John Carroll was the son of an old and distinguished Maryland plantation family, who had become a Jesuit priest and toured Europe extensively before returning to America in 1774. His sympathies were with the colonists. He accompanied Benjamin Franklin on a mission to France to seek its neutrality or, at best, its alliance. Their success helped Carroll's status among the other Founding Fathers. He was one of them, espousing their thoughts, and not an agent of a foreign temporal power called Rome. Carroll detailed the difficulties confronting American Catholics in a *Report . . . Concerning the State of Religion in the United States of America,* which he submitted to his superiors. The number of Catholics in the population was less than 1 per cent.

Carroll estimated their number in Maryland at 15,800, including children and slaves. In Pennsylvania there were 7,000, "less scattered" and "living nearer to each other." In Virginia there were 200, visited "four or five times a year by a priest." He added: "In the State of New York I hear there are at least 1,500. [They] have recently at their own expense sent for a Franciscan Father from Ireland. . . . [There are also] many Catholics, formerly Canadians who speak French, and I fear are destitute of priests . . . on the river called Mississippi and in all that region."[9]

The element of foreignness was reflected in the comment about sending to Ireland for a priest, and in that about the frontier inhabitants. Other distinctions were beginning to arise also, as when Carroll reported that "a few of the leading families still profess the Catholic faith introduced at the very foundation of the province by their ancestors," in referring to Maryland, where the greater number of these families were planters.[10] In Pennsylvania, on the other hand, nearly all the Catholics were farmers except for merchants and mechanics living in Philadelphia.

"As for piety," Carroll said, "they lack that fervor which frequent appeals to the sentiment of piety usually produce. . . . Many congregations hear the word of God only once a month and sometimes only once in two months." These difficulties were even more pronounced, he said, among "the Catholics who in great numbers are flowing here from different countries in Europe."[11]

He added: "the abuses that have grown among Catholics are chiefly those which result from . . . more free intercourse between young people of opposite sexes than is compatible with chastity in mind and body; too great fondness for dances and similar amusements; and an incredible eagerness, especially in girls, for reading love stories which are brought over in great quantities from Europe [and] a general lack of care in instructing their children. . . ."[12]

Carroll generally reflected in his judgment the virtues of thrift, industry, and piety that uniformly characterized many religious colonists regardless of faith. Yet there was also the free-wheeling, informal social life that existed free of orthodoxy and stern restraints. Catholics following such habits hardly stood apart as foreigners, and were reportedly well treated so long as they didn't seek to proselytize.

That was the scene as the Constitutional Convention met in May, 1787, with every leading religious group except Baptists represented among the delegates. It was a time when religious sectarianism was of less influence on the people than it had been in many years. The winds of rationalism and deism were blowing hard across the Atlantic, and many religious leaders were concerned with their reputation among influential men.

Despite the legal disenfranchisement of Catholics in some states, there was little animosity now. There were still relatively few Catholics. Moreover, they simply avoided unfriendly civil localities. These bars were to continue in one state (New Hampshire) as late as 1852, and were to figure prominently in the presidential campaign of that year. Meanwhile the influence for removing or countering them came only from a small circle of men among the Founding Fathers.

It was Charles Pinckney, of South Carolina, who, at the convention, proposed the addition of a clause stipulating "No religious test or qualification shall ever be annexed to any oath of office under the authority of the United States.[13]

Pinckney, born in South Carolina, had been a fighter in the Revolution, then a member of the Continental Congress. At the age of twenty-nine, he was the author of a major number of provisions incorporated in the final form of the Constitution. A friend and associate of Jefferson and others, Pinckney later served in the United States Senate, and as minister to Spain, after successive terms as governor of his home state.[14]

His proposal to the convention was withdrawn, modified in its wording, and reintroduced ten days later. It read, "No religious test shall ever be required as a qualification to any office or public trust under the authority of the United States."[15] One of the two delegates supporting the motion was Mr. Gouverneur Morris, of Philadelphia. Roger Sherman, of Connecticut, rose to express the view that it was "unnecessary, the prevailing liberty being a sufficient security against such tests."[16] Nonetheless, the delegates approved the clause, and it was incorporated.

The wording of the religious-test clause as passed did not bind the states. In the prevailing spirit of confederation more than in that of federalism, the states did not welcome tampering with their internal affairs. The clause bound only Congress and federal office.

Madison, Hamilton, and others felt that federal interference in religion would be a flagrant usurpation of the new government's authority. Yet the pressure for a more specific spelling out of rights in this area persisted. A week after Washington's inauguration Madison told the House that he was soon to offer a number of amendments to the Constitution, a "bill of rights." But he was doing so, he had said earlier, chiefly because they were "anxiously desired by others," and not because the Constitution had a "material defect."[17]

Jefferson, it appears, was one of those who anxiously desired such amendments. He had written some time earlier to Madison supporting "a bill of rights, providing clearly and without the aid of sophisms, for freedom of religion, for freedom of the press. . . . A bill of rights is what the people are entitled to against any government on earth, . . . and what no government should refuse."[18]

Madison noted the controversy surrounding the religious-test clause in some states, and this only made him more hesitant about a proposed bill of rights. The role of the federal government in state affairs was very much an issue, and this would exacerbate it. Madison wrote: "There is great reason to fear that positive declaration of some of the most essential rights could not be obtained in the present latitude." Moreover, he declared, "I am sure that the rights of conscience in particular if submitted to public definition would be narrowed much more than they are ever likely to be by an assumed power."[19] He noted that even in Virginia the state's bill of rights had been "violated in every instance where it has been opposed to popular current."[20] Only the fact that the majority of Virginians were no longer of one sect prevented the continuance of an established religion there. He saw this reciprocal toleration as the greatest guarantee of religious freedom. But to others, this meant simply an armed truce, if not subdued warfare.

Roger Sherman, who earlier had felt that the times no longer necessitated the inclusion of the religious-test clause, thought the amendment forbidding Congress from making any laws regarding the establishment of religion was "altogether unnecessary." Congress had no such authority. He had said he would move to have it struck. It was Samuel Livermore, of New Hampshire, who suggested that it might be altered to read, "that Congress shall make no laws touching religion, or infringing the rights of conscience."[21] This was largely the sense of the final wording, and Livermore's motion was carried by a vote of 31 to 20.

Madison was named by the Senate and House to a committee studying the text of the clause establishing free exercise of religion. He was the chief author of the final version that became part of the First Amendment: "Congress shall make no law respecting an establishment of religion, or prohibiting the free exercise thereof; . . ."

Some years later Jefferson wrote of the establishment of professorships for each religious sect at the University of Virginia: "By bringing the sects together, we shall soften their asperities, liberalize and neutralize their prejudices, and make the general religion a religion of peace, reason and morality."[22] Washington added a postscript a short decade later, while the country still was beginning the long fight to establish itself as a sovereign nation. In a reply to American Catholics who had written congratulations to him on his unanimous election, Washington had expressed the hope that their "fellow citizens will not forget the patriotic part which you took in the accomplishment of their revolution and the establishment of their government." He added the hope that Catholics would, "animated alone by the pure spirit of Christianity, and still conducting themselves as the faithful subjects of our free government, enjoy every temporal and spiritual felicity."[23]

In 1796, less than a decade after the ratification of the Constitution, and in the very first campaign to choose Washington's successor, the religious issue arose for the first time. Roman Catholicism was not involved. Jefferson's documents on religious freedom and church disestablishment labeled him sharply among some clergymen in Virginia and New England as a sympathizer of the French Revolution with its anticlerical terrors.

Jefferson was born an Anglican. He had condemned "priest-craft" and maintained that religion was "a matter between man and his Maker." He believed in the ethical teachings of Jesus and in God, but eschewed denominational creeds. Federalist opposition attacked this thinking, and claimed he was outside the pale of even liberal religion.[24]

The election that followed, in 1800, was characterized in political cartoons of the period as one between the forces of law, order, and religion against the irreligion of Voltaire and his ilk. The fact that Jefferson had been a vestryman for some time in earlier years was lost in the turmoil. After three days of close balloting in the House of Representatives, Jefferson was selected over Aaron Burr. Jefferson's declaration in his 1801 inaugural address of intending "equal and exact justice to all men, whatever state of persuasion, religious or political, . . ." did little to assuage militant religionists. Again in the election of 1804 he was attacked as he had been in 1796 and 1800.[25]

For all the efforts to protect against it, the question of religion was to rise immediately. And it was to figure prominently in an average of *one of every three* campaigns for the Presidency through 1960.

CHAPTER TWO

ANDREW JACKSON

*"Rivaling the bold but impious pretensions of
King Henry VIII"*

BEFORE 1824, ONLY ONE OF EVERY TEN PERSONS WAS ELIGIBLE TO vote. In addition to early qualifications of church membership there were new requirements: ownership of land—acreage in the country, or village real estate, or in town—or personal property above a certain value, on which taxes were paid. In 1787 in virtually every colony this had meant ownership of fifty acres or eligibility in the other two categories, church membership and personal holdings.[1] But then the country expanded. During Jefferson's administration Lewis and Clark had broken through to the shores of the Pacific. The other side of that seemingly unlimited horizon had been reached. Between lay thousands of miles, a continent, room to grow. People began to break out through the Cumberland Gap across the Alleghenies to the land that lay beyond, and as the country expanded, so did the electorate, the huge tracts of free land providing the means.

New frontier states soon were added. Gradually, under the hard, equalizing conditions of the life of frontier enterprise, property qualifications were reduced in many of these newer states. A man became worthy by his character, deeds, and merits, not by crusty traditions. By 1820 the farmer, grocer, blacksmith, and shoemaker could all vote in great numbers along with the gentry.

The selection of candidates for the Presidency, however, was a matter exclusively the property of each state's electors. The distance between people and electors was great. In 1824 only half of the twenty-four states chose electors through a direct popular vote. In other states they were chosen by members of the legislature. Moreover, the party candidate was recommended to the electors, not through a convention, but through a caucus of party leaders in that state.

Until 1824 there had been a string of Presidents from only two states, Virginia and Massachusetts. But the Virginia dynasty, which had given the young nation Washington, Jefferson, Madison, and Monroe in succession, was ending. In its place the nation began to change from an aristocratic commonwealth not much removed from the evolving English scene into a republic in practice. Then out of the new western states came Clay of Kentucky and Jackson of Tennessee to face the New Englanders and the Tidewater aristocracy. With them came a new era.

The expansion of the electorate in the 1820's meant more people, more voters, more raucous campaigns, free-wheeling, less deliberate and stately appeals—a circus to cajole the people rather than a forum. It also was to create a setting on which the religious issue would arise in the framework of modern democratic government.

Jackson received a popular mandate in the election of 1824, according to the haphazardly kept records of the day. But since no man had received a majority of the electoral votes, the election went into the House of Representatives. There Henry Clay released his votes to John Quincy Adams, giving the New Englander the victory.

The campaign of 1828, among Jackson supporters, began almost the very next day. They charged that Clay had sold out to Adams in return for his new job of Secretary of State, seemingly strengthening his next attempt at the Presidency. Over the next three years a circle of Jackson supporters worked steadily to enlist county leaders throughout the states, keeping a card file of reliable ones and of potentials. As election time grew near, men traveled for weeks from one locale to another, staging bonfires, processions and rallies in an effort to drum up interest among the populace.[2] By the 1828 election, all but two of the states had switched to direct popular voting for electors, with New York about to do so for the first time. With the expansion of the electorate, it was almost inevitable that campaigners would appeal to sentiments and prejudices, aside from issues.

There were signs of Pennsylvania's moving its support to the frontier, to Jackson. There and in New York there were heavy concentrations of Germans and growing numbers of Irish Catholics.[3] Meanwhile a religious revivalism had been sweeping Baptist and Methodist churches in southwestern and western communities. Rumblings of this theological conflict were felt in New England, and grew to a pitched controversy. It was a time of revivalism versus old New England Puritanical sentiment. The country consisted of sections, loosely joined; and personalities stood out strongly.

Here were Jackson, the tall, lean, bony brawler of the frontier, a hearty man, proud, with a broad forehead, deep-set eyes, intense, strong cheekbones; and Clay, full of invigorating dash, serious, resourceful, strong, heavy intent brows, dignified, almost arrogant in his bearing, with great powers of oratory that could hold even opponents spellbound; and Adams, the stern New Englander.

The injection of morality, tapping religious sentiment, began early. The religious issue became an issue in earnest, woven out of personal morality and out of antagonism between groups. Much was directed at the quiet schisms that existed between the overwhelming majority of Protestants and the still tiny minority of Catholics. There were new words, but they were to find their way into campaign talk for more than a century—first blatantly open, then in literature for the masses, then as an undercover appeal.

In a speech in Baltimore some years earlier, Adams had characterized the Catholic Church as a "portentous system of despotism and superstition."[4] Now the Jacksonian partisans threw this in his face. To counter it, a letter was produced from a Catholic layman, stating that Adams, as President, had made generous contributions to priests for the building of churches and had named Catholics to federal posts.

Emotional appeals to sectarian sentiments persisted, partially because church membership was proportionately higher among the voting population than in the population at large. The exchanges flew. It was charged that Jackson, while governor of Florida, had tried to "regulate the due observance of the Sabbath," thus "rivaling the bold but impious pretensions of King Henry VIII."[5] Some frontier churchmen praised Jackson's encouragements of prayers by his troops before wartime battles, but Jackson's travels on the Sabbath were held against him and publicized in New England. It was rumored, too, that Jackson's belief in the Trinity and Incarnation left much to be desired in the way of fervency. He was even called a deist, as had been Jefferson. During wartime, Jackson once had ordered the execution of six militiamen. The fact that one had been a Methodist preacher was dragged up and hammered upon.

A paper in Pennsylvania reported that ministers of the General Conference of the Methodist Episcopal Church had overwhelmingly opposed Jackson. Of 197 ministers, the paper said, only seven were for Jackson, and all seven were from his home state of Tennessee. A New York paper took the trouble to answer this claim, which predated the so-called "Peale Manifesto" by 132 years. It said first of all that there were only 167 members in the organization and that no effort had been made to determine their political preferences.[6]

Little or no objection was raised to the content of these declarations, nor was their substance challenged. The important thing was simply the fact that these ministers were against Jackson— almost as if a solemn, irrefutable judgment had been passed. The propriety of such a judgment was not questioned. It wasn't seen as "meddling." This power of endorsement or condemnation was accepted and even regarded as a right or obligation. Yet in their content the declarations were not sensitive to issues of church-state separation; they were sensitive reactions to alleged victimization of a religious minority. As such, they reflected what was considerable unrest and a sense of threat that caused some religionists to speak out so harshly.

A great effort was made by the religionists against what they perceived as an essentially secular society arising permanently around them. Involved was an attempt by leading sectarian religionists to maintain a more or less direct influence on the policies, activities, and make-up of government. The "alliance between religion and politics" that De Tocqueville had seen existing from the beginning of the young American Republic up to the time of Jackson seemed to be loosening.

Monarchy and its customary affiliation with religious authority simply did not exist. (A debate had quickly developed during the Constitutional Convention over the official acknowledgment of "belief in the existence of a Deity" and distinctions between "professors of Christianity and downright infidelity or paganism.")[7] Now it seems that with the advent of Jacksonian democracy any hopes of establishing even some modified form of such joint authority were disappearing permanently. It was a hard pill to swallow for the orthodox, militant religionists.

Theodore Frelinghuysen, of New Jersey, then chancellor of New York University, a highly respected educator and a deeply religious man, was a particularly stanch advocate of a close alliance between religion and government. Frelinghuysen's warnings about widening Jacobinism and his decrying of the loosening ties between government and religionists were prompted by a serious contemporary trend. From a situation before the Revolution in which states with established churches barred certain religious sects' members from holding office, the pendulum had unexpectedly swung to the other side. Several state constitutions now contained provisions barring clergymen from holding public office.[8]

As the campaign warmed in 1828, the charges seemed to be having some effect. Martin Van Buren, a Jackson supporter, wrote to ask whether Jackson had prayers in his own house, and requested that if he did, it be mentioned "modestly."[9]

Other moves were made to utilize religious sentiment or antag-

onisms. A Catholic bishop acquainted with Clay was approached
in Baltimore on his return home from Europe by a friend. It was
indirectly suggested that it might be viewed as a religious duty
for the bishop to advise his parishioners on their political preferences. The bishop made no response, "grew increasingly grave
in his expression," and the matter was dropped.[10]

Baltimore was a major port of entry for Irish immigrants, and
Adams was accused of trying to win Catholic votes by paying
visits to churches there and by his earlier appointments of Catholics. At the same time, his accusers said, he was not only ignorant
of the religion's doctrines but was also flippant or even hostile
toward them.[11]

Many of the clergy involved in the charges were aligned with
the Whig party, and assailed a rising wave of irreligion. Democracy was labeled by some clergymen as a "branch of atheism,"
harboring those with atheistic sentiments under its wing. These
sentiments were hammered at again and again by some speakers
and lecturers before the citizens of some communities. Democratic campaign speakers, on the other hand, lambasted "priest-
craft," calling it an instrument, a tool of the rich, of the Whigs.[12]
There were political meetings every day as the bitterly fought
campaign came down to the wire.

At its conclusion Jackson won by some 140,000 votes. For the
first time more than a million votes were cast. And for the first
time the religious issue had flared as a force to be reckoned with
among thousands of voters. The people had cast their vote with
Jackson, however, on a much more tangible sentiment, in many
cases, than that of religion. Greater tides were running. In New
England, the old domestic system of manufacturing goods, in-
herited from the Middle Ages, was being replaced by the growth
of the factory system, just as in England.

The country was still overwhelmingly agricultural outside the
large centers of the East. Communities remained relatively remote. Canals opened the way, and rivers provided links, but the
stage was the mainstay. Railroads were yet to come. The Baltimore & Ohio Railroad ran between Baltimore and Washington

over rails, but drawn by horses. The trip from Philadelphia to the capital took two days by boat. In the election, voting results in Ohio had been transmitted to Washington in eight days.

National government, indeed the nation itself, was a loose entity. There was little genuine national identity in social traditions beyond the formal pronouncements of government. The national culture was most noted for its rugged heterogeneity, and there was as yet no consolidation of strength. The great powers of Europe remained dominant and immediate threats. The United States was coming into conflict with them, directly and indirectly, as it pushed its expansion westward into Texas, California, and New Mexico. The country was not unassailable. The closeness of the Old World continued to be felt in other ways, too. Into the country were coming large numbers of people from Germany and Ireland. Although there were tradesmen, skilled craftsmen, and farmers among them, fully half had no occupation.[13]

In 1816 a total of 6,000 Irish arrived; in 1820 another 20,000 came; and this was only the initial trickling of a major flow that was to total a million by 1850.[14] Arriving in squalid craft for as little as five dollars per person, they quickly ran into disillusionment. Boardinghouse runners met them at the docks of New York, Philadelphia, and Boston, leading the unwary to wretched quarters hastily erected by the fleecers, who milked them of their last funds any way they could. Phony steamship and rail tickets were sold to illiterate immigrants who then often found themselves at the mercy of whoever could offer them work. Sometimes they were sold tickets that moved their families just a few miles inland toward the promise of better conditions. Oftentimes the "tickets" turned out to be spurious coupons, adorned with a picture of a steamship or railroad.[15]

The hapless immigrant found himself in a strange country, without funds and without a skill to offer, fair game for a dozen schemes. His first goal was to earn a livelihood, and he took what work he could get. He cleaned stables, swept streets, and became the menial laborer of the day. And if he could avoid the schemers, disease, poverty, and waves of helplessness and despair, he could expect to live perhaps fourteen years in his new land.[16]

There was one steadying influence to which he could cling, however, and that was his church, with its familiar Latin liturgy and consistency of ceremony and taste of home. It offered him the one link that wasn't completely foreign, and he clung to it tenaciously.

The native countryman could hardly be expected to show anything but contempt for this new breed of American. Even an objective look would show squalor beyond the comprehension of the relatively secure workingman and his family. When inevitable direct contact came, it was likely to be on the working level. The immigrant was there, eager to work for lower wages, unmoved by the fact that the native American might be put out of a job in the process. Naturally, the rivalry grew stronger. And as if these factors weren't enough, the immigrant also worshiped in a strange manner. His statues and crucifixes and ornate vestments and processions stood in sharp contrast to the austere, individualistic worship of the Protestant American. Atop that, his "foreign" religion sought openly to convert the world, to bring the "errant" Protestant back to its fold; history was studded with such examples. In short, the immigrant was a threat to everything the native held dear. What better atmosphere for hatred?

Not surprisingly, outbreaks of violence occurred in several larger cities and communities among workingmen of different ethnic or sectarian groups. In 1833, in Boston, as the result of allegations that a band of Irishmen had beaten a "native" American, a crowd marched on a heavily populated Irish sector and burned or smashed several homes. It was merely an inkling of the violence to come.

The fighting even filtered into the ranks of the Irish themselves, spurred by the drive for higher wages. On one occasion President Jackson had to use federal troops to quell riots among rival Irish working gangs on the Chesapeake and Ohio Canal.[17]

At this time daughters from a number of wealthy non-Catholic families attended one of the better area schools in Charlestown, an outlying community of Boston. The school, affiliated with an Ursuline convent, was in a community mainly inhabited by the working class, and shady tales circulated about life in the convent on the hill. Many of the parents who sent their children to the school were Unitarians who had left their congregational fold to which many older inhabitants belonged. When a Protestant school was set up nearby, and parents of the children in the convent school did not remove them, suspicions were aroused. It was rumored that the young daughters and their parents were being converted by the Catholic nuns.

A young girl from a workingman's family had been employed there in a menial position, and taken as a candidate for the order. But she soon left, and gossiped darkly about life behind the convent walls. Shortly thereafter one of the nuns left the convent, emotionally upset, asking to be released from her vows. But after a talk with Bishop Fenwick she decided to return. This further stirred local sentiment, and made the dark tales seem more credible. At the same time the bishop was engaged in a controversy with local authorities over being granted land in a cemetery on Bunker Hill. He had approved the burial of two children there, despite protests by town authorities. A prominent Boston clergyman, Dr. Lyman Beecher, was in the process of delivering a series of sermons on the evils of foreign popery. This served to legitimize resentments in the mind of the townsfolk. A hard-core group of men, organized for that purpose weeks earlier and abetted by a mob of youngsters, toughs, and down-and-outers, burned the convent to the ground.

The sisters hurriedly shepherded the children out a back way. The mother superior, unnerved and helpless before the malice and intent of the milling, ugly mob, and at the same time fired by anger and frustrated defiance, shouted that the throng should not forget that the bishop had 20,000 Irishmen at his command in Boston.[18] At the very least, the hasty remark failed to daunt the crowd. For days afterward, gangs of "foreigners" and nativists roamed the neighborhood. But only one man was convicted and sentenced as a result of the fire, from among several arrested and tried.

In 1834 a series of newspaper articles was written under pseudonym by Samuel F. B. Morse,[19] just back from Europe. While in Vienna, he'd learned of the existence, in that Catholic Austro-Hungarian capital and elsewhere, of Catholic lay societies dedicated to advancing the Catholic religion in America. While attending a papal procession in Rome, innocently standing with his hat on, he'd had it knocked off by a bayonet fixed to a soldier's rifle, and was rudely admonished for not showing due reverence. Morse came to be convinced that the countries of the Holy Alliance then recently formed had become aligned with the Papacy in a grand plan to advance Catholic power in America. These empires had purely nationalistic designs on us, he maintained, and were joined with the church in order to do by gradual infiltration and subversion what another country had been unable to do by force of arms. He was to maintain the same thing again during the Civil War in regard to England.

As a means of blocking this infiltration, Morse advocated the denial of voting privileges to future immigrants. He also demanded that the Roman Catholic hierarchy make public its administrative affairs as Protestant churches were expected to do.[20] "We are politically attacked," wrote Morse, "under the guise of a religious system." He characterized the Papacy that had existed in the Middle Ages as "the cunningest political despotism that ever cursed mankind."[21]

Several weeks after the last of the Morse articles, a meeting of the Protestant Association in New York was called to discuss the question, "Is popery compatible with civil liberty?" Catholic clergymen were among the participants. The meeting was interrupted by a band of Irish Catholics who moved roughly front and center and began to heckle the speakers in a disturbance that quickly erupted into a free-for-all.[22] A similar incident occurred in Baltimore. The Catholic clergy repudiated the incidents, but the damage had been done. The patience of jobless, poorly educated, newly arrived Irish Catholics also grew increasingly short.

Within a few weeks after these outbursts, a political alliance was formed between those motivated by antiforeign and anti-Catholic sentiment and the Whig party in New York. In 1836 it ran Morse as its candidate for mayor.[23] He polled less than 10 per cent of the total vote. The great mass of the people, it seemed, still were unreceptive to warnings of a Catholic threat.

Meanwhile the influx of Irish immigrants quickened. The home country was racked by poor economic conditions, and famine itself was setting in. People were leaving their homes to chance the New World. As they flocked in, their immediate center for organization continued to be either the parish church or social groups set up by politicians. These societies began to mobilize the vote of the new arrivals. In Boston, the number of qualified voters among the Irish rose by 50 per cent in one five-year period, then jumped by 300 per cent in the following five years. In that same time, the number of native voters grew by only 14 per cent.[24]

State legislatures in the next few years rang with earnest debates over the extension of suffrage to newly arrived foreigners, as well as to Negroes. In 1841 a bill was proposed in the Pennsylvania Legislature to prevent all foreigners coming into the state after July 4, 1841, from voting or holding office. A similar bill there had singled out Catholics before the Revolutionary War.

By 1817 the Society of St. Tammany in New York, founded by Aaron Burr a quarter of a century before, had come to be considered hostile to newly arriving Irishmen there. A short time earlier it had rejected an Irishman as a candidate for Congress. One night in April of that year more than a hundred Irishmen, after assembling at Dooley's Long Room, marched in on a meeting at the hall, precipitating fist fights that became a free-for-all in which furniture was smashed and many were bloodied.[25]

This method of protest began to enjoy a certain vogue. Gang clashes were numerous throughout the first decades of American city politics. In one year (1839), it was estimated that there had been a $7,000,000 property loss as a result of clashes, as well as twenty-three killed in rioting.[26] One Tammany club in New York about this time was headed by Isaiah Rynders, a former

New Orleans gambler who had survived numerous bowie cuts and pistol fights and a brawl on a Mississippi steamboat in which he fought a pug with a red-hot poker during a gambling salon melee. On the way north he stopped long enough in Washington to bring about his arrest in connection with a theft of treasury notes.[27] Now he was a "politician." Such was the state of much of the country's politicking as it moved into the campaign of 1844.

CHAPTER THREE

JAMES K. POLK
The Emergence of Americanism

"Foreign Catholics have defeated us"

AMERICA WAS LAYING CLAIM TO ITS SOVEREIGNTY ONCE AGAIN IN 1844, as it had been doing almost steadily since the Revolution. Spain and even England were regarded darkly as belligerents, preventing us from taking hold of what was rightfully ours.

In the forefront for the Democrats as 1844 standard-bearer was James K. Polk, withdrawn, formal, deliberate, plodding, punctilious, with little personal magnetism. Against him once again ranged the tall Henry Clay, swaggering, charming, who could castigate, intimidate, and hypnotize with his wondrous gifts of oratory. Clay, the son of a Virginia preacher who owned a large farm and a dozen slaves, had as his running mate stern, pious, zealous Theodore Frelinghuysen, senator of New Jersey, who earlier had lashed out at Jackson and other Democrats for furthering the separation of religion from politics and contributing to what was described as an irreligiousness that was overtaking our institutions.[1] His viewpoint had helped him gain a Senate seat in Washington.

As the election neared, a wave of tragic violence rocked Philadelphia, precipitated by a continuing conflict between Catholics and Protestants over the use of a Protestant Bible in the public schools. The riots began when a crowd of some five hundred "Native Americans" planted a flagpole in the middle of a busy market place on Friday, May 3rd. A small encounter at the rear

24

of the crowd touched off shooting and brawling. Mobs attacked Irish-occupied homes nearby, then turned their attentions to a Catholic schoolhouse, where they set fire to a wooden fence while Irish families fled.[2]

Probing rioters claimed they found caches of guns in Irishmen's houses. On Tuesday morning another Native American rally was held, and the crowds marched in procession bearing the tattered flag from Friday's riots. On it was a sign that read, "This is the flag that has been tramped upon by the Irish Papists." That afternoon nearly three thousand nativists crowded into Independence Square. An organizer led them to another spot, and mounted an outdoor stage to speak. As he did so, a shot rang out from the direction of a nearby firehouse. A volley of fire followed, and six persons were injured. The mobs continued to surge that night, setting fire to twenty-nine houses. Firemen, when they weren't hampered by rioters, were hesitant to battle the flames.[3]

Later in the day a brigade of Pennsylvania militia was called out. Contemporary newspaper accounts said it was "very possible that several Irishmen were killed in the houses which were afterwards burnt and the bodies consumed." On Wednesday the mobs burned St. Michael's church, school, and rectory, and that night they set fire to St. Augustine's church, rectory, and library, and nearby houses. Troops guarded nearby St. Mary's, St. Joseph's, and St. John's churches. For a time, Catholic masses had to be suspended. Then peace volunteers from each ward helped to stop the violence. The toll stood at seven dead, thirty-seven wounded. Despite a $1,000 reward offered by the mayor, only a single arrest was made.[4]

Throughout all the the incidents, a single distinction was sharply evident. The religious issue was being complicated by other issues, which made it more difficult to isolate and combat. The Catholics were attacked as lower-class foreigners by people who called themselves nativists. But immigration, while heavy, still was only a minor problem in America. The country still had room to grow, and immigrants did much of the moving. In the next few decades, however, millions who arrived stayed on the

East Coast, and the problem of their assimilation took a different form. The religious issue was there in all its complexity as the campaign of 1844 got under way.

Handbills were distributed among Catholics, claiming that Clay had offered his congratulations to anti-Catholics for their work in Philadelphia.[5] Meanwhile, Whigs asserted that the Democratic candidate for governor in Pennsylvania had marched in a Catholic parade. Mass meetings were held in several cities in which inflammatory speeches were made against Catholics—foreigners. There were appeals to Protestants to close ranks against the "Jesuit band" by supporting Clay and the right local candidates. In rebuttal, a letter was offered, allegedly from a Protestant minister who had been with Clay on a riverboat and had witnessed his extensive drinking and swapping of bawdy yarns while he gambled away the night.[6]

The Whig platform included a plank that favored "discriminating for the protection of the domestic labor of the country." In New York and New Jersey, Frelinghuysen served as spokesman for these views.

The continued influx of Catholic laborers into eastern seaboard cities contributed to greater friction there than anywhere else. Clay's candidacy prompted New York Whigs with abolitionist sentiments to bolt the party and present their own candidate. Whig leaders in New York fatefully wrote off the bolt, and sought to offset it with support from those Democrats who harbored enough anti-Catholic sentiment to move into the Whig camp. There was agreement among politicians, in areas where that sentiment was heavy, to work for the Clay ticket while the Whigs in turn would help those local politicians in their own efforts.[7] As the campaign moved into its final weeks, it promised to be a close race.

In 1839 a bill had been passed by the New York State Legislature providing for the first time that voters in New York City should register, and making fraudulent voting a felony. But in 1843, because of its emphasis on New York City alone, it had been repealed as discriminatory.[8] Now, as the voting began, cries of fraud went up from Whig headquarters in New York. A letter to an associate of a Democratic politician described Tammany Hall as a jam from eight in the morning until past midnight, with naturalization of new arrivals proceeding at a fast pace. In one day, more than 250 immigrants received naturalization papers. And they were all Democrats.[9]

Although qualified voters in the city totaled just 45,000, the vote finally recorded there was 28,216 for Polk and 26,970 for Clay—a total of 10,000 more than were eligible! With this went the state's thirty-six electoral votes, and victory in the national election for Polk.[10]

In a letter to Clay a week later, Millard Fillmore in New York said firmly that "the abolitionists and foreign Catholics have defeated us in this state. . . . Our opponents, by pointing to Mr. Frelinghuysen, drove the foreign Catholics from us and defeated us."[11] Right or not, the emphasis had been put again on the "religious" issue. And it is noteworthy to record Fillmore's phrase "foreign Catholics." The river of hatred, flowing from separate streams of antiforeign and anti-Catholic sentiment, had conjoined with distrust and fear over the economic threat, to grow into a sea of opposition.

From the election of 1844 emerged a solid new issue that an office seeker could use to arouse and mobilize the electorate. The election had proved the issue's power and attraction, either as a legitimate sentiment or as a trumped-up piece of demagoguery, to summon a broad base of uniform appeal. It was something that seemed to transcend all fears. For our purposes, we can term it "national concern," in a nation far from fully established. National concern was to have a more unifying effect 116 years later in a nation more sure of its identity than it was in 1844.

Meanwhile it had become clear that the "religious" issue was not based solely on religious differences. It was not wholly a matter of religiousness versus irreligiousness, although it often expressed itself as such. It was basically antiforeign motivation. The issue also involved the practical matter of economic competition among older working-class citizens. Essentially it represented the beginnings, the stirrings of a manifested national consciousness.

A sense of the country's destiny had begun to filter down from the removed councils and pronouncements of government, into the life and thoughts and culture of the people. It was the concern that found articulation in the epochal "American Scholar" address delivered by Emerson in 1837, when he declared:

Perhaps the time is already come . . . when the sluggard intellect of this continent will look from under its iron lids and fill the postponed expectation of the world with something better than the exertions of mechanical skill. . . .

Our day of dependence, our long apprenticeship to the learning of other lands, draws to a close. The millions that around us are rushing into life cannot always be fed on the sere remains of foreign harvests.[12]

Emerson's was a feeling that sprang from predominantly positive, even idealistic elements in many instances. An American ethos, an American culture was forming. Dr. Johnson's often quoted comment that "patriotism is the last refuge of scoundrels" was as true then as it is in too many instances today.

But among the politicians who rode into office on the crest of this newly activated power were amiable and upright men. Many of them sometimes finished an antiforeign or anti-Catholic diatribe with a renewed statement affirming their belief in the practice of religious freedom. Not a few of the immigration and naturalization reforms originally advocated by these men have since become law, accepted and approved. Others, advocated by extremists, did not. The withholding of the right to vote was felt justified because newly arrived aliens in their lack of understanding and responsibility were so often the tools of demagogues. Election frauds occurred blatantly and outrightly. It was charged, too, that, as she had done in earlier times, England was deliberately unloading her paupers and criminals on the United States. Many of the earlier colonists had been honest debtors, but many criminals and paupers entered too.

Sam Houston, the hero of the Alamo later to serve in the

Senate, was to seek the nomination for President with these sentiments as part of his position. Houston, with characteristic individualism, stood rather apart from the Know-Nothing element in the American party. His strongest point, in fact, seemed to be that southern strength in the Union, and the nation's noblest traditions of democracy, were being adversely affected. At a time when native labor faced competition from incoming foreigners, chiefly German and Irish, Houston, in a speech at the Democratic convention in Austin, Texas, in 1852, was characterized as "an advocate of the rights of labor and the interests of the masses . . ." and "against the oppression of tyrannic absolutism."[13]

"Until recently," said Houston in 1855, "a large portion of those who came to our shores were prompted by a desire to improve their condition. They were men of sobriety . . . of enterprise . . . of character . . . of intelligence. The crowned heads of Europe had formed no conspiracy against our institutions or at least did not attempt its accomplishment. Of late they have determined to empty the convicts from their penitentiaries and paupers from their poorhouses. . . ." And there was another element already making itself felt. Immigration, continued Houston, "is constantly diminishing Southern representation in the Councils of our Nation and increasing the proportionate ratio of the representation of North and Western states. This gives the abolitionist more power. It is greatly to the interests of the South to stop it and increase the naturalization period to twenty-one years."[14]

Nativism, with its expression as a "religious" issue, was one of the first dramatic manifestations of Americanism. In its long-run effect it promoted assimilationist rather than separatist currents. After having expressed their eagerness to become citizens, it had been charged, the new arrivals remained as separate clannish communities, closer to the old country than to the new. Ethnic identification was still more vivid than national identification. The immigrants' great concern for their Old World relatives and countrymen underscored this.

The Irish potato crop, a bulwark of the tottering economy

there, had failed. Hundreds of thousands were starving, and without even the meager hope that the immigrants had of success. On wages of perhaps fifty cents a day, the Irish sent $800,000 to their countrymen in the year of the famine. A few years later the total reached $8,000,000; it was to reach $65,000,000 between the years 1848 and 1864.[15] Before the famine Ireland had a population of eight million; after it she had six million. A million had died and another million had emigrated—most of them to Canada and the United States. It was at this time that Patrick Kennedy left his family homestead to seek a new life in America.

With the consciousness that was emerging tentatively and proudly in the inarticulate spirits of many ordinary citizens there smoldered transmitted remembrances of old foes in circumstances and spirit. The seed of hatred was there amid the emerging spirit, and the spirit drew to it all kinds of political opportunists as well as extremists and bigots. Emerson observed in his journal shortly after the election of 1845:

I hate the narrowness of the Native American Party. . . . Man is the most composite of all creatures. . . . In this continent—this asylum of all nations—the energy of Irish, Germans, Swedes, Poles and Cossacks and all the European tribes—of the Africans and of the Polynesians—will construct a new race, a new religion, a new state, a new literature which will be as vigorous as the New Europe which came out of the smelting pot of the Dark Ages. . . .[16]

The men who carried the sentiments we spoke of in the early nineteenth century sometimes took pains to distinguish between temporal higher allegiance and spiritual higher allegiance in their warnings against foreigners and popery. But they pointed out that in the Middle Ages, under the revised doctrine of the divine right of kings, which declared the voice of God through the voice of the people, Catholic populations were told by Rome that they had a right under a higher allegiance to overthrow heretical kings, which usually meant Protestant kings. A representative speaking in Congress in the middle of the nineteenth century emphasized this point as he related the Catholic struggle and accession to power over the English kings. It was declared that

Catholics were tolerant only while still a minority, until they became a majority, and that they would move into power by the
democratic process itself.[17] Then they would reveal their true
despotic colors, it was warned. Clearly, as the Founding Fathers
had often acknowledged themselves, all high-flown pronouncements aside, the best plain and simple reason for gradual colonial
tolerance had been the diversity of sects. Once a relatively solid
majority emerged, it was feared, the balance would be upset.

During the years when this cry was raised, the ratio of Protestants to Catholics was about twenty to one in the United States.[18]
It was the sudden influx that was alarming. In 1850 just 2.2 per
cent of the country was foreign born. But of these, nearly half
were Irish. And they bore the brunt of nativist dislike.

Any distinction between temporal allegiance and spiritual allegiance was lost on many citizens who lived in close touch with
these newcomers. Their reaction was largley an undifferentiated
emotional one made in response to the rowdy, squalid, clannish
strangers who moved among them or grouped nearby, and who
competed with them for jobs or who created disturbances among
themselves involving innocent citizens.

Thus by their actions some well-meaning men summoned into
being, like an explosive, rambunctious jinni, the deep prejudice
against the Papacy. It was there, waiting to be activated amid a
host of pressures and discontents that marked the changing
character of American society and its assertion of sovereignty.
As had been the case in the Charlestown convent disgrace, the
streams were conjoined, and the stream of the pulpit legitimized
the pitiful sewerage of mean despair. Educated, earnest, zealous
men were speaking out from the pulpit against popery; ignorant,
suspicious, resentful lowlifes were listening to every word.

As an indication of the sentiment of emerging Americanism, it
should be pointed out that some Catholics counted themselves
among those who subscribed to antiforeign sentiments against
newly arrived aliens. It was even suggested that if Catholics
would openly support Know-Nothing proposals on immigration

and naturalization, they might thereby "allay Protestant apprehension" and even conceivably "win additional converts."[19]

In earlier years, and in large measure even in the 1830's and 1840's, there had been few or no native-born Catholic priests. Now the first ones were appearing, ministering to other native-born Catholics. One, Father Isaac Thomas Hecker, became the founder of the Paulist Fathers, then the "sole religious congregation of clerics of American origin." Father Hecker was born in New York in 1819.

But divisions were occurring in the Catholic community itself. Some Catholics gained grudging acceptance among Yankees and flourished among their fellows. A Catholic representative from Pennsylvania gave voice to a new assertive sentiment when at about this time in the course of a House debate he stated that were the Bishop of Rome to invade United States territory with a host of ships or men, or otherwise attack the rights of the United States, there would be no opposition stronger than that of Roman Catholics in America. Moreover, he added, he would be earnestly praying to God to repel the invaders—if he were not actually engaged himself in armed opposition.[20]

His protestations were prompted by specific national sentiments reflected in Congress itself. One representative, from Alabama, in strongly urging passage of immigration and naturalization measures, said: "Suppose, sir, that England, France or Russia or any other Government have a desire to make war upon the United States . . . before any act of hostility should be committed they could land upon our shores in merchant ships, in the form of immigrants, any number of soldiers, from one hundred to a million. How easy it would be for the Czar to send 100,000 Russians to this country as emigrants. One hundred thousand immigrants arriving in New York in a month would create no excitement. Their promenading Broadway would not so swell the tide of that immense population as to be perceivable. They would go and equip themselves with American rifles, furnish themselves with American powder, and American bullets, and go in American cars to any portion of the country and be ready at any time, to exhibit themselves as an armed force, in the heart of the country.[21]

"This may never occur," added the representative, but he re-iterated that existing laws "enable an enemy to flood the country with his soldiers in the form of emigrants."

Bishop John England declared, concerning the American Constitution, "Let the Pope and the cardinals and all the powers of the Catholic world united make the least encroachment on that Constitution, we will protect it with our lives. Summon a General Council—let that Council interfere in the mode of our electing but an assistant to the turnkey of a prison—we deny the right, we reject the usurpation."[22]

The bishop's spirited statement reflects the sentiment that had existed among a number of American Catholics, beginning with John Carroll himself when he urged Rome to permit itself to exercise control only to the extent of approving a choice of bishop made not in Rome but in the United States. The unique conditions of American society almost made absolutely necessary certain modifications in traditional Church doctrine, it seemed.

It was about this time that a convert to Catholicism, Orestes Brownson, sounded a new note. Brownson, who had been a Presbyterian, then a Universalist, then a Unitarian, shifted the focus from the rights of man to the *duties* of man in discussing the place of Roman Catholicism in American democracy. "Here is our hope for our republic," he wrote. "We look for our safety to the spread of Catholicity."[23] He continued:

We render solid and imperishable our free institutions just in proportion as we extend the kingdom of God among our people and establish in their hearts the reign of justice and charity. And here then is our answer to those who tell us Catholicity is incompatible with free institutions. We tell them that they cannot maintain free institutions without it.[24]

It is not a free government that makes a free people, but a free people that makes a free government; and we know no freedom but that wherewith the son makes free. You must be free within before you can be free without.

The Roman Catholic religion . . . is necessary to sustain popular liberty because popular liberty can be sustained only by a religion free from popular control, above the people, speaking from above and able to command them. . . . [25]

Brownson's sincerity was praised more than the substance of his views. The book fell quietly amid the ferment of the times. In his views, though, Brownson was reasserting a number of implicit premises.

For one thing, again, as the Founding Fathers had said, the individual was the key to free government. And the individual factor was drawn primarily in terms of religious and, inferentially, ethical strength. The difference was this, however: Liberty was becoming increasingly confused with license or apathy. Leadership had to be provided.

It was at this time—1848—that modern socialism was being born in Europe, that Karl Marx was about to give the world the support of his theory and driving intuition in *Das Kapital*. With the Industrial Revolution, big capital was coming into being, and, shortly thereafter, big labor. Liberation seemed to be sweeping through, the results of the Enlightenment finally reaching fruition. In America, these currents had come with the Jacksonian Era. Brownson, not far from being under the shadow of the medieval time, was sounding the first modern call in America for a consensual escape back from this new "freedom." He was boldly asserting that this was the only hope for maintaining the traditions out of which democracy drew succor and flourished. Amid these vast stirrings the religious issue was to rise to new heights of prominence in the presidential campaigns of the 1850's.

CHAPTER FOUR

FRANKLIN PIERCE and JOHN C. FRÉMONT

"Religious persecution and free trade"

In 1852 THE POLITICAL AND SOCIAL LANDSCAPE WAS A SENSE OF *national* destiny rather than international destiny. The use of "American" sentiment as a convenient and greatly successful device was carried into the 1852 conventions and campaign for President. London newspapers were reporting that "in their present political condition immense territories of North America resemble those of Europe in the days of Charlemagne, imperfectly stocked by barbarous tribes, degenerate races, rising communities and powerful states."[1]

Meanwhile, a New York paper was commenting, "One of the most striking features in the history of the times is the fact that public opinion in England and to a certain extent throughout Europe is gradually conceding to the United States a power and position on this Western continent far higher than our most sanguine statesmen have ever claimed."[2]

Politicians who were strongly identified with militant nativist sentiment were much in evidence at both nominating conventions. At the Whig convention they supported Millard Fillmore in an unsuccessful drive. At the Democratic convention they supported Lewis Cass. They were playing both sides of the fence.

Neither man was selected to run. Instead, Winfield Scott emerged, tall and proud, of magnificent bearing, a national hero who had said of his campaign in Mexico, "I went to sustain the high tide water mark of our own American civilization in all its moral and civil virtue."[3] And opposing him was Democrat Franklin Pierce, sociable, buoyant, gracious, somewhat vain, and occasionally lacking in self-confidence, a "gentleman lawyer" and son of the quiet back country of New Hampshire.

Just a few days before receiving news of his nomination, Pierce had summoned friends and called a town meeting in his village of Concord, New Hampshire, for "friends of democratic equality and religious tolerance."[4] Most of those appearing at the meeting were Democrats, but a few Whigs came too, curious. The meeting condemned a state ban against Catholics for office, one of those technical religious "tests" that was as effective as an old colonial law.

The ban stood, however, as the voters of the state declined to pass an amendment that would have eliminated it. The situation was bound to cause trouble, and it did. As the campaign opened, public statements were circulated accusing Pierce of anti-Catholicism and linking him to the state "test." Charles O'Conor, a prominent New York Catholic attorney, asked Pierce about the facts surrounding the constitutional clause and Pierce's relation to it.

Apparently Pierce's reply satisfied O'Conor, who defended him. But the matter continued to mushroom. Campaign sheets were circulated, in an effort to exonerate Pierce and show that it was the voters of New Hampshire who had refused to remove the test, but the onus remained.[5] After all, Pierce was a son of that state, which in turn was a stronghold of anti-Catholicism. Stumping speakers took up the issue immediately. In New York in September, at a mass rally complete with bonfires and brass bands, a speaker addressing himself to the Irish and Germans present exhorted his listeners to back Scott because he was "a representative of the principle of protection . . . to the laborer and mechanic the means of support from his toil."[6] Moreover, the speaker continued, it had been his misfortune to live ten years in New Hampshire, and he knew that the policy of Pierce was "religious persecution and free trade," which would flood this country with the produce of "England's pauper labor." This was the policy that had sent forth the Irish from the hearths of their fathers and the graves of their ancestors, he declared, to seek a home in this country. Now the same policy would be adopted here that had caused their ruin at home.

Pierce wrote to a friend in Baltimore who was close to Archbishop Purcell, and to another friend in Boston who was influential among several Catholic newspaper editors. He replied to an invitation to a Fourth of July celebration in Philadelphia, in which he sang the praises of the "foreign-born" in the cause of the American Revolution.[7] The letter was publicized. In Pennsylvania there was pitched campaigning in the face of alleged anti-Catholic sentiments attributed to Pierce. The state attorney general, Catholic James Campbell, went all out in an effort to stem the tide on Pierce's behalf.

The "issue" was employed as a calculated device by both sides. Protestants were told that one of Pierce's daughters had become a nun. Among Catholics, Scott was accused by Democrats of being hostile to foreigners, and characterized as a threat to their well-being because during the Mexican War he had approved the hanging of deserters who had happened to be Irish Catholics. At the same time, among Protestants, Scott was presented as being a Catholic sympathizer because he too had a daughter who had become a nun.

The issue reached such proportions that Scott was advised to take to the hustings to counter these charges by speeches and personal magnitude. He took a swing through the northeastern states. In Rochester, he used a theme he was to repeat in other cities where necessary:

I recognize before me persons of different parties, of different creeds, and of different countries. . . . I am proud to address native and adopted as American citizens. . . . (cheers). I am proud to belong to the same country with you all (cheers). I detect in those cheers, gentlemen, a brogue I am always happy to hear. I have been in many tight places in my life, but I have never been deceived or betrayed by that brogue (cheers). I have always been sustained by the natives of the glorious Emerald Isle. . . . We had a goodly number of Irish soldiers who fought bravely in the Mexican War, and as I said, they never disappointed me—always brave and faithful (loud and prolonged cheers).

I must be allowed to speak here of a miserable slander I understand is circulating among you. It is said I have misused Irishmen. Whoever utters this calumny lies (cheers). I would advise my Irish friends around me to give it the lie whenever they meet it. . . .[8]

In the closing stages of the campaign, attempts were made to get Archbishop Hughes of New York to urge a protest vote among Catholics against the New Hampshire religious test by casting their ballots for Scott.[9] It was reported darkly in the final week that August Belmont, a special agent and representative in New York of the great European bankers, the Rothschilds, and also the Austrian Consul General in New York, was an "active advocate" of the election of Pierce.[10]

After it was all over, the Democrats had won by a landslide. The plurality was over 28,000 in New York. Baltimore and Chicago, heavily Catholic centers, had gone for Pierce. Only Massachusetts, Vermont, Kentucky, and Tennessee went for Scott. The electoral vote was 254 to 42.[11]

Pierce named James Campbell, his Pennsylvania campaigner, to his cabinet as Postmaster General. The outcry that followed the appointment was a strong indication of the continuation of anti-foreign sentiment and also of its continued rise. A letter sent by the Pope to the new President fanned the fires. Rumors were circulated that Pierce was under the influence of the church, and articles were published to that effect. After being called anti-Catholic, Pierce now had moved to an alleged position of pro-Catholicism. The instability of the charges only serves to reflect the quick and easy political opportunism it was intended to serve.

Before the democracy was two generations old, four Presidents, Jefferson, Jackson, Polk, and Pierce, had had to face and overcome challenges based on religious grounds, and the issue seemed to be gathering force. At first it had been seen as irreligiousness versus established religion and morality. As vociferous advocates had urged closer ties between religion and government, it had become a matter of the principle of separation between church and state.

The issue developed further with the expansion of the electorate—and the appeal to sectarian animosities. Then, as people began to sense a national identity, the issue became linked to threats by foreign powers—and an alien religion. By the middle of the eighteenth century, the religious issue had become a full-fledged, double-edged device for political agitation.

In a sense, the history of sentiment against the Catholic in this country can be concentrated in the swing of a pendulum from one extreme to the other in a single century covering the years from about 1856. At that time seven governors, eight senators, and one hundred and four representatives were in office after campaigning largely on anti-Catholic sentiments. Almost exactly a century later, the nation could count nine governors, twelve senators, eighty-seven representatives, and a President who professed the Roman Catholic faith.

But midway through the nineteenth century, the nation was growing past older factional issues that had their roots in Old World soil to grapple with crises rooted in its own. Before the generation passed on, this was sharply to change the way in which the religious issue was dealt with. In 1853 a papal emissary named Bedini arrived from Rome. Bedini was here to settle controversies within the Catholic community, centering on whether church property in Buffalo and Philadelphia should legally be held in trusteeship by laymen or by the clergy. Also in America at the time was an Italian revolutionary, Gavazzi. Touring and lecturing, clothed as a monk, a blazing cross woven on the breast of his garb, he called for the "absolute destruction" of popery, and dubbed Bedini a "bloody butcher, . . . an advance agent of the Inquisition."[12] Americans took notice. Here was an actual foreigner (Bedini) in this country to settle affairs among American citizens. Who was he? Where was he from? What right did he have? He was an official of the Roman Catholic Church, a direct representative of the Pope. And who was listening to him, obediently abiding by his decisions? His subjects, citizens who were Roman Catholics, as well as priests of the church!

Bedini, after finishing his business in the two cities, decided not only to stay but also to tour as many American cities as he could. In Cincinnati he was threatened and mobbed. He was manhandled by irate crowds as he went through Wheeling, Baltimore, and other cities. As he moved into the South, threats of violence were directed at him, forcing changes in plans to visit several cities. A veritable craze swept the land, the disordered expression of a variety of sentiments connected with antiforeign and anti-Catholic feeling.[13]

A band of men in Washington one night removed a block of marble from a shed and managed to cart it to the Potomac, where they threw it in. The marble had been a gift from the Pope to the American people, to be placed as part of the Washington Monument, then being constructed.[14]

This was the high point of the Know-Nothing movement. The American Republican and Native American forces, striving for removal of the immigration threat, had got that name years earlier when they repeatedly answered queries about their activities by saying, "I know nothing." The name appeared on tea, candy, toothpicks, a stagecoach line, and a new clipper ship.[15]

In 1854's off-year elections for Congress, amid rioting in cities in Missouri, Kentucky, Massachusetts, Louisiana, and other states, candidates campaigning on the strength of Know-Nothing sentiments had occupied a majority of seats in the Houses of Massachusetts, Delaware, Pennsylvania, Maryland, and Kentucky.[16] In the national Congress there were eight senators out of sixty-two, and one hundred and four representatives out of two hundred and thirty-four, who had made these sentiments the predominant theme of their campaigns.

The national spectacle prompted a young lawyer in Illinois to write* to a friend: "As a nation, we began by declaring that 'all men are created equal.' We now practically read it 'all men are created equal except negroes.' " Continued Lincoln: "When the Know-Nothings get control, it will read 'all men are created equal except negroes, and foreigners, and catholics.' When it comes to this, I should prefer emigrating to some country where they make no pretense of loving liberty—to Russia, for instance, where despotism can be taken pure, and without the base alloy of hypocrisy."

* Letter to Joshua Speed, August 24, 1855. *The Collected Works of Abraham Lincoln*, Basler, Roy P., ed., New Brunswick, 1953, II, p. 323.

Of almost four hundred members of the Massachusetts Legislature in 1855, fewer than forty had served before or had any kind of real political experience. Many were farmers, mechanics, teachers, and tradesmen. All but several had declared themselves antiforeign and pro-American sentiments studded their platforms. A committee formed by the legislature to investigate convents, academies, and boarding schools to uncover any sinister activities or conspiracy whirled through its chores, intimidating nuns, running up a big bill for food, drink, and other pleasures, and uncovering nothing.[17]

Once elected to their positions, many legislators made occasional antiforeign speeches that were read into records and had the effect of placating the well-meaning citizens who had believed they would stem the "great conspiracy." But the only unity among legislators in any chamber seemed to be on matters of immigration.

In 1854 a bill providing for a twenty-one-year-period requirement for naturalization had been introduced in the United States Senate. The bill had died in committee. A similar bill met a like fate in the House. Occasional speeches on the subject were publicized. Support for immigration reforms came from the South and from labor groups in northern cities. When a bill was reintroduced in 1856, it was reported out by the committee but with the recommendation that it not pass. It did not. The House had a similar experience.

Now that antiforeign sentiment had prevailed, it became incorporated in a body of strangers and self-seekers surrounding a small core of conscientious proponents. In some quarters it was felt that a man might even be swept into the Presidency on the strength of the antiforeign, anti-Catholic feeling that continued to be effective as a vote-getting appeal. For the country could hardly unite on any other matter.

As the campaign of 1856 neared, there was a profusion of splinter parties, and the land was slowly being ripped by sectional controversies over the role of slavery in institutions and economy. Throughout much of the South, the anti-istic sentiment was traceable to the fact that continued immigration meant a growing predominance of the North in political strength and in manpower for its economy. Foreigners were doubly condemned, because they were "Northerners."

Sam Houston appeared in the running on a pro-American ticket. The nomination, however, went to Millard Fillmore, who reportedly received the news in Europe at about the time he had been granted an audience with the Pope. For the Democrats, it was noncontroversial James J. Buchanan, in sympathy with the South though a Northerner, on the seventeenth ballot. There was a strong tinge of crusade in both platforms.

The Democrats had approached John C. Frémont for the nomination for President, but Frémont demurred, saying he was against the extension of slavery. Slender, wiry, and tall, with Gallic eyes revealing a driving energy and poetic spirit, Frémont had trail-blazed into California, rousing the national imagination while still young, and had fought to retain the Territory for the United States. Following a military squabble over jurisdiction and obeying of orders, he had been court-martialed and then granted a presidential pardon by Polk. He had gone on to become a millionaire following the discovery of gold in California, and to serve in the United States Senate. Now, with slavery eclipsing everything else as an issue and looming even greater, the Republicans acclaimed Frémont. He became their candidate on the first ballot. United behind Frémont were many professional men and clergy, the eggheads of their day. William Cullen Bryant, Henry Wadsworth Longfellow, and Ralph Waldo Emerson all campaigned and involved themselves, out of moral sentiments, in the issue of slavery.

With Robert Emmet, an Irishman, as its chairman, the Democratic convention adopted a platform that criticized the "adverse political and religious test which has been secretly organized by a party claiming to be exclusively American."[18] It said the United States had been established and built upon the principle of "entire freedom in matters of religious concernment . . ." and declared, "no party can be justly deemed national, constitutional or in accordance with American principle which bases its exclusive organization upon religious opinions and accidental birthplace.

And hence a political crusade in the nineteenth century and in the United States . . . against Catholics and foreign born is neither justified by the past history of the country nor in unison with the spirit of toleration and enlightened freedom which particularly distinguishes the American system of popular government."[19]

Immediately, Frémont became the major object of abuse. Although the Democratic platform seemed to be quickly forgotten in the heat of a vicious campaign, and although it had been essentially a political document, it was significant. It represented an effort to redirect and guide what had become misdirected nationalistic zeal fallen prey to political opportunism. It tried further to channel political reality into the ways of the national ideal that had been established by declaration eighty years earlier.

Local Democratic stump speakers in some areas immediately charged that Frémont favored the Catholics, an interesting tack in the light of their party platform. At the same time, in other areas, Catholics were told that Frémont was sympathetic to the Know-Nothings. Know-Nothings, in turn, were told that he was a Catholic. Frémont indirectly aided the charges by refusing to deny that he was a Catholic, although he was really an Episcopalian. He maintained that to issue the denial would be to play into the hands of his enemies by participating in their tactics—seeking votes on a religious appeal.

A letter written by the editor of the *Freeman's Journal and Catholic Register* to a friend purported to confirm that Frémont was in reality a Catholic. If he denied it, the editor said, he "would brand him as a liar as I know the whole story of his life in Washington, and know that daily and for years he professed to be a Catholic and nothing but a Catholic."[20] The letter brought charges of "an open coalition" between the Jesuits and the Know-Nothings. That at least was a *new* twist! Then Archbishop Hughes of New York denounced the letter. That led to charges that he was secretly supporting Frémont.

While on a speaking tour Frémont was finally asked, "Are you or were you ever a Roman Catholic?" He "was not and never had been," the questioner reported. The report said Frémont had claimed that he "and his wife are members of the Episcopal Church; that his children have been baptized and confirmed in that Church, and that his daughter, instead of being educated in a Catholic cloister, received her entire education under his own roof."[21]

How many times had Frémont been in a Catholic church? "Possibly twelve or fifteen times—not more—and never except from motives of curiosity," was his reported reply.[22] Reports such as this one, ostensibly designed to counter the charges, were widely circulated. The abuse continued unabated. Pamphlets circulated in which Frémont's "Romanism" was allegedly established, and were quickly followed by refutations. "Frémont a Catholic," said one. "Frémont not a Catholic," proclaimed another. Political cartoons depicted Frémont standing before a line of various individuals, including a Negro, a Catholic priest, a "free lover," a laborer, a "women's righter," and a "Puritan prohibitionist"—all of whom were being told that they would be granted their wishes.[23]

In a lead editorial early in October a New York newspaper observed:

> Col. Frémont's religious sentiments have been canvassed with far more bitterness and ferocity than his political opinions . . . he is pronounced a liar . . . and the blackguardism is caught up and echoed by every Know-Nothing organ and orator in the country. The virulence and malignity of party politics seems to have let loose the vilest passions of the worst men in the whole community —and the whole atmosphere is polluted by their exhalatives.
>
> We are not in the least degree fearful of their effect upon the public mind. If they have any result other than to bring contempt upon their authors and render the man they aim to injure still dearer to the public heart, we shall have sadly mistaken the character of the American people.[24]

A scheme was advanced to depose Frémont if he was elected. It was to be "just as in the medieval days of popes and antipopes," by having Virginia, Georgia, the Carolinas, and other southern states join with President Pierce and with the Roman Catholic Church to deny his election and maintain the *status quo*, with the President (Pierce) to "possess himself of the treasures and archives of government." The scheme was proposed by a writer to a South Carolina newspaper who signed himself "A Devout Roman Catholic."[25]

In the middle of October, a report circulated that a "well-known Catholic priest" had himself administered the Eucharist to Frémont. The priest rapidly repudiated it.[26] In the closing weeks of the campaign, a man who had made a trip to Montreal to check once for all the allegations as to Frémont's Catholic birth declared that he had irrefutable evidence that Frémont had been born in Montreal of a Catholic father. Within several days a letter appeared from a Montrealer who had lived for thirty years in the neighborhood across the street from the house in which Frémont was allegedly born. It refuted the report entirely.[27]

The day before the election, a report said that the latest mail from California contained a charge by a United States Navy lieutenant that Frémont had been a Roman Catholic while in that state, and had told many people so. This too was denied. In a closing editorial, under a headline referring to "The Catholic Question," the New York *Daily Times* condemned the Whig-American party of Fillmore as a "tyrannical proscription against race and religion, unworthy of the greatness of our country."[28] In a postscript it lamented the immense "expense in cash" of a presidential contest, estimated at more than $75,000,000.[29]

Rumors circulated of bankers and brokers contributing heavily to the effort to block Frémont, in anxious anticipation of a rupture between North and South, causing the bottom to drop out of the stock market if he should win. Economically motivated sources promoting the "religious" issue were to be revealed in large scale as being at work in 1960. Meanwhile, it was clear that the "religious" issue had become a device involving more than honest differences or similarities in religious views.

At the conclusion James J. Buchanan had received more than 1,800,000 votes, nearly half a million more than Frémont. Although it had taken twelve years for the presidential vote to increase from two million (in 1840) to three million (1858), the total vote cast in the election now exceeded four million.[30] The electorate had been aroused. And Irish immigrants had entered the country at the rate of approximately 300,000 a year between 1845 and 1855.[31] Changes were coming, as signified by the greater increase in the popular vote. Fillmore captured about 875,000 votes, or 22 per cent of the total.[32]

The attacks on Frémont centered on the question of whether he was a Catholic. Nowhere can we find a trace of his being asked what *difference* that would make, and this is an important facet. The mere fact that Frémont was a Catholic—or was not— apparently would sway great numbers of voters. For the moment, the words "Catholic" and "foreign" meant conspiracy and potential tyranny. Charges inspired highly emotional and frequently irrational reactions. Catholicism automatically inspired rejection.

The sense of America as a pluralistic society was yet to take hold. Horace Greeley was striking this note when he declared in 1860, "He who votes in our election as an Irishman or a German has no moral right to vote at all."[33]

The pattern of Fillmore's voting strength reflected or suggested the diffused pro-American sentiment he and his party attracted. More dramatically, that sentiment on which his party had built its strength had switched to another party.

Much of the balloting for Fillmore merely represented a compromise position between the Democratic and new Republican parties. Fillmore's vote was spread out more or less evenly across the country. It was strongest in Louisiana, weakest in New England. He captured the electoral votes of only one state, Maryland.[34] Only in such areas as New Orleans and Baltimore was intense antipathy to Catholics probably the overriding motivation for voting for Fillmore's "American" party. New Orleans, where Fillmore was strong, had approximately 25,000 Catholics at the time. There also were that many in Missouri and Tennessee, the border states where Fillmore did best.

A sense of the state and of national destiny was beginning to grow, but the question now was what *kind* of state, what *kind* of destiny, a question that was just on the verge of being resolved. The Civil War loomed, "testing whether that nation or any nation so conceived and so dedicated, can long endure."

CHAPTER FIVE ✓

From HAYES
to GROVER CLEVELAND
The Catholic Vote

BEFORE THE CIVIL WAR AND THE CRUCIAL PERIOD OF TRANSFORMA-
tion into the industrial urban pluralistic society that followed,
religion in the United States seemed to be closer to Old World
roots than to modern America, despite the beginnings of epochal
advances. It was rooted in the antagonisms and conflicts of the
Old World and Middle Ages with their feudal territories and
wars and systems in which the church was bound closely to government.

The nativist sentiment was based on contemporary attitudes and
a picture of the world that was rooted in earlier generations, when
reverberations of old struggles were slow in dying. America was
still close to England and, in fact, to medieval religion. The Catholic Church was not then an "American" church. It was, in the
thinking of the nativist (and his English counterpart), an alien,
temporal power. Moreover, America was far from established as a
strong, independent, self-assured, self-sustaining industrial power.
And in its wobbly decades of slow struggle, it still was prey to
towering older forces and institutions, and countries. It was prepared to go to war for these aims, with Mexico, Spain, or any other
nation—even England.

The pre–Civil War clashes involving Irish Catholics continued,
and for a time flamed even higher in that great crucible. Negroes
had come into New York with almost the first Dutch settlers.
Usually they were found as household servants in twos and threes

47

at the better residences. It was a friendly kind of slavery, and even had its comforts. It was John Jay who, in New York before the turn of the century, had organized a group for the gradual emancipation of Negro slaves. Alexander Hamilton succeeded Jay as chairman. An emancipation law came about in 1799 chiefly through Federalist support, and in the first decade of the century eligible Negro freedmen were voting for the Whigs. As early as 1813 a legislator in Albany, New York, had declared that several hundred Negro votes in that state had determined an election in favor of the Federal party.[1]

From the first, some opposition to freeing the Negro had come in many instances from unskilled laborers, workers, mill hands, mechanics, and small tradesmen, who saw in them potential competitors. In early elections through 1830, Negroes usually voted Whig, and against Tammany. When drawings for the draft began in New York in early July, 1863, Negroes recently had been strikebreakers in a dispute on the docks where many strikers were Irish. The war was being dubbed "The war for the Negro." Many of those chosen in the draft were Irish workers, who could not pay the $300 that would have exempted them.

The friction erupted in several days of rioting. Mobs predominantly Irish wrecked the draft headquarters, raided homes, fought the police, destroyed a Negro home for orphans, and beat and hanged several Negroes. The draft was suspended; a regiment of troops aided police, many of whom were Irish, in restoring order. Archbishop Hughes sought to end the disorders by personal pleas. After four days the riots subsided. But in the election of 1864, Irish wards in New York went heavily for McClellan against Lincoln.[2] Several thousand Irishmen fought in the Army of the Confederacy, spurred by anti-Negro feelings and joblessness.

Great numbers of soldiers fighting in the Union Army were Irish, in greater proportion to their population than "native" soldiers. Many were recruited immediately upon their arrival in America, and many took up arms willingly in the hope that it might in some way eventually advance the cause of home rule in their native land. This hope most dramatically manifested itself in the fiasco of the Fenian expedition immediately after the war's end. In that episode, several thousand Irishmen "invaded" Canada from Buffalo, trying to free it from English rule. They were quickly dispersed with little harm.[3]

Out of the war came a stronger Roman Catholic Church in America. Most of its membership had been in the North, in the large cities. It had not been split by sectional or sectarian strife.

Protestant denominations, on the other hand, in many cases had suffered a splintering among themselves. Because of many factors, Irish Catholics had ceased to be a negative element to the degree that they had been in both North and South. These factors included their assimilation into the national strife, fighting often side by side with men who had had antiforeign sentiments before 1860, and their sharing what was a current rise of northern hostility to England as a result of her role in the war.

In 1872 the first Catholic candidate for President of the United States was nominated. Charles O'Conor, prominent in New York politics and counsel to Jefferson Davis in his trial for treason, was selected by an offshoot group of Democrats who had gathered support from a smattering of labor and states'-rights groups opposing the nomination of Horace Greeley, the regular Democratic candidate. In the national balloting, the first election in which a popular vote existed for presidential electors in every one of the thirty-seven states, O'Conor, who had not campaigned, polled just over 29,000 votes as Grant was swept in with 3,600,000 to Greeley's 2,800,000. In Georgia, O'Conor polled approximately 4,000 votes. In Illinois, around Chicago, he gained about 3,000. In New York, opposed by the regular Democratic Tammany organization, he received fewer than 1,500. The remainder of his total was spread throughout Iowa, Michigan, Kentucky, Missouri, and Texas.[4]

By 1876 the complexion of American society had radically changed from that of the decades before the Civil War. Transportation and industry began to mark the once rural land of great stretches outside the cities. The blight of unemployment began to hover, disappear, and return with a frequency that portended and reflected new currents. Yet the issues that marked the impending election were rooted in the past. The Civil War remained smoldering in the evils of Reconstruction as two million more people went to the polls in 1876 than had in 1872. Graft, corruption, lawlessness in high places gripped the country, caught in an economic depression in the very midst of the stirring of industrial expansion.

Samuel J. Tilden, governor of New York and recent prosecutor of the Tammany ring of Boss Tweed, was selected by the Democrats over the opposition of John Kelly, new Tammany head. In his drive for the nomination Tilden had been helped by a New York advertising concern that presented the results of a poll of "public opinion" among responsible citizens throughout the country.[5] Opposing Tilden was Rutherford B. Hayes, who won the nomination over James G. Blaine of Maine.

In the course of the campaign a "denunciation of the Romish Church" was issued, reportedly with Republican backing, in which the church was charged with trying to undermine the Republican party and the "free school system." James A. Garfield, who was to become President in 1880, wrote that "the combined power of rebellion, Catholicism and whisky" was defeating his party. He termed it "a trinity very hard to conquer; what the future of our country will be no one can tell."[6]

The campaign turned on other matters as the race drew closer. Eventually it was to be won by Hayes. The religious issue—now clearly the Catholic issue—had refused to die in the transition of the country. Its spark had been saved to light new fires in modern America. But a greater flame was to spread and counter these fires of bigotry across the new land.

As America advanced into the 1890's, class interests based on economic levels seemed to intrude into the very web of the affairs of daily society. Some even feared revolution.[7] Labor was agitating for a vote in the higher councils. It was the time of the robber barons and the building of the great American fortunes. Extremes of wealth and poverty existed sometimes almost side by side.

Democrats, representing themselves as the poor man's party, gained control of the House but had been unable to elect a President since before the Civil War in 1856. They too had their internal warfare. In 1882 in New York, downstate Tammany had clashed with upstate political leaders who had prevailed and cleared the way for a new reform mayor of Buffalo to move into the governor's chair. Grover Cleveland, "who talks well on any subject with which he's familiar and on any subject with which he's not familiar does not talk at all . . ."[8] had for two years as mayor brought money-hungry politicians up short with his successive vetoes of sewage and street-cleaning contract proposals. He served both Republicans and Democrats as a liaison peacemaker with the people.

Now he was being pushed as a candidate for President. For the Republicans, the "plumed knight" James G. Blaine, who had been with Garfield when he was assassinated in the Washington, D.C., railroad station, was the foremost contender. At the convention, Henry Cabot Lodge worked busily behind the scenes, and young Theodore Roosevelt addressed the assembled party stalwarts for the first time. Blaine had almost made it in 1876 and again in 1880. By 1884 he'd been senator, Speaker of the House, and Secretary of State. Miss Frances E. Willard came to the Republican convention with a petition signed by 20,000 persons urging prohibition. Brewers and distillers there ridiculed the petition, and party chieftains, anxious for their major support, obliged. The petition was discarded and left to gather dust.

At the convention the enthusiasm that had built up for Blaine over the years burst loose. But there were strong misgivings about his nomination in some quarters. Blaine had lobbied for railroad interests in Washington, and a scandal had developed in 1876 in which he had been accused of preferential treatment in return for his services. Democrats at the time had moved to have him expelled from the House, but an impassioned defense plea helped forestall the maneuver.

Blaine also had a longer history that was referred to by opponents. In 1861 he had recommended a particular manufacturer's rifle to the Secretary of War. The company received an order for several thousand from the government, and Blaine received stock in the company. While Democratic opponents of Cleveland called him a friend of capitalists, Blaine's detractors labeled him an enemy of the workingman. A group of Republicans threatened to bolt if Blaine were nominated, and even appealed to the Democrats to give them a candidate they could support.

At the Democratic convention Tammany fought the nomination of Cleveland. A delegate from Wisconsin arose to proclaim that the convention was fed up with Tammany's squabbles and greed. Cleveland was loved, declared the delegate, not only for his character but also for the enemies he had made.[9] A Tammany leader replied that on behalf of Cleveland's enemies, he reciprocated the statement. Tammany John Kelly's opposition at the convention stemmed from rocklike Presbyterian Grover Cleveland's alignment with the upstate element in the party that Kelly was fighting. Cleveland had refused him much patronage upon assuming the governorship, and had vetoed a bill appropriating state funds for a Catholic shelter in New York City, maintaining that it was a bad precedent and that it was the city's business anyway. Tammany claimed that Cleveland would not be able to carry his own state of New York because he had alienated Roman Catholics and Irish and the laborer.

"The cry has gone up," reported the New York *Times,* "that Mr. Cleveland is against the Irish, therefore the Irish of his state are against him."[10] Two Catholic state officials whom Cleveland had appointed as heads of their departments went with a former Catholic senator from New York to counter these charges. Tammany continued to speak against him. Said one, "I do not believe he has the mental qualifications."[11]

The charge of alienating the workingman grew out of Cleveland's veto, as governor, of a bill proposing a five-cent fare in New York. This made several New York bankers and corporation heads sit up and take notice, thinking that he might not be such a bad fellow after all.

Most of the New York delegation favored Cleveland, but he still needed every vote he could get. Tammany's faction in the delegation sought to lift the unit rule (in which a delegation's entire vote goes to the candidate preferred by a majority of that group), so that it might have its votes counted against Cleveland. But the rule was upheld, and Cleveland was assured of the nomination.[12]

So here was James G. Blaine, charming, able, magnetic, facile, son of once-wealthy parents, sarcastic and quick as a debater, yet with dignity and polish . . . and Grover Cleveland, scrupulously honest, beefy, burly, steady, deliberate, the "hangman of Buffalo" who as sheriff once had hanged a condemned man himself; stolid, blunt, caring little for social amenities; a generally immobile face, mute but resolute, sincere; his mother the daughter of an Irishman, his father a Presbyterian minister.

Blaine too had Roman Catholic antecedents. His mother was a Catholic, and a cousin was then the mother superior of a convent. Moreover, as Secretary of State at a time when Parnell and the Irish Land League were struggling against absentee English landlords, Blaine had exhibited some animosity toward the British. All this stood him in good stead now with Irishmen. The *Irish World*, an influential paper, backed him early in the campaign. Another, the *Irish Nation*, followed suit shortly. Some Irishmen declared that if Blaine were elected, Ireland would be free within thirty days. Veterans of the Irish Fenian "invasion" of Canada and of battles in the old country worked for him in the Midwest, and in Chicago.[13] Suddenly half a million Irish votes were at stake. It appeared that the Irish Catholic vote, which for several decades had been a mainspring of Democratic strength, was not at all a sure thing in the election.

In New York in July there was a Blaine rally at which prominent Tammany men appeared on the platform. John Kelly, the Tammany head, had been slow in coming around to Cleveland. He was still reportedly weighing it in August when he expressed a wish that Cleveland withdraw. Tammany, meanwhile, campaigned only halfheartedly for Cleveland. For their part, the Republicans aimed strongly for "the Irish vote," Blaine himself intimating strong steps against Britain if he were elected.

Now undercover charges were circulated to the effect that Cleveland was in fact anti-Catholic, that he was a "Presbyterian bigot." The bishops of Albany and Buffalo immediately issued condemnations and denials.

Cleveland conferred with a prominent Irish Catholic from Boston, Patrick Collins, who subsequently made a series of speeches in his support. Campaign headquarters for the Democrats saw to it that they received wide dissemination among Irish Catholics. Michael Corrigan, Archbishop of New York, in a letter to James Cardinal Gibbons of Baltimore, noted that he was being approached by Democrats asking his help in holding the Irish votes. He expressed "amusement" at the thought that he held any such sway over the voters.

Blaine's campaign took him through New York and out into West Virginia, Ohio, Indiana, and Illinois. There was a wave of thefts of watches and other valuables in the campaign crowds. In Brooklyn, Blaine was greeted in a driving October rainstorm by "a wild shrill, almost deafening scream from 3,000 female throats,"[14] and went on to tell his audience that he attributed the conduct of his young male supporters to the counsel of their mothers. The Republican party, he said, owed a great deal to the women of the United States, maintaining that women wielded an influence greater than votes. Meanwhile, Cleveland stayed in Albany most of the time, occasionally speaking at county fairs, sometimes in New Jersey or nearby Connecticut. As the election campaign entered its final weeks, it remained close, and Tammany's opposition and the vote in New York took on increased significance. The Republicans had bitter second thoughts about the defection of the highbrow independent Republicans opposed to Blaine.

As Blaine returned East from a strenuous speaking tour in the last week of October, he went to New York City to attend a fund-raising dinner given by a group of the most powerful figures in banking, finance, and business, and to make one more swing of the Irish Catholic territories. On the morning of October 29th, at the Park Avenue Hotel in New York, several hundred clergymen gathered from in and around the city. Invited by word of mouth or by a printed, unsigned card sent by a minister working with the Republican National Committee, they were there to meet the candidate and to present him with a number of resolutions. They selected the Reverend Samuel D. Burchard, pastor with the longest consecutive service in the city, as chairman. James King, well acquainted with Blaine, was asked to bring the candidate down to meet his guests. King introduced Blaine to Dr. Burchard and the assembled ministers, and then Dr. Burchard made a short welcoming statement.

In it he said: "We expect to vote for you next Tuesday. We are Republicans and don't propose to leave our party and identify ourselves with the party whose antecedents have been *rum, Romanism and rebellion*."[15] Newsmen present did not hear the few short words, but a shorthand reporter on the pay roll of the Democratic campaign committee took the entire statement down verbatim as part of his general coverage chore.

The party then moved into the ballroom, where various ministers addressed the group. It was after the third or fourth of these speeches that Blaine, sitting next to King, turned and said, "That 'rum, Romanism and rebellion' remark of Dr. Burchard's is exceedingly unfortunate."[16] Blaine suggested that King see the editor of one of the papers, a close friend, and with his aid get reporters to suppress the remark. After several more speeches, Blaine made a brief address and the session concluded. The shorthand reporter took his notes to Democratic headquarters and began reading them to Arthur Pue Gorman, head of the campaign executive committee.

When Gorman heard the rum, Romanism and rebellion phrase he exclaimed, "Write that out!"[17] Within a few days handbills carried the remark to almost every Roman Catholic parish in the East.

James King called on Dr. Burchard, who was "crushed under the consciousness of having been the declared instrument of injury," and tried to get him to write a letter to the newspapers which was to have read:

In addressing Mr. Blaine on October 29, I used the phrase rum, Romanism and rebellion in characterizing some of our political opponents. I would desire simply to say that perhaps the remark was inopportune and under the circumstances it would have been more politic not to have made it. But I also desire to say that while the utterance might have been in timeliness inexpedient, it embodied historical and painful truth and as an individual citizen I assume the responsibility for its accuracy.[18]

Dr. Burchard "declined to place himself on the record in this way," King said later.[19] For his part, Blaine issued a firm denunciation and repudiation of the statement almost immediately. "An unfortunate expression of another man," he said, calling himself incapable of making "a disrespectful allusion to that ancient faith in which my revered mother lived and died."[20]

On Sunday, November 2nd, priests spoke from their pulpits. Said one, the Reverend Edward McGlynn, already pro-Cleveland, "Few Catholics will vote for the old Know-Nothing who to this day is but too willing to avail himself of Know-Nothing prejudice, and what makes it worse, not from anything like honest passion or prejudice, but from cold-blooded self-interest."[21] He alluded to a circular Blaine had sent as editor of the *Kennebec Journal* in Maine, expressing Know-Nothing sentiments against a "reputable Irish American and candidate for Congress" just a few years earlier.

A priest in Hartford assailed Blaine's "bribery and corruption" in contrast to Cleveland, the "embodiment of honesty." Noting Cleveland's moral taint in a paternity scandal, however, the speaker advised his listeners to "choose the lesser of two evils," and denounced "Blaine's renunciaton of the Catholic religion."[22]

Republican campaigners distributed millions of sheets attempting to offset the effects of the remark during that Saturday, Sunday, and Monday. But the Democrats had done such an effective job of distributing copies of the Burchard phrase that nearly every Roman Catholic family heard of it. And the election was just a few days away.

Before leaving New York, Blaine attended a fund-raising banquet where it is reported he "turned down his glass and did not taste wine."[23] He was met with a disconcertingly cool reception in the coffers, although all heartily applauded in his presence. Several bankers and businessmen had contributed much to Democratic funds, heartened by Cleveland's moderate declarations and actions on labor, and feeling more assured with his rock-bound character than with a facile and brilliant opportunist. The banquet was given a big play in the morning newspapers. Cartoons depicted a starving, scrawny workingman and his family on the outside looking in. It seemed dramatically to polarize the issue. Moreover, prohibitionists were stirred to new heights of condemnation by the event.

Election day dawned cloudy, and it rained torrents in upstate New York. Late in the day, after dinner, Cleveland and several close associates retired to the library. No telegraph was hooked into the circuits of the house, and the telephone was out of commission because of the rainstorm. As results began to arrive by messenger, it appeared that in Irish Catholic districts Blaine was running ahead of what Garfield had polled four years earlier.[24] After a late group snack at nearly midnight, Cleveland said he was going to bed. His associates stayed, and began notifying county leaders to keep a close watch on the returns. In New York's Madison Square, in the drenching downpour, a stereopticon flashed the returns by projected slides, mixed with occasional advertisements.

The election remained undecided for three days. Cleveland was certain he had won, although the Associated Press claimed Blaine was victorious. New York's secretary of state told reporters, "There is no chance of stealing this state, not so long as I have charge of the affair."[25] Blaine, at his home in Maine, expressed the judgment that a majority of the voters in New York State had "cast their ballots for the Republican electoral ticket. To quote my own saying on an important occasion, 'Any party in the United States can bear to be defeated, but no party will bear to be defrauded.' "[26] He had full confidence that he had been elected, and fairly so.

The *Tribune* in New York refused to concede the election, and the people waited. On November 8, as a Fourth Avenue streetcar passed the *Times* office, a newsboy hopped aboard shouting, "Extree, Extree!" A fine-clothed gentleman plunged hand into pocket and drew forth some change. But as he reached for the paper a sudden thought made him pause in mid-gesture.

"Who's elected?" he asked.

"Cleveland," said the newsboy.

The prospective customer put the change back in his pocket and sat down. "I won't buy it," he said. "It's a lying sheet anyhow!"[27]

Angry crowds milled about the Western Union Building in New York, charging that results were being deliberately delayed. Financial wizard Jay Gould wired his congratulations to Cleveland as the crowds threatened to dispense violence against his company's premises.

In another few days it was declared official, although results from some districts still were being contested. Cleveland had carried New York State by 1,149 votes, and its bloc of electoral votes gave him a total of 183 to Blaine's 182. Nationally, of a total of 10,000,000 votes, the Democratic plurality was 68,299. A switch of 600 votes in New York could have changed the outcome.

There is no question about the importance of the Irish Catholic vote. But although it never can be pointed to infallibly as *the* decisive factor, it is significant because of its effect. It was seen as the single most responsible factor by many contemporary observers. When men see things as real, whether they are or not, they are real in their consequences. And the matter of the Burchard remark and its effect on the voting was real in its consequences as a consideration in presidential politics during succeeding campaigns.

Both parties, realizing early in the campaign that the Irish vote was far from assured, saw this group not only for the first time as one to be zealously courted, but also as one they could not afford to offend. If there had been any doubts about this before, they were now abruptly discarded. For the first time, the disjointed and sometimes scattered vote of the immigrant was turned into an effective bloc. The minorities had found a new weapon, their first really effective one in a hostile land. Even if the bloc was not actually a reality, it was treated as one, and that produced the same results. The weapon was displayed, demonstrated, and respected from that day forward.

The dictates of practical politics were joined for the first time with democratic ideals, although representing only a tentative and grudging alliance. The form of the issue also should stand close scrutiny. Just as the differentiation between spiritual and temporal allegiance was lost on many in the early part of the nineteenth century, the issue of Catholicism in 1884 actually was linked more closely to foreign national sentiments than to any domestic relevance. Romanism, and all that it implied, had been described as "antecedent."

And once American Catholics became just that—American—and the controversy became one without any significant foreign complications, the pressure was all toward resolution under this society's principles and practices.

CHAPTER SIX

ROOSEVELT, WILSON,
and the Shaping of Modern America

"The spirit of the country has changed much"

IN 1884 A COUNTRY ON THE THRESHOLD OF AN INDUSTRIAL REVOLU-
tion had seen a potent minority wield for the first time a weapon
rightfully granted—the vote. Forty-four years later a changed
country witnessed a member of that minority group in a bid for
its leadership. In the interim the entrenchment of capitalism, the
firm establishment of an organized labor movement, a major
world war, the rise of modern mass media and aviation, and a
"noble experiment" in legislated morality had combined with the
addition of nearly 25,000,000 immigrants to forge on the mighty
anvil of industrialism the beginnings of modern America.

No single factor was more crucial than the coming of the immigrants in unprecedented numbers over a shorter period of time
than ever before. In several single years more than a million came
annually. They arrived fresh from the Old World in a vast new
land that reeled dizzily from a wealth of growing pains. Recognition had come with practical and dramatic suddenness in
1884. Chastened by the swift decisiveness of the issue, politicians
sought to make their peace with the giant. Cleveland's administration named a prominent Fenian, William Roberts, as minister to
Chile. The dispensing of patronage in Minnesota through two
Irishmen led to rural opposition. The Minneapolis *Tribune*
dubbed them the "pro-consuls of the province."[1]

As early as the first decade after the Civil War the *Catholic*

World had observed the tenement packing and "vice, immorality, pauperism, disease and depravity" in New York, and was moved to declare that "the physical wants of these unfortunate classes should awaken in us serious consideration."[2] In the church the immigrant found a ready-made organization, eager to help him in his quest, anxious to minister to his whole person. Shortly after the middle of the century Orestes Brownson noted that the "conversion of bad Catholics, the proper training of Catholic children, the correction of the vice of intemperance, and other immoralities prevalent in a portion of our Catholic population . . ." would do more than any other efforts to prove "the practical moral efficiency of our religion."[3]

In a natural formula, the nativist resistance increased as the number of immigrants multiplied. In 1900 there still were 46,000,000 rural residents against 30,000,000 urban ones.[4] But the threat was plain to the nativist. Long-time resentments still lived. The newly arrived man was still alien; more than ever, it seemed. Atop that, he brought with him allegiance to his European church. Also, the threat was more serious than ever that the long-time working-class inhabitant would be priced out of the labor market. And now a new threat—bloc voting—added to his worries. The melting pot was coming to a boil, heated by the flames of domestic troubles. The fact that each lived in his own America helped delay the inevitable test of strength. If each stayed in his own place, things might turn out all right. It was a country of separated areas, in which railroads were the only link and "mobile" was a word to describe an agile horseman.

But the two Americas were growing, each with its own class of inhabitants, and becoming more unavoidably involved each day. Each was not staying in his place. Interdependence increased at a tremendous rate. Strikes, for example, such as the great Pullman strike of 1894, now had repercussions throughout the entire political and social body. Today the diet of an African in the Congo is accepted as a matter of legitimate concern to Americans. In the late nineteenth century Americans were yet fully to accept even their responsibility for a starving miner in Illinois or a sweatshop worker in New York City. Social welfare movements were just beginning. The economy was still largely agricultural, but the rapid rise of industrialism after the Civil War was bringing great changes.

The old days when a man earned what he got by honest, plain hard work were giving way to speculation, investment, and profiteering. Individual initiative, enterprise, and self-reliance, traits that had seemed to mark the heart of the American character, were now seemingly growing anachronistic as a complex new industrial society billowed. The old individualism was even coming to be viewed as irresponsible in view of the interdependence and complexities of arising social problems. Social consciousness became a new virtue. In contrast to the old individualism there stood the city masses, the huddled poor, the refuse of teeming foreign shores who, despite strong drives to make their fortune and their place, however large or small, in this new land of individual opportunity, stood rather helpless and in need of aid. The Catholic Church was moving with increasing swiftness into the breach. Protestant churches remained identified with the old virtues, the old individualism, and the fortunes it had produced.

Protestantism was now the religion of the rural resident and of the rich. It had been withering into a social religion sans competition, growing out of touch with the new society, as it had at first in the colonies. Now it committed itself on an unprecedented scale to social involvement. It was the era of the social gospel. Seminaries began to offer courses in labor, the family, penology, charity organizations, and municipal reform. Gymnasiums and sewing groups and community centers thrived. Church leaders fought for shorter working hours, industrial controls, civil liberties, public works, unemployment insurance, old-age pensions, child-labor laws, and later even a "better distribution of wealth and income."[5]

The urgency of the problem was recognized politically in such doctrines as that cited by Colonel Edward House, Woodrow Wilson's close adviser: "No war of classes," House had written, quoting Mazzini in a book describing the new order, "no hostility to existing wealth, no wanton or unjust violation of the rights of property, but a constant disposition to ameliorate the condition of the classes least favored by fortune."[6] In Wilson's social legislation, the "social gospel" achieved recognition on a new scale. Here was the birth of the new concept for a new society that eventually found full expression in the programs and philosophy of the New Deal.

Following the rise of Theodore Roosevelt's progressivism in 1912, Woodrow Wilson's 1916 victory was significant as the first in which the modern Democratic coalition jelled.

Wilson "carried 200 counties that had never been Democratic in a two-party contest prior to that time."[7] The location of these counties across the country was noteworthy. In Ohio they included Cleveland, Columbus, and the Shore counties, all industrial, with heavy concentrations of ethnic minorities. In Pennsylvania, they consisted of mining, oil, steel, and railroad workers in many sections throughout the state. In New York State, Kings and Bronx counties joined Manhattan as a Democratic stronghold. In Rhode Island, Providence went Democratic for the first time. In Minnesota, areas around Minneapolis and St. Paul, and the ore fields and ports of Duluth and Hibbing in the north, went into the Democratic column.

The Socialist and the Progressive votes had dwindled by hundreds of thousands. After volatile and massive changes in the electorate through the nineteenth century, the shape of modern Democratic power had arisen.

Wilson seemed to many immigrants in his idealism to represent the first clear ringing voice of opportunity and of America's founding conscience since Lincoln.

The old America was passing forever. In the new America that was emerging, Catholicism began to seem better suited to cope with conditions and problems. Individual contacts gave way to remoteness, to a mass society, to collectivism and the vying of interests. "Neighborliness" and "charity" as early rural America had known them were growing less effective in relations between men. Systems—even systems of charity—were replacing individual responsibility. From a society in which relations were run largely on custom and habit we were becoming a society run by contract, by law.

The Catholic Church, increasingly striving to aid its children, now seemed an order that retained some regard for the individual, as had Protestantism in earlier American society. Wilson readily acknowledged the relevant role of the Roman Catholic Church in the new America. He left little doubt about his attitude when he said in 1912: "The only reason why government did not suffer dry rot in the Middle Ages . . . was that so many of the men who were efficient instruments of government were drawn from the Church—from that great body which was then the only Church, that body which we now distinguish from other religious bodies as the Roman Catholic Church. . . . [It] was then, as it is now, a great democracy."[8]

Wilson was, in effect, according the highest possible degree of public recognition and acceptance to the Roman Catholic Church in America since perhaps the Revolution. The implication was clear. The church "belonged." It was not a foreign church, an alien church, or the immigrant's church. It possessed the most central characteristic of the new nation—democracy. The threat, however, was by no means all alien.

To add to the frictions, the first great national conflicts between science and religion began to appear. Science was acclaimed by Robert Ingersoll as "the only true religion, the only savior of the world."[9] This from the man who placed James G. Blaine in nomination at the Republican convention in Chicago in 1876. In 1885 the Congregationalist minister-author Josiah Strong published a thesis, called *Our Country*, in which he foresaw no limit to American expansion because of the natural superiority of the Anglo-Saxon. To support his theory he quoted religion's biggest thought threat of the generation—Darwin.

If Protestantism thrived on challenge, it was in for much more, too. Crooked political machines were running at full speed on the oil of indifference. Huge power trusts were operating, too, and the rich were getting richer as they rode atop the unparalleled expansion of manpower. One set of statistics showed that 1 per cent of the nation's population had more money than the other 99.[10] The New York *Tribune* in 1892 compiled information on the millionaires of the country, who were sprouting like spring seeds. It showed that there were sixty-five lawyers among the country's millionaires, but only twenty-six farmers—and most of these were absentee landlords.[11]

And still the immigrants kept coming. New York now had twice as many Irish as Dublin, as many Germans as Hamburg. In some of its slum sections, the population density was over 1,000 per acre—greater than in Bombay.

Nationally, in the closing decades of the nineteenth century, the economy was sliding. Farm prices were skidding, and the workingman was underpaid. It was the time of the Haymarket riot in Chicago. This is what the Protestant community and the country faced as the century was ending.

The Roman Catholic Church was consolidating its position as an American church rather than a foreign one. Its priests were now Americans, born and bred in the texture of its society. Germans and Italians and other Catholics arriving in America began to confront an American Catholic Church that increasingly wove itself into the social currents of the new society, not the Old World's. Increasingly the church came to the forefront in the social struggles of the day. Irishmen were often prominent among the leaders of labor movements that sometimes employed extreme measures in combating powerful bosses. Hope for reward in the next world "is not the doctrine to preach the honest laborers of this century," said Father Edward McGlynn.[12] In 1886 Rome issued a condemnation of the Knights of Labor in Quebec. The action was met with loud protests from many Catholic workers. To church fathers, the Knights, with its unholy alliance of Protestants, atheists, communists, and socialists, meant danger.

The workers saw it in a different light. The newly appointed Cardinal of Baltimore, James Gibbons, appealed to Rome to lift its condemnation, maintaining that the issue involved "the fundamental interests of the Church and of human society for the future."[13] "To lose the heart of the people," said the Cardinal, "would be a misfortune for which the friendship of the few rich and powerful would be no compensation."[14] The church could emerge as a religious alternative to socialism, which was on the rise, feeding on labor unrest and social inequality. (In 1912 the Socialist party candidate for President was to poll more than 800,000 votes.) A new doctrine, that of "social justice," began to find receptive ground in the hierarchy.

In May, 1891, Pope Leo XIII issued the *Rerum novarum*. It proclaimed that social justice was to be found in mediating between relatively unchecked laissez faire, on one hand, and socialism—which held the threat of statist tyranny—on the other. In contrast to the socialist tenet of communal goods, the "inviolability of private property," and of every man's right to hold it, was to be a guiding principle.[15] Social justice involved the maintenance of harmony between capital and labor, both of which had an important role in the state. Moreover, relief of poverty and philanthropy was deemed desirable activity on the part of those who enjoyed a surplus of private wealth. The *Rerum novarum* called for a shorter working day, no Sunday labor, and regulation of child and woman labor, all with an eye to making possible "reasonable comfort" on the part of the individual.

The theories on land reform advanced by one of the new radicals of the day, Henry George, were well received by the Irish Land League, a powerful contemporary group that sought to abolish the absentee landlordism that was ruining Ireland. Cardinal Gibbons appealed to Rome when George's work *Progress and Poverty* was about to be placed on the Index of prohibited books of the Church, and was successful in his effort to prevent the inclusion. In a series of strikes in the final decade of the century, Archbishop John Ireland, in Minnesota, acted as a mediator, and made frequent appeals for social reform.

Clearly, the time was ripe for an alliance against the newcomers. Several were to come, riding the spirit of fear created by the foreigners. They were different from earlier movements in that they lashed out almost exclusively at the religion. But they were of the same ingredients as their predecessors, using some of the same old weapons and appealing to the same prejudices. Inevitably, people began to fight back at the forces that seemed to be inundating them. Outside the cities, a host of groups grew by 1891 into the People's party, the Populists. In the larger cities reform movements led by clergymen sprang into existence, battling Tammany Hall and other machines. As these forces began to move, they gathered together in a new spirit of unity, forming an alliance.

In searching for grounds for consensus, the older Americans found it in things spiritual or tinged with morality. The old, minor differences faded. Now again it was Protestant versus Catholic, and the word Protestant itself took on a new meaning. Progressive religion was out, and in its place came fundamentalism, doctrinaire belief. Firmness was needed. "I am a Know-Nothing in politics," declared Sam Jones, a leading revivalist of the day, in 1889. No longer was it temperance versus intemperance. Now it was prohibition versus the liquor craze. Temperance was sufficient for normal times, but here was a major threat. A moral crusade was under way.

Almost simultaneously, bigotry again took shape as a potent, coldly employed tool. Its wielders began to reveal some more or less uniform characteristics. Several men and women who billed themselves as ex-priests and nuns are good examples. A French-Canadian named Chiniquy was one of these "ex-priests." Then in his eighties, he claimed to have known of a Jesuit plot to assassinate Lincoln. Chiniquy said he had warned Lincoln after hearing of the plot from Samuel F. B. Morse. Then he claimed he heard of it again from Jesuits. Later, he said, he'd been told by priests that Lincoln was dead and that they had told him hours before the actual assassination![16] (Old canards die hard; this one was still being told a half-century later, when John F. Kennedy was campaigning.)

Then, as is frequently the case today, isolated, poorly educated and endowed individuals with sociopathologic family situations were preyed upon by the ministers of hate. They found ready followers in these victims of what they regarded as a world at large rapidly becoming alien, threatening, and unfathomable.

Hate literature flourished in an intense effort to stop or at least slow down immigration. Ottmar Mergenthaler's new Linotype machine arrived just in time for the venom writers. Bigotry became a profitable business.

Leading the attack was the American Protective Association, headed by Henry F. Bowers out of Iowa. Grasping at every available incident, the A.P.A. told the nation in millions of printed words of the "papal threat" to destroy democracy. Priests in confessionals were said to be baiting traps to lure young women; convents were "dens of horror" where unwanted infants were murdered and carnal abuses were rampant.[17] The charges now did not retain quite the impact they had made when first issued. The country and its people had moved forward somewhat since then. The foreign conspirator had become more an American instigator in the eyes of the fearful. Yet Irish still were characterized in this hate literature as members of a vast papal army that was awaiting only the inevitable Vatican signal before rising up with arms to overthrow the government in the name of Rome.[18]

After all, the Irish were already entrenched in nearby Chicago, some claiming that it had a Catholic mayor, police chief, and fire chief, and that more than half of its policemen and teachers were Irish.[19] And Irish elements also led political movements in other cities: Boston, Milwaukee, Brooklyn, Jersey City, Indianapolis, Cleveland, Philadelphia, and Buffalo.

The political machines drew the brunt of nativist condemnation. And in turn, the nativist drew the political wrath of the newcomers. The diatribe wouldn't be stopped even in the face of truth. At the peak of its power the A.P.A. claimed to be responsible for abolishing political regimes in several states, and for helping to elect dozens of congressmen. Hundreds of pamphlets and speeches went unchallenged, although an irate public sometimes protested at the obvious lies of the bigots. A woman claiming to be a former nun was greeted with a shower of overripe fruit in upstate New York when she unfolded her tale of convent eroticism. A former priest and his new wife with a similar story needed the assistance of armed militia in Georgia to escape a furious crowd of Catholics. The A.P.A. immediately attacked these demonstrations against what it called "free speech."

Responsible Protestant voices were nearly useless. Spurious "revelations" were common. One blatant mind even invented a papal encyclical, reportedly issued by Pope Leo XIII, in which American Catholics were ordered to burn the houses of heretics.[20]

Most popular of all the disclosures was that of the Knights of Columbus "oath" which pledged "relentless war, secretly and openly, against all heretics, Protestants and Masons." In a subsequent repudiation before Congress, the "oath" was read into the *Congressional Record*. Hatemongers turned that around, quoting the *Record* for proof of the oath's existence.

An especially virulent anti-Catholic, Senator Thomas E. Watson, of Georgia, was responsible for many attacks upon the newcomers. He helped spread the infamous *Awful Disclosures of Maria Monk*, originally published in 1836. On the frontispiece of the book was the dedicatory reference: "Come out of her, my people, that ye be not partakers of her sins, and that ye receive not of her plagues."[21] In the preface, Maria says: "The mere recollection of it makes me miserable . . . sometimes I think I can hear the shrieks of helpless females in the hands of atrocious men. . . ." While full of innuendoes, the book did not fail to specify the "horrors" of the convent, even including the penances required. If unable to answer a catechism question correctly, for example, the nuns were "obliged to kneel down upon as many dry peas as there were verses in the chapter out of which they were questioned . . ." and this felt after a time like "needles running through the skin."[22]

Maria told of her alleged mistreatment by a priest: "In a private apartment he treated me in a brutal manner; and from two other priests I afterward received similar usage that evening," after which she was, with the first priest, "compelled to remain in company with him until morning."[23] She then described a secret passageway, linked to a seminary across the street; a macabre "coffin-warming" ceremony and other "recollections." She told of infants born in the convent who were "always baptized and immediately strangled . . . [to secure] their everlasting happiness," and described a triple suicide of nuns.

Finally Maria related an episode in which several nuns, she among them, were allegedly sent to drag before the bishop a "beautiful young nun . . . about twenty, with light hair, blue eyes, and a very fair complexion and . . . a look of meekness." When confronted by priests, questioned, and told to repent for some comments she was reported to have made, the nun said she "would rather die than cause the murder of harmless babes."[24]

"That is enough, finish her," the bishop is reported to have said. Then, according to the book, the young woman was set upon by nuns and priests, gagged, and put face upward on a bed. Another bed was thrown upon her; priests and nuns jumped and stamped on it, up and down, to trample her without leaving a mark. After some minutes of this, "no motion" was seen, and the priests and nuns began to laugh and joke aloud.

The lifeless young form then allegedly was dragged down to the cellar and tossed into a pit described earlier as "a hole dug so deep into the earth that I could perceive no bottom . . . twelve to fifteen feet across," with lime spread on its sides. "This must be the place," she decided, "where the infants were buried after being murdered."[25]

Such obvious discrepancies as the no-evidence murder scene, followed by burial so that the slayers' marks wouldn't have made a difference, apparently went unnoticed. Aroused investigators had examined the purported center of this activity, the Hôtel Dieu Nunnery at Montreal, and discredited her story when it was first published, fifty years before Watson. But thousands read the book, and the stories no doubt increased in horror as the accounts spread. This type of hate literature grew more popular because it offered rationalization; if this were true, here was a good, solid reason to hate the Catholic hierarchy (and also its followers, those same foreigners who threatened a way of life). And with little organization to combat the disclosures, they spread quickly.

Throughout the book a pattern is evident. Nuns and priests were repeatedly described as "rough," "gross," and "ignorant." The book was going to a relatively homogeneous public, Protestant upper-class gentry more than lower-class readers. The threat of the Roman Catholic Church was equated with that of a band of uncouth roughnecks, thus arousing class sensibilities.

It propagandized baldly. Maria described the gift of a large, richly woven rug to the King of England "as an expression of gratitude for the money received annually from the government,"[26] and told of other convents that had "received funds from the government." In 1836 this had been an explosive issue. We were then at loggerheads with England. Even now, in the tempestuous 1880's and 1890's, it retained some sting.

The image of the church as a secret conspiracy continued, and found currency in such passages from Maria Monk as the following: "Go where I might, I should meet men informed about me and my escape . . . fully empowered to seize me wherever they could, and convey me back to the convent from which I had escaped. . . ."[27] Maria reported that "cases in which citizens of the United States were said to have been converted to the Roman Catholic faith were sometimes spoken of, and always as if they were considered highly important."[28]

Apparently written for women readers, the book carried a soap-opera quality about its thrills and suspense and eyelash-aflutter references to sin, full of coy innocence and horrendous innuendo. In doing so it reflected to a point the literature of its time. The enthusiastic interest and warm reception accorded a more recent *A Nun's Story*, first as a best-selling book and then as a film starring Audrey Hepburn, strikingly conveys the changes in America since 1836.

Tom Watson later published a sequel to the book, entitled *Maria Monk and Her Revelation of Convent Crimes*. Watson enjoyed some success in his efforts to gain recognition by aligning himself with the People's party. In the election of 1896, during which leaflets were circulated as part of a whispering campaign to create the belief that William McKinley was a Catholic,[29] Watson ran for Vice President on the Populist ticket under William Jennings Bryan. Bryan simultaneously got the Democratic presidential nomination. His backers found themselves with a choice of two vice presidential candidates. The Democrats had chosen Bryan and J. W. Sewall, of Maine. On the Populist ticket the candidates were Bryan and Watson. McKinley outdistanced all competitors. Eight years later, in 1904, the Populists nominated Watson for President. The dying movement ran him again in 1908. But in those two elections he polled a total of only 150,000 votes.

Fighting for the same moralistic principle that their rural brethren espoused, the urban clergy turned naturally to reform movements. In New York the effort was concentrated on Tammany, which recognized the value of the immigrant's vote and soon became a haven for him. It frequently fed him, helped him find a job and a home, and guided him toward quick naturalization (and, incidentally, voting rights). Often the immigrant would stroll into a strange courtroom holding a printed card that read, "Common Pleas Court: Please naturalize the bearer," and signed by a Tammany official.[30] The machine didn't stop at legal vote-getting, though. The abuses that had been charged in 1844 and subsequent elections continued despite the passage of voting registration laws. Now there were other abuses. As the country got bigger, so did its vices.

In its heydey, under the iron hand and voice of Boss William M. Tweed, the Tammany-run city received such bills as one for $179,000 for three tables and forty chairs, to be used in a new courthouse. The cost for nine months' plastering work at the new courthouse was an incredible $2.8 million. Thermometers cost $7,500.[31] Into this type of corruption and outright theft stepped the Reverend Charles Henry Parkhurst. His popular sermons so spurred the city's voters that they swept a completely new reform ticket into office. An insurgent candidate backed by young Al Smith and others was among those winning. Smith's reward was a political job that eventually led to the state legislature.

The skirmishes continued. In 1909 James Cardinal Gibbons of Baltimore could write, "Catholics feel at home among their countrymen—they are conscious of no barrier separating them into a class apart. . . . The spirit of the country has changed much in half a century, and it would be very difficult to arouse such fanaticism as I saw in the Know-Nothing days."[32] Yet the cardinal's article was prompted, ironically, by statements attributed to two synods of Protestant ministers to the effect that "Catholics cannot be trusted with political office."

When the federal government had to settle with the Vatican for land taken from friars in the Philippines late in the 1890's, Protestant America screamed in anguish against William Howard Taft, who had negotiated with the Holy See while civil governor of the Philippines. This, coupled with Taft's religious views, created much animosity when he ran for President in 1908. President Theodore Roosevelt wrote during the campaign, "I have received hundreds of letters . . . protesting against him on this ground."[33] Later in the campaign Roosevelt believed the issue was strong enough to warrant public pronouncements, while privately he advised Taft against making a declaration of his beliefs. "If there is one thing for which we stand in this country," said Roosevelt, "it is for complete religious freedom, and it is an emphatic negation of this right to cross-examine a man on his religious views before being willing to support him for office."[34]

Two weeks before the election, Henry Cabot Lodge wrote to Roosevelt that the situation in Ohio was "quite dismal" because "the religious issue has been revived on Taft's Unitarianism." Added Lodge: "Good heavens, are we to elect Presidents on a creed? The mere reviving of the issue is intolerable."[35]

Taft had written a letter in 1899 that said in part, "I am a Unitarian. I believe in God. I do not believe in the Divinity of Christ, and there are many other postulates of the orthodox creed to which I cannot subscribe."[36] Had this letter been made public in the campaign, it might have had disastrous results for Taft, for it was as much a repudiation of organized, omnipresent Protestantism as the "rum, Romanism and rebellion" statement had been against an embittered minority. And in a sense it was even more heretical, as Jefferson had seemed more than a hundred years earlier. But the reaction, such as expressed emphatically by Roosevelt and Lodge, signaled a strong new current.

Taft at the time was merely echoing ever growing sentiment. Crisis-prone American man was thinking the same free thoughts that had led to a great Renaissance generations before. The growth of Unitarianism and, later, Christian Science was reflecting liberal tendencies. The Protestant Church reacted to the threat vigorously, with every weapon at its command. One weapon was expulsion, and it was used against a professor at Andover Theological Seminary in Massachusetts after a spectacular trial in which five professors were charged with theological liberalism. A similar case in New York was widely publicized. William Jennings Bryan stirred things to an even higher pitch by calling Darwinism a "program of infidelity masquerading under the name of science."

The modern fundamentalist movement planted its roots in this shifting soil, publishing *A Testimony to the Truth* with its five basic truths of Christianity: the Scriptures, Virgin Birth, Resurrection, First Atonement, and Second Coming of Christ. Almost simultaneously, fundamental-like satellite groups gained impetus. The Christian Endeavor Society in Missouri opened a campaign to ban all motion-picture kissing scenes between non-relatives. Father Divine drew national attention with a Long Island "Peace Mission" to soothe the troubled world. An obscure onetime professional ball player named William Ashley (Billy) Sunday was winning fans as an evangelist after early training with the Y.M.C.A. The Salvation Army was establishing itself in America, after having arrived here in 1879. And the General Assembly of the Presbyterian Church ruled evolution "untenable."

This war against theological liberalism, and especially Darwinism, was inevitably to reach what seemed a climax, although few novelists in their wildest plots would have dared pit William Jennings Bryan himself against the theory in open court. And to make the script even more sensational, the magic name of Clarence Darrow was added. The young defendant, John T. Scopes, of Dayton, Tennessee, had been arrested for illegally teaching Darwinism. Bryan, the prosecutor, matched wits with Darrow, the brilliant master of impassioned defense, as the nation watched.

The high point came on a hot July afternoon when Bryan himself condescended to take the stand to be questioned by Darrow on fundamentalist doctrine. Bryan, who was to die just a few days later, suffered his last defeat when the shrewd Darrow pointed to the absurdities of literal Bible interpretation. Just five years earlier, Westinghouse's experimental radio station KDKA in Pittsburgh had begun the first regularly scheduled radio broadcast. Now an estimated 2,500,000 radio receivers crackled the news that Scope's conviction and $100 fine had been set aside on a technicality. (The law that had precipitated the clash remained on the books in Tennessee in 1960, despite later efforts to remove it.)

In 1915 a long-smoldering menace had arisen. Originally taking its name from the Greek "kuklos" (band or circle), it had become known simply as the Ku Klux Klan. From a small but violent and relentlessly anti-Negro group formed in 1866, it grew to a wealthy, powerful, 9,000,000-member force. Riding its crest, Klan leaders prospered. One case is reported in which a Klansman sold his interest in the organization for $90,000.[37]

The Klan now claimed jurists, legislators, and other highly placed people as members, as it went about its task of eradicating the fourfold "menace" of Catholics, Negroes, foreign-born, and Jews. It mixed a baseless stream of printed and spoken hatred with unrecorded thousands of cases of violence in its early days. Its apparent influence in politics extended to all areas of the country, and at its pinnacle in the early days of this century it claimed members in forty-eight states, Alaska, and elsewhere.

Much of the Klan's support came covertly from fundamentalist-minded churchmen. The power of this group dedicated to a war against the common enemy apparently was too great a temptation for many embattled clerics to resist.

The country, coming out of the World War with a new set of problems and a new position as a world power, was concentrating on its internal troubles and rejecting its responsibilities in the communal League of Nations and the World Court. Henry Cabot Lodge, a revered symbol of Yankee Protestantism and isolationism, overcame a threat to his Senate seat in 1916 by defeating warm-spirited, canny Irishman John F. Fitzgerald, mayor of Boston, by 33,000 votes. Years later the Lodge and Fitzgerald traditions were to face each other in a series of fateful contests that dramatized the transition of a nation.

Labor unions were no longer conspiracies but a legitimate means of battling organized postwar attempts by industry to kill the movement. The powerful American Federation of Labor under Samuel Gompers led the drive which by then had enrolled 5,000,000 members. While they organized cooperatives and labor banks and undertook education and research moves, another 4,000,000 unemployed were being helped by new government weapons, including relief checks and unemployment compensation.

With Henry Ford pioneering reforms, the twelve-hour sweatshop day was dying along with child labor and skimpy pay checks. A new holiday, "Labor Day," was recognized. The passing of the abuses heralded a new school of emphasis for the common man. Ford's Model T's, priced at about $300, were so common that New York had been forced to enact a speed law (10 mph in the cities, 15 in the villages, and 20 on the open road).

Meanwhile clergymen on a higher level formed a plane of cooperation to attack jointly the abuse of the workingman. The Federal Council of Churches of Christ in America, the National Catholic Welfare Conference, and the Central Committee of American Rabbis issued manifestoes, testified at hearings, and made radio appeals. Brakes were being applied to big business, too. The powerful industrial trusts had been somewhat shredded by government action after having invaded the fields of sugar, whisky, oil, and grain.

Klansmen, beset by scandal and new-law enforcement, still resorted to tar, feathers, and bombs. But now they faced a National Association for the Advancement of Colored People.

Revivalism, the World War, and the spectacular growth of the Roman Catholic Church had caused a dramatic upturn in churchgoing. In 1880, 20 per cent of the population attended church; by 1930 the figure was 47 per cent. America also counted another hundred religious sects and an additional 50,000 church buildings.[38]

But "moral decay" continued apace, and reached into the highest places. The double standard had many takers. Teapot Dome headed the scandals, and gangsterism flourished. The cities did, too. For the first time, most Americans lived in an urban environment. The mighty Anti-Saloon League gathered dozens of weaker temperance groups into its fold, and finally won national prohibition, touching off a whole new concept of crime. Churches fought the crime menace with all the artillery they could muster. *The Presbyterian Magazine* quoted Isaiah:

Oh, sinful nation, a people laden with iniquity, a seed of evil doers, children that deal corruptly! . . . The whole head is sick, and the whole heart is faint. From the sole of the foot even unto the head there is no soundness in it; but wounds, and bruises, and fresh stripes; they have not been closed, neither bound up, neither mollified with oil.[39]

A new instrument of morality achieved recognition. After a dozen abortive attempts, New York had finally granted the vote to its females. That and Teddy Roosevelt's Bull Moose suffrage plank in 1912 gave national women's suffrage its final push into reality. And now women's temperance groups assumed new power. Mother's Day was born, with momism as the midwife. The distaff Americans presented a new set of national heroines: Mary Baker Eddy, Gertrude Ederle, Margaret Sanger, Clara Barton, Amelia Earhart—and Clara Bow. Churchmen quickly discovered the power of women, too. A Methodist Episcopal Conference dropped its ban on dancing and theater attendance, and Protestant Episcopal bishops voted to delete the word "obey" from the marriage ceremony.

In politics, Mrs. W. H. Felton became the first woman senator, named to fill the unexpired term (a single day) of the late Thomas E. Watson. Jeannette Rankin, a Republican from Montana, had become the first woman in the House of Representatives, and had won further recognition as having voted against the 1917 declaration of war. (She also voted against war after Pearl Harbor.)

Older America still looked with apprehension and distrust at Ellis Island, the immigrant welcoming station in New York's harbor. In the decades between 1880 and 1920, 23,000,000 new citizens had arrived, and with them the United States population soared past the 100,000,000 mark.[40]

Nativist pressure had been great on Congress to stop the tide. Woodrow Wilson had followed William Howard Taft in vetoing immigration limits based on literacy tests. But an inevitable trend was clear as early as 1882, when Chinese laborers were denied admittance. Bans against Japanese workers and undesirable aliens followed. And in 1917 Congress overrode another Wilson veto and passed a literacy qualification. Four years later, the quota system was established. It limited newcomers to 3 per cent of the number of their countrymen residing in the United States in 1910.

Sporadic opposition failed to offset organized pressurers, who won their biggest victory when, in 1924, an act of Congress established a "national origins" plan, and limited the annual quota of European immigrants to 150,000, mostly dispersed among northern Europeans. The result was to be that, compared to more than 4,000,000 in the 1920's, only 500,000 would arrive between 1931 and 1940.[41] The great immigration to America was ended.

Now, with the incoming tide under control, the battered old-line American braced for a showdown with this other half of the country. The new citizens were everywhere, it seemed, and breaking down tradition after tradition as they grew. Roman Catholic church rolls had swelled by millions; Catholic parishes, schools, colleges, and hospitals were opening by the score, and church-oriented movements sprang up. More and more Catholics entered medicine, the law, and other professions, and amassed wealth in business. They seemed to the entrenched but grumbling conservative to be aiming at control of every occupational field. A Catholic middle class was now coming into existence in America. No longer was the word "Catholic" able to summon up solely a lower-class stereotype.

The time was fast approaching when a resolution of the conflict had to occur. The old front had won prohibition and suffrage and immigration restrictions. It had failed in an effort to force all children into public schools, though, when in 1926 the Supreme Court ruled unconstitutional an Oregon effort aimed at curtailing parochial school attendance.

That case reflected a beginning. The battle had moved into the courts on at least one front, to be settled according to the laws of the land rather than in lawless and violent strife. The Constitution thus became a guide in practice.

At the moment, however, the old front was at the crest of its power. And so were the new citizens, as the country moved through the Roaring Twenties. Drawing the wrath of one of these Americas grew dangerous. And when both sides were aroused, it was disastrous, as it was in the aftermath of a Massachusetts murder, when the helpless defendants were immigrants Nicola Sacco and Bartolomeo Vanzetti. While they were branded as apostates and despised by many of their fellow immigrants, they were regarded as foreign agitators by nativists. They were condemned and executed on the most minimal evidence, arousing bitter controversy in a conflict of national conscience.

This was the era of personalities. Radio made it easier to recognize the feat of the individual, and individuals performing new and exciting feats were cropping up. The youth, courage, resourcefulness, and technical mastery of the machine exemplified by Lindbergh elevated his personality into a national symbol, an embodiment of national aspiration; Babe Ruth's power and skill, his warm humanity, and struggle against odds gave him a special place in a competitive society. Jack Dempsey's seeming invincibility commanded the same kind of attention.

In pinpointing a national personality, at least, the two Americas sometimes seemed to be in accord in a kind of inarticulate consensus. When the person proved to be a man or woman of virtuous merit and honest achievement, the honors flowed.

Most honors, it seemed, were to be had in the city, headquarters of the new dynamic society. And in one of these cities, the country's greatest, was a man who had won the hearts of his city neighbors and had made it stick throughout his whole state. An antiprohibitionist, he lacked youth (he was fifty-five) and education. But he had virtue, he had merit, he had achievement—and he was the immigrants' own in a time to test their power of choice on a national scale.

His name was Alfred E. Smith.

CHAPTER SEVEN

ALFRED E. SMITH
A New Kind of Candidate

"The allegiance of a 'Catholic conscience'"

IT WAS A BRIGHT AUTUMN DAY IN 1928, AND WAS GOING TO BE AN important one for the eleven-year-old boy fresh from private school in Boston. He faced what promised to be a difficult transition to New York's public school classrooms, and the disappointment of leaving all his friends in Massachusetts didn't make it any easier. It had its compensations, though: At his home in Bronxville, the boy was close to an exciting city that was extracting every ounce of prosperous joy from the verve and action of boom times. Young John F. Kennedy paused to glance at the morning newspaper before it went up to his father.

The newspaper was heavy with advertising. A seven-passenger Minerva limousine was for sale at $5,000. Silk net stockings were selling for $3.75 a pair. Six persons were indicted in a baseball pool that grossed millions. Prohibition enforcement officers seized forty-three bottles of liquor from visitors and the crew of the liner *Ile de France*. And stocks were booming. Radio Corporation of America closed at 232, Pierce-Arrow preferred at 63.5, Johns-Manville at 168, and R. H. Macy at 179.

On the political side, the first Roman Catholic to run on a major party ticket for the Presidency, Democrat Alfred Emanuel Smith, was preparing for his campaign. But there were ugly portents. Smith's campaign manager charged Republicans with helping the anti-Catholic forces, offering as proof an intercepted letter containing "red hot stuff." Evangelist Billy Sunday, leaving Ocean City, New Jersey, declared that Smith "has no more chance of being elected than the Pope has of being named Imperial Wizard of the Ku Klux Klan." The preacher's prediction, of course, was right. The Pope was not named Imperial Wizard; Al Smith was not elected President.

A newspaper in Salt Lake City hailed the election in quick retrospect as a "victory for Prohibition." The W.C.T.U. was even more emphatic on that score; in a post-election statement it said it hoped and believed that prohibition would now be taken out of politics forever.[1] The tremendous vote, it claimed, proved that the nation was dry to stay. A daily newspaper in Ohio opined that Smith had been "too candid." Other papers summed it up this way:[2]

"A vote against Tammany."

"Bigotry effect discounted."

"Religious question is to be regretted."

"Religious issue deplored."

And finally,

"Protestants defeated Smith."

Smith from the start was deeply disappointed at the considerable religious target shooting that his candidacy provoked. But had he known to what extent his campaign was helping the country over an obstacle in its path toward political maturity, his wounds might have been somewhat salved. His losing battle became a guide for the future, and his mistakes became well-marked pitfalls. Ironically, it can be argued that had Smith won, John F. Kennedy's election might never have come to pass. We can only guess at how much blame for the Great Depression would have been heaped upon a Catholic President.

Al Smith was born in a third-floor tenement on New York's Lower East Side. The cobbled streets of the teeming Fourth Ward became his playground, and the nearly 20,000-member Roman Catholic Church of St. James constituted his early social world. Smith's early years were spent as an altar boy and then organ pumper at St. James, a newsboy, laborer, trucker's helper,

Fulton Fish Market worker, pumps works employee, and real-estate man. He was elected to the State Assembly in 1903.

In eight years as governor, Smith forged the elements of the political image that were to identify him during his coming bid for the White House. He emerged with a reputation for efficiency, liberalism, and a clownish humor. Yet he continued to be thought of upstate as a city man who knew or cared little for the needs of the rural citizen.

His progressive-liberal reputation was bolstered by his support for state maternity insurance and other welfare bills. Although Smith was probably the most individualistic prominent politician of his time, the image as a Tammany man persisted despite instances where he bucked the Hall—and won. It was Tammany that put Smith in the favorite-son role that won him a few token votes and heavy applause as early as the 1920 Democratic convention. Again it was Tammany that raised him to the forefront in 1924 in the effort to capture his party's nomination. Both Cleveland and Wilson, in 1884 and 1912, had won crucial votes from the South and West by attacking Tammany Hall. It was doubtful in 1924 that a machine-led politician could win. Yet Smith remained stubbornly in the running.

Earlier, Smith had taken his stand on what now were two prominent 1924 issues: the anti-Catholic Klan and fundamentalist-inspired prohibition. At the 1920 convention in San Francisco he had clashed with William Jennings Bryan on prohibition. As the Klan developed huge power centers in Oregon and Indiana, supporting the platform against moral decay, Smith had said dryly, "This spirit of unrest is an unnatural consequence of war, and will soon subside."[3]

Tammany won an initial victory by having the convention scheduled for Madison Square Garden in New York, Smith's back yard. His opponent, William Gibbs McAdoo, had a majority of votes, but not the required two-thirds, as the convention opened. Caucuses buzzed with rumors about the "Romanistic" candidate. The aging orator, Bryan, son of the Midwest, aligned himself with McAdoo.

Facing each other as the convention opened were Klan and prohibitionist elements versus the citified wets, Tammany men, and liberals. The Republican convention had ignored the Klan issue, thereby tacitly approving it. Delegates to the Democratic conclave now were faced with an early problem of whether to make the hooded order an issue. Representatives of the West and South wanted to ignore it, but the Smith faction favored bringing it out into the open, and finally forced a showdown vote, which proved disastrous. The final count was 546.15 for the Klan and 542.82 against.[4]

As the convention progressed, with radio carrying his voice to millions across the land, Bryan preceded the balloting with one of his classic golden-throated speeches. But his living-room audience soon heard jeers in the background, as the Tammany-packed galleries began heckling. Catcalls and shouts soon flooded the huge auditorium, and finally Bryan was reduced to an unaccustomed role, that of just another politician screaming in order to be heard. The radio audience couldn't see Bryan's right index finger suddenly point to his tormentors, but they heard his deep voice boom the retort, "You do not represent the future of our country!"[5] A new flood of boos and abuse drowned out his next sentence, but the big question remained unanswered: Who did?

As the balloting began, it became obvious that a stalemate was developing, and several deals were offered. Finally Smith agreed to withdraw (after the hundredth ballot) on the condition that both men release all pledged delegates. Three ballots later the convention named John W. Davis for the task of welding the strife-torn party into a winning team to beat Coolidge.

Smith made several speeches in behalf of Davis while campaigning again for governor. Despite the fact that Coolidge won New York State by 869,000 votes, Smith won the gubernatorial chair, running a million votes ahead of his party. Another heavy-margin victory two years later clearly established him as a favorite when the 1928 convention opened. Here then was the Al Smith who faced his party in that convention: a liberal-minded governor, a top-notch administrator, a proven vote-getter with a record of progressive legislation.

Smith's laboring background, his supporters believed, would be of inestimable value in the growing cities. Of one thing they were certain: they could not hope to win the Presidency unless they won New York State. And Al Smith had certainly demonstrated an ability to win in New York. Still, there were handicaps. His progressiveness would not appeal to the Midwest. His wetness might draw a flood of protests. He would be running for President in times of great national prosperity. He was a new kind of candidate. He was a Roman Catholic.

Smith's forces, well oiled and anxious, got off to a good start by agreeing to hold the convention in Houston, Texas, on June 6th, in an apparent move to placate the South.

Prohibition, not religion, was the big worry of the platform writers. The country had come a long way since 1856, or so it seemed. Then, the Democratic platform had put great emphasis on the "adverse political and religious test," condemning the "political crusade . . . against Catholics. . . ." Now, seventy-two years later, other concerns were paramount. After a knotty wrangle, they finally agreed to an inoffensive prohibition plank that promised "an honest effort" to support the Eighteenth Amendment, while chiding the Republicans for laxity.

Franklin Delano Roosevelt described him as the "Happy Warrior" in making his third consecutive nominating speech for Smith. The balloting began. Smith's total rose to 742½ votes—just ten short of the required two-thirds. Then the Ohio delegation chairman jumped to his feet and switched the state's votes to Smith. Others waved their placards in a frantic effort to be recognized. The vote-switching bandwagon rolled onward. The new count showed Smith nominated with a total of 849⅔ votes.

It was a joyful day in the life of the East Side immigrant governor, and a boisterous night at Tammany. But the Hall's new hero found himself in controversy within hours. In a telegram to the convention he said he thought that "fundamental changes" were needed in the prohibition laws, in effect rewriting the

Democratic platform.[6] Ignoring the hard-fought prohibition plank, he spoke up for what he thought was needed. That gesture and others like it were to hurt him where it counted most: in the ballot box.

Embittered by his attitude, southern delegates sought retribution. It came later in the campaign with their formation of the "Hoovercrats," and was to cost Smith thousands of votes. At the moment, however, the vice presidential selection of a dry Southerner, Senator Joseph T. Robinson, of Arkansas, who was enormously popular in most of the South, appeared to have appeased the wounded delegates.

The real battle, for Smith, had taken place four years earlier. Bryan had died in 1925. The Klan was in trouble from repeated scandals and legal entanglements.

Smith wasted little time in getting started on the campaign, although it was several weeks before he read his notification speech, one of the few he ever delivered that wasn't given from notes scratched on the back of envelopes. Smith named General Motors industrialist John J. Raskob, a Catholic, as national campaign chairman. The appointment brought almost immediate charges of a "Catholic plot" from the bigots.[7] It served as a springboard for the venom dispensers waiting impatiently in the background. Raskob was labeled a "private chamberlain of the Pope," a man who had contributed at least half a million dollars to the Church over the years.[8]

The American Protective Association and the Know-Nothings had seemed just memories, but a briefly resurgent Klan and other groups continued to carry the spirit in many individuals. Senator "Tom-Tom" Heflin, of Alabama, whose Senate harangues against Rome had drawn bitter protests, helped stoke the fires.

Heflin claimed that the papal ensign was placed on battleships, that the cross and rosary decorated dollar bills, and that the papal color, scarlet, was on the White House. The Cincinnati *Catholic Telegraph* wrote: "He has strangely overlooked what is probably the most striking proof of the papal invasion of the United States. The telegraph pole bears the form of the cross from one end of the country to the other. . . . The plan was devised by none but a master mind."[9] Even Heflin, the acid-tongued enemy of everything Catholic, seemed behind the times. His Senate colleagues either laughed or walked out as he braced for battle. Indeed, the issue now carried overtones of a different kind of plot.

Women, granted the vote just a few years before, were beginning to play an outspoken part. A pamphlet issued by the "Sons and Daughters of Washington" charged that Smith was out to "Romanize" the schools. A Democratic national committee-woman from Virginia urged citizens to "save the country from Rome." Mabel Walker Willebrandt, an assistant attorney general of the United States, pleaded with Methodists to unite to keep Smith out of Washington. She was backed up by a young New York clergyman, Daniel A. Poling.[10]

The Klan, now operating as the "Knights of the Great Forest" and "Knights of the Midnight Mystery," staged a comeback. Its magazines, the *New Menace* and the *Kourier*, led organized attacks, printed and distributed literature, and spread a whispering (and sometimes shouting) campaign.

Other anti-Catholic publications sprang into existence. Their greatest fears had come true: a professed Roman Catholic was actually trying to take over the Presidency! Tracts, handbills, leaflets, and posters once again were entitled *Crimes of the Popes, Roman Oaths, Convent Life Unveiled, Convent Horrors,* and *Popery in the Public Schols.*[11] Up to ten million of these found their way into circulation in one-week periods. In them, old issues were once again revived. One magazine, purporting to examine Smith's "un-American activities," advertised itself thusly: "Nothing like it in America . . . 'Skins' the crook . . . Anathematizes the Hypocrite . . . Exposes the Grafter . . . Turns the Light on Romanism . . . Makes War on the Liquor Machine."[12] The author of this tract, a West Coast Methodist preacher, maintained not only that Lincoln had died as the result of a "Romish" plot but also that Garfield and McKinley had been murdered by "Romanists."

Although the immigrant tides had ebbed, in 1928 the question of "whether the ports of America shall be thrown open without restriction to foreign immigrants" was again posed as a burning issue. Smith, it was maintained, "has throughout his political career stood . . . for the flinging of our gates open to the foreign hordes." It was no wonder, though, observed the accuser. Smith himself had been "born and reared in a foreign atmosphere." Attempts were made to publicize the "strange and meaningful . . . relationship that has grown up between the New York governor and Mussolini."[13]

Here, again, an explicit foreign conspiracy loomed, a throwback to almost a century earlier. Smith, it was implied, was the agent of a "clandestine, international empire of hidden darkness [and] secrecy."[14] Inevitably, the charges embraced the ludicrous. It was claimed that two ancient cannons outside the Catholic-owned Georgetown University in Washington were pointed at the White House. Even Episcopalian J. P. Morgan became a target, vilified as a "rich Catholic banker."[15]

The remains of bitter sectional antipathies were seized upon as a noble cause. "The South is still American and fundamentally honest," declared the pamphleteer. It was "the land of chivalry, and the center today of the purest Anglo-Saxon idealism in America."[16] The reader was given a choice of virtues to champion in case he was unable to identify adequately with any single one. Smith's "relationship to organized and commercialized vice,"[17] to gambling, liquor selling, and prostitution, was "proved" as the author asked his reader, "What is a lie to the Vatican if it takes a lie to win?"[18] There were cryptic references to the Jews and Jewess (*sic*) aiding or aided by Smith. The challenge was flung at the reader in a final flourish of righteous exhortations: "Shall America elect a Bowery-produced, Tammany-trained, Roman-owned, liquor-dominated champion to the Presidency of the United States? . . . Not since the Civil War has this Republic faced so sure a decision for or against those assets that belong to the very soul of a people's government. . . . Americans, this is your hour. God have mercy on us if you fail!"[19]

In the offensive against Smith, the devil could quote scripture. The theme that a lie was employed by Catholics as a permissible device began to emerge. One writer noted: "Lying for the truth's sake" has long been a fine art, and respectable. Said the Apostle Paul: 'For if the truth of God hath more abounded through my lie unto His glory, why am I also yet judged as a sinner?' "[20] But lying was merely an incidental means to cover true allegiance. It was asserted that "in certain imaginable crises his [Smith's] allegiance to the Pope would outweigh his duty to the American people.[21] That's the whole thing in a nutshell," said the opposition, "the danger that in a crisis he will react first as a Roman Catholic and then as a man and an American citizen."[22] The same charges of Roman allegiance were to be hurled at John F. Kennedy a generation later, surrounding such issues as birth control and aid to parochial schools.

The twenties marked the rise in America of the new science of psychology. Still in its early stages, the new thinking found ready adaptation to the uses of the campaign against Smith and against Catholicism. Smith, it was stated in a jumble of pseudo-science, "had his religion bred into his bone and sinew and brain cells long before he got his politics. The reflexes of childhood are well-known to be stronger than any inhibitions of later life. How could he be expected to repudiate the strongest impulses of his nature? It isn't done."[23] Said the writer: "In certain vital issues on which his church has taken a stand, he has already forfeited his freedom of choice . . . his mind is already made up for him. . . ."[24] This new twist was pursued throughout the challenges to Smith's candidacy.

Some church leaders now judiciously questioned the intentions of the Roman hierarchy, citing old pronouncements by Pope Leo XIII that said the church was opposed to the "wall" separating it from the state. Leo XIII had made two statements before 1900 concerning Catholicism in America. In one, he had said it would be "erroneous" to think that it would be "universally lawful or expedient for the state and church to be disservered and divorced," and said that the church would "bring forth more abundant fruit if, in addition to liberty, she enjoyed the favor of the laws and the patronage of the public authority."[25] In his other statement, Leo had said that the church deemed it unlawful "to place the various forms of divine worship on the same footing as the true religion."[26] He had added, however, that the church did not necessarily condemn leaders who did so. Smear spreaders, of course, seized upon these two pronouncements as evidence that the Holy See was indeed plotting a Constitutional revision, if not an outright revolution.

But something new was happening: theologians and responsible Protestant churchmen were taking a quieter view, if not actually making appeals against bigotry. The *Christian Century* lashed out at the bigots at least thrice in 1928, specifically naming Heflin on at least one occasion. "It remains to be seen," said the magazine as the race began, "if the Southern drys vote in November as they pray in June." In November it extended "our apologies to the tens of thousands of Southern drys who voted as they prayed."[27]

Perhaps most indicative of the stands taken by the Catholic press was an editorial carried by the *Catholic World*. It asserted that no one had a *right* to question Smith on his religion, a tack somewhat more aloof than the one taken by the Catholic press during the Kennedy campaign.[28] Another Catholic magazine, *Commonweal*, carried advertisements throughout the campaign for a *Handbook of Catholic Facts*, intended to repudiate the bigots' charges.[29]

On an unprecedented scale, religious leaders now were repudiating the charges themselves. In earlier days it had taken an outspoken and sometimes fearless leader merely to protest against *violence;* few Protestant leaders would have explicitly urged that the would-be rioter judge the "papal threat" in the cold light of reality. Over the decades of America's growth, clergymen had developed a new view toward the invading Catholics. Many had been forced by circumstances to reexamine their outlooks. Immigrants who had successfully detached themselves from poverty had begun to win the empathy of their "hosts."

Even the simple, selfish desire to increase a church's membership sometimes forced a pastor to look upon the "foreigners" and their faith in a new light. It was one thing to deem something "undesirable" or "unlawful" (as Leo XIII had done), they reasoned, and quite another to change the situation. They were more interested in Smith's intentions and in the over-all picture of American tradition than they were in distant proclamations. The mainstream of Protestant clerical opinion was not taking issue with Smith simply because of his faith. It opposed his Tammany affiliations and his wet philosophy.

Moreover, for the first time a faint defensive note could be heard in their utterances. The *Christian Herald* said, "We deny that those who question" Smith as a Catholic are bigots.[30] Later, it said that the Catholic question was really a political one, that questioning Smith as a Catholic pertained to his political feelings and motivations, and not essentially to his right to be a Roman Catholic.[31]

Laymen, too, shared this sincere interest in Smith's position. One prominent New York attorney, Charles Marshall, questioned Smith's allegiance (and that of his fellow Catholics) in an "open letter" in the *Atlantic Monthly*. Marshall sprinkled the piece with liberal quotations from papal encyclicals, and the material was widely reprinted. Smith, with the help of World War I Chaplain Father Francis P. Duffy and Joseph M. Proskauer, drafted a reply that was cleared by Patrick Cardinal Hayes of New York. The reply, a seven-page letter, appeared the following month and received wide publicity. The exchange had taken place a full year and a half before the election. Smith said:

> You seem to think that Catholics must be all alike in mind and in heart, as though they had been poured into, and taken out of the same mould. You have no more right to ask me to defend as part of my faith every statement coming from a prelate than I should have to ask you to accept as an article of your religious faith every statement of an Episcopal bishop, or of your political faith every statement of a President of the United States. . . . I have been taught the spirit of toleration. . . .
>
> What is this conflict about which you talk? It may exist in some

lands which do not guarantee religious freedom. But in the wildest dreams of your imagination you cannot conjure up a possible conflict between religious principle and political duty in the United States. . . . And if you can . . . how would a Protestant resolve it? Obviously by the dictates of his conscience. That is exactly what a Catholic would do. . . .[32]

The old and rather shrill charges no longer seemed to make inroads. The world was changing. The *Awful Disclosures of Maria Monk* was almost an anachronism, even at the turn of the century. The issue now was set in the fabric of American institutions. Only the most unreasoning opponent could deny the reality of the melting pot. The influx of foreigners had occurred. It was now largely at an end, and the principles of the Constitution remained unsullied.

The focus became one in which democracy was threatened in more insidious ways than by a far-flung band of conspirators alone. No longer were there concrete demands of specific instructions allegedly relayed or executed by the priesthood. The priesthood had too much sense for that. Said a pamphleteer: "Well-trained orthodox Roman Catholic consciences probably need no specific instructions. . . ."[33]

The making of a Roman Catholic state out of America did "not mean a State in which *all* citizens accept Roman Catholic theology, morals and ecclesiasticism as binding . . . nor . . . a legally acknowledged union of states with the Roman Catholic Church. . . ." Instead, it was now said, "such an ideal Roman Catholic State would be one in which the Roman Catholic Church's *social polity* would approximate closely to a complete legislative expression and effectiveness." The Protestant would become simply a minority influence in this regard. Such a condition could come about as a result of indifference in the face of "active cooperation of . . . non-Catholic politicians, together with some aggressive aid from ambitious theocratic Protestants."[34]

The concept of social justice as enunciated by Pope Leo XIII already was virtually indistinguishable from the most central concerns and demands of the time among labor and management.

Catholic politicians were joining with representatives of other minorities in new coalitions of political and social strength.

In Syracuse, New York, four years earlier, Smith had pinpointed the issue as one of national scope. Referring to bigotry at that time, he had said: "The Catholics of this country can stand it, the Jews can stand it; our citizens born under foreign skies can stand it, the Negro can stand it. But the United States of America cannot stand it."[35]

Hoover himself decried the bigotry on several occasions, beginning with the words of his notification speech: "In this land, dedicated to tolerance, we still find outbreaks of intolerance. . . . By blood and conviction I stand for religious tolerance both in act and in spirit."[36]

Smith, meanwhile, refused to believe that all the venom could be directed at him, and frequently said he doubted if it would hurt his chances. On only one occasion did he lash out at his critics. In a nationally broadcast speech from Oklahoma City, he said: "I have been told that politically it might be expedient for me to remain silent on this subject. But so far as I am concerned, no political expediency will keep me from speaking out in an endeavor to destroy these evil attacks."[37] He spent five minutes talking about other more general matters before probing the issue of religion; he "briefed" his audience, as he had done many times before (enough to establish the Smith trade-mark phrase, "Let's look at the record").

Yet the speech represented perhaps the most forthright public expression ever made by a presidential candidate concerning the religious issue in the midst of a campaign. Of the argument that by voting against him a citizen would be upholding the ideals and institutions of America's forefathers, Smith said: "Nothing could be so out of line with the spirit of America. Nothing could be so foreign to the teachings of Jefferson. Nothing could be so contradictory to our whole history. Nothing could be so false to the teachings of our divine Lord Himself. The world knows no greater mockery than the use of the blazing cross, the cross upon which Christ died, as a symbol to instill into the hearts of men a hatred of their brethren, while Christ preached and died for the love and brotherhood of man."[38]

In the speech, Smith had first repeated what an imposing list of prominent people had said about him. All on the list were easterners, and many were intellectuals who had little appeal to his audience; they included Nicholas Murray Butler, John Dewey, and Charles Evans Hughes. He noted that the Grand Dragon of the Arkansas Klan had publicly opposed him. Then he debunked a charge that he had driven down Broadway at fifty miles an hour while drunk (he didn't know how to drive), and mentioned Mrs. Mabel Walker Willebrandt's charges, noting that she had been chairman of the credentials committee at the Republican national convention.

As he covered other towns, he made no further mention of religious bigotry. Only in Milwaukee nine days later did he briefly remind his audience that he had spoken on the subject in Oklahoma.

For their part, his fellow Irish Catholics appeared to see in Smith a home-grown hero, one of their own who had pulled himself up by his bootstraps and proved that an Irish Catholic could make a mark on the world. In 1918 Smith had opened campaign headquarters opposite Grand Central Station in New York. The office, maintained for a decade, was described as "a kind of club, halfway between the Bowery and Albany."[39] Certainly Smith's visits back to his old Fourth Ward neighborhood helped endear him to his fellows, as did his picnic excursions and his repeated references in his campaign speeches to the sights and sounds and smells of his home. He used to say he had a degree, F.F.M. (for Fulton Fish Market). He was the self-made man, and gloried in the role, his leathery face breaking out in smiles as bands across the country played *his* theme, "The Sidewalks of New York."

Throughout the campaign trips, several demonstrations were held against Smith, and on at least one occasion, near Helena, Montana, a flaming cross was within view. At another time, in Alabama, Klansmen hanged him in effigy.[40]

While the anti-Catholic drive was characteristically poorly

organized, however, the antiwet one was concerted and power-ful; there seems to be little doubt that the Anti-Saloon League and its satellite groups cut far deeper into Smith's vote totals than did religious bigotry. But in some cases the two merged. Many engaged in a whispering campaign in which bigotry hid behind righteous indignation, over Smith's stand on prohibition.

The mighty league, fresh from an impressive national drive that had put across the Prohibition Amendment and the Volstead Act, had growled in 1920 and in 1924, when Smith's name had come before nominating conventions. Now it made ready to bite.

Organized in 1895 with the help of about fifty temperance groups, the league had grown into a fearful political machine that chose candidates strictly on the basis of their stand against liquor. After 1911, about 30,000 churches across the country supported the League, which reportedly turned out about 300,-000,000 pieces of literature in the push for prohibition.[41] In 1928, placards, broadcasts, advertisements, leaflets, posters, books, and handbills by the millions were thrown into its drive. And this time church support was forthcoming from scores of de-nominations. Against this tide the Smith backers spent an un-precedented total of more than $5,000,000, relying on Smith's "common man" touch in speeches in contrast to Hoover's sedate style, and also on his popularity in the cities.

From the earliest returns on election night, however, it became evident that the weight of the handicaps was going to fall heavily on candidate Smith. When the night ended, the fate of only four states (with 55 electoral votes) was in doubt. Hoover already had won 407 electoral votes, far above the needed 266. Smith's total the next morning was 69 votes. Later, Massachusetts' 18 votes gave him a total of 87. The other three states, North Carolina, North Dakota, and Texas, went into Hoover's column. Hoover received approximately 21,320,000 popular votes to Smith's 15,000,000.[42]

Smith had lost New York, the upstate vote defeating him there. As was the case in many eastern states, Smith's soaring totals in the cities were more than offset by conservative feelings of rural voters. He did win Alabama, Georgia, Louisiana, Mississippi, Rhode Island, and South Carolina; nearly all his few electoral votes had come from the "solid South."

It was natural for contemporary observers—especially Catholic Democrats—to smart, and blame the loss on bigotry. This widespread feeling was to present John Kennedy with a major obstacle in his drive for a place on his party's ticket in 1956 and again in 1960. Even if the bigot vote did not defeat Smith, the feeling among many voters was that it had. This was to have practical effects, particularly among some Catholics, on their voting choice in 1960.

The 1928 election proved that Catholic and bigoted anti-Catholic voting elements continued to exist in twentieth century democratic America, and that a morality-tinged wet-dry battle had been strong enough to influence many voters in a country that many clergymen had claimed was speeding down the road to perdition. And the results held significant portents.

The metropolitan and New England votes (heavily Catholic) had given Smith a major show of strength. It was the first time since the Civil War that a Democrat had carried Massachusetts, with its heavy concentration of immigrants. All told, Smith got 40.8 per cent of the total national vote, more than any losing Democrat had drawn in any previous twentieth century election.

Had Smith had something more than Tammany, wetness, and Catholicism to offer the rural voters, he might very well have come much closer. But contrary attributes formed an obstacle far too high for the native conservatism of the nonimmigrant town and country citizens. As expected, it was in the cities that Smith showed his real power. His plurality in the twelve largest cities was 38,000 votes. In contrast, the Democratic candidates in two previous elections had *lost* the same dozen cities by 1,638,000 and 1,252,000 votes.[43] Much of Smith's urban total was credited to women, who swelled vote counts; but paradoxically, the distaff vote was probably heavily responsible for his rural losses, especially in temperance-group areas.

A survey by Professor William F. Ogburn, of the University

of Chicago, covering 173 counties at random in Massachusetts, New York, Ohio, Illinois, Wisconsin, Colorado, Montana, and California, displayed an analytical picture of the results.[44] The ratio of electoral votes from these states (121 Hoover, 18 Smith) was just about the same as the total winning figures (444 to 87). The study found the vote slightly in favor of Hoover after statistically "removing" the issues of drink, religion, and immigration from the urban sphere. Numerically, Ogburn found the wet issue nearly *three times as important* as the religious one. Apparently, regardless of his faith, Smith had been doomed to failure.

The 1928 election had been keyed to the dividing line that existed across the country, separating conservative, rural America from Al Smith's more liberal cities. The religious issue had become a matter of social forces operating beyond the scope of control by any central conspiratorial plotting center. It was no longer a conspiracy or a plot. When it arose again, it was to involve the social composition of a nation. And its national purpose.

Had Smith been a Protestant, he very likely would have lost anyhow, perhaps by an even greater margin (as Hoover himself later wrote in his Memoirs). But with the Happy Warrior, who so many times had run ahead of his ticket, it was merely a case of running a little ahead of his country.

CHAPTER EIGHT

FRANKLIN D. ROOSEVELT
The Testing of America's Ideals

"We have learned . . . the spiritual strength of our people"

BIGOTRY WAS ABOUT TO TAKE A BACK SEAT IN PRESIDENTIAL CAM-
paigns for a generation after Smith's defeat in 1928 before coming
back with new trappings and old fervor in 1960, in a changed
country from the one that roared through the bubbling twenties
toward near chaos. Meanwhile, the fever pitch of materialism
rolled on to greater heights, propping common stock averages on
the New York Exchange from 100 in 1926 to 191 in June of 1929.

Prohibition spawned a host of children, in all walks of life,
who looked upon this law as a kind of harmless game that even
added relish to the enjoyment of old pastimes. Nearly everybody
was doing it. But was it really so terrible to break the law when
it seemed as ridiculous as this one? And what about those other
laws? Just who made the law, and on what ground? Booze,
money, and sex sounded the note. Enjoy life! "Hi, sucker!"
smirked Texas Guinan merrily, and it endeared her even more.
The red-hot mommas set the beat.

And the gray ones came back in force. In New York the
Margaret Sanger clinic was raided on complaint of the Daughters
of the American Revolution. But it wasn't a clear-cut issue. The
Federal Council of Churches of Christ in America took a stand
defending birth control. It was all too confusing for most people. The President could be depended upon, and those behind
him, the pillars of the national community, the businessmen, the

clergy. But when respectable people start breaking the law, something must be done. President Hoover asked Congress to strengthen prohibition enforcement. Meanwhile, gigantic bootleg rackets thrived and served as a step up for "businessmen" who had been denied other means of entry into the affluence of the new society. Millions of dollars were spent, jingling in a roaring cascade into the underworld till.

Then it was October, 1929, and the party was over. Rolling along the road to prosperity, the country suddenly skidded crazily off and headed downhill. By 1932 thirteen million unemployed waited aimlessly. Wages were off 60 per cent from only several years earlier. The $35-a-week salary was only $14 now, if you had the job. Nearly two million school children no longer attended class. No teachers. Gone. Those who did attend were often found suffering from malnutrition.

The 1932 Democratic convention found Al Smith seeking a second try at the Presidency. Aligned against him were powerful new elements in the party. Their candidate was the ebullient, energetic, skillful, inspiring governor of New York, Franklin Roosevelt.

A pitched convention fight resulted in the nomination of Roosevelt. Smith, embittered, left without releasing his 190 ballots to make the choice unanimous.[1] "Al Smith had created Franklin Roosevelt," said one commentator, "by picking him for the nomination as governor of New York, and had backed him throughout his two terms."[2] Now it seemed to Smith as if a breach of an unwritten political ethic had been perpetrated.

Addressing the convention, after a plane ride from Albany, Roosevelt pledged himself and his listeners and his fellow Americans to "a new deal for the American people."[3] Around F.D.R. now were some of the same men who had championed Woodrow Wilson's progressive legislation in 1912: Senator George Norris, of Nebraska; "Young Bob" La Follette, of Wisconsin; Felix Frankfurter, Bernard Baruch. Roosevelt himself had served under Wilson as Assistant Secretary of the Navy. The Roosevelt force set about reforming in order to preserve the system that ran

America. Abuses of power by concentrated interests or particular sectors were to be curbed. Government regulations increased sharply, as the interdependence of society's parts spread, and grew more delicate. Into existence came the SEC, the NLRB, the FHA. The WPA sought to mobilize manpower for the general good. TVA promised a new concept in public power for the common welfare, for businessman and farmer. Social security promised aid against the threats of old age. The "New Freedom" of Wilson was being put in motion, on an unprecedented scale.[4]

Setting the pace and providing the mortar for this new coalition of the many groups and interests that made up the American society was the new aristocratic Democrat in the White House. Roosevelt used the office of the President to spur, cajole, or subtly threaten where necessary. Buoyant, congenial, sensitive to people, a magnificent practical political craftsman, F.D.R. often aroused antipathy, but not apathy. Leading the way for all the people, Roosevelt talked with them, across the land, in one "fireside chat" after another. And the people wrote to him in a flood of mail, sharing their personal troubles, their anguish, and their hope—for themselves and for his mission.

Gradually farm prices came up; metals and commerce rose, slowly; the output of autos increased; there were five million fewer unemployed. But the effort continued, straining against enormous odds. Throughout the country a consensus moved the people to save the society that meant their families, their loved ones, their way of life that once had been. It gave dignity and meaning and useful purpose to themselves and others. Faces brightened, but others darkened. In the 1936 election Roosevelt observed to an aide that all the issues that crowded in were summarized in one overriding issue—himself.[5] The people were either for him or against him, and the way he brought the country forward.

Al Smith took an increasingly active role in national affairs. In December of 1932 he was a member of the Transportation Commission that studied the plight of the railroads. He was still the same jocular Smith, though, even through his defeat. After extensive testimony before the RFC for a loan for Jones Beach on Long Island, Smith solemnly requested permission for one question. It was: "Where do we go to get the check?" But the rift between the two former governors, Smith and Roosevelt, grew wider. Smith, ardent patriot and faithful Catholic, wrote an article quoting from his favorite speech by Richard L. Sheil in the House of Commons: "Partakers in every peril, in the glory are we not to be permitted to participate? And shall we be told . . . that we are estranged from the whole country for whose salvation our lifeblood was poured out?" Smith joined the conservative American Liberty League that boasted such members as Irénée du Pont, James Wadsworth, and John W. Davis, and gradually withdrew from the political tides of the times, against the New Deal.

In 1936 the CIO was organizing the auto and steel industries, and outbursts of bloody violence seemed to mark almost every step. Strong opposition to liberal elements again sprang up. There were other kinds of fireside chats besides the kind Roosevelt held. In Detroit, Father Charles E. Coughlin regularly used the great new medium of radio to gather around him in weekly broadcasts many thousands of listeners. He assailed Roosevelt's policies and preached many of the sentiments that had moved the Klan and, before it, the American Protective Association.

About the same time, a Catholic League for Social Justice was formed, not related to Coughlin's Union for Social Justice. They declared that "the social, financial and industrial dislocation that has overwhelmed the world demands that we conform our human relations to our spiritual ideals."[6]

In 1936 Al Smith campaigned for Alf Landon. An irremeable split seemed to have occurred in the Democratic party. The dissident elements within it sought in 1936 to set the brakes to what they saw as runaway power in the hands of the federal government—and one man. In the most resounding presidential victory of the new century, the people returned F.D.R. to office. His support came from every sector and from all levels.

In his 1937 Inaugural Roosevelt again echoed the fusion of the social gospel and the predominant strain of Wilsonian democracy, declaring, "The test of our progress is not whether we add more to the abundance of those who have too much; it is whether we provide enough for those who have too little." He saw "one-third of a nation ill-housed, ill-clad, ill-nourished."[7]

It was indeed a nation, perhaps more so than it had been in years. All faced a common threat and a common purpose. The nation was mingling, by station, by region. It was not only the migratory worker: 160,000 trailers were on the road as the nation looked for work, or went where there was work to be had. Now began the mobility of the labor force, a phenomenon that was to be accentuated as the nation girded for war in later years. It signaled an increasingly mobile America; more companies grew nation-wide in their operations, and began to move men, to rotate them, following plant relocation. Men were coming off the farms, into the cities; entire families plucked up roots.

Radio, with the same voice, the same music, spanned the continent. By 1940 nine of every ten persons owned a set. Four out of five said they'd sooner give up movies than give up the radio.[8]

The airplane shortened the distance between most outlying sections, and necessitated the establishment of a new government agency, the CAA. The Twentieth Century Limited made the New York–Chicago run overnight in an almost giddy new high of sophistication: one long party and the trip was over. The Super Chief picked up the steel thread and bore it to Los Angeles in less than three days. The country was woven together in unprecedented ways as the thirties drew to a close.

The reluctance with which we had faced our new role as a great nation among the world's great nations in the decades after the Great War continued. But the ill winds that blew from abroad spoke of change. In 1935 the Senate had rejected the World Court as a mortal threat to national sovereignty. Neutrality was the order of the day among people and in the harassed councils of government. The country had been preoccupied for years, first with prosperity and then not merely with the preservation of prosperity but with the prospect of actual dissolution. And it was dissolution translated into the most personal terms: family, homestead, self. National principles were remote. It was the daily reality that spelled America's challenge and its promise in the thirties. The rest of the world was far away. Yet great shifts in thinking had occurred too.

Was the system worth saving? Were there only empty principles in the Declaration of Independence? And in the Constitution? And in the Bill of Rights? Had our democracy been, in the final analysis, a cover for a headlong race for profit, for keeping one foot on the masses as the capitalists gained ever new footholds of greater wealth and power? To whom did the country belong, anyway?

It was because of events during the long reign of Roosevelt, too, that secularism increased apace. Throughout the long hard years the government provided social action—and brought deliverance. And who was the government? More than any other, it had been one man. Franklin Roosevelt was a kind of savior, a great and towering presence, and a strangely personal reality to his people. Throughout the world, in fact, great personalities were to bestride and identify great events: Gandhi, Hitler, Stalin, Churchill, Einstein.

Suddenly our internal struggles seemed to pale, as across the oceans other nations moved against one another. What stake did America have in all this? Most seemed to think America had little: In 1937 a national public-opinion poll found that 70 per cent of those queried still believed it a mistake for the United States to have entered the First World War.[9]

Yet most listened when the man in whom they had monumental faith starkly stated the crisis in 1939:

Storms from abroad directly challenge three institutions indispensable to Americans now as always. The first is religion. It is the source of the other two—Democracy and international good faith.

There comes a time in the affairs of men, when they must prepare to defend not their homes alone, but the tenets of faith and humanity on which their churches, their governments and their very civilization are founded. The defense of religion, of democracy and of good faith among nations is all the same fight. To save one, we must now make up our minds to save all.[10]

In 1940, as Europe trembled and then collapsed into new mechanized rumbling warfare, and helpless millions slid into the holocaust of "total war," the American people returned Franklin Roosevelt to the White House by a plurality of 5,000,000 votes.

As Roosevelt addressed the nation in his 1941 State of the Union Message, he reminded it of its heritage, articulating the Four Freedoms, but expanding them to include in their scope the peoples outside the borders of the United States, "everywhere in the world."[11] Once again the humanitarian principles of the nation were being articulated for all humanity. The first of these freedoms was freedom of religion—"freedom of every person to worship God in his own way, everywhere in the world." With it came freedom of speech. But superseding the all-important freedoms of the press and assembly now were freedom from want and freedom from fear.

Amid swirling currents of isolationism, the nation was forced into a role of world responsibility. But the intense opposition soon was removed by the Japanese bombs that shattered the peace of an early Sunday morning. In the next four years, the necessity for working together joined the nation into a powerful functioning instrument. Differences remained, but they were overcome by the greater necessity of facing the threat to national survival. Unity was actively generated and promoted in thousands of different ways. Frank Sinatra took time away from thronging bobby soxers to bring the lyrics of "The House I Live In" to the country, explaining, "That's America to me," as he sang of its diversity and neighborliness. Everybody belonged now. Everybody was needed. That is, almost everybody. Japanese were shunted into camps as a precautionary measure, while Nisei troops, fighting in the high snows and bare hills of Italy, won repeated citations for bravery. Comrades in arms all.

Irish-Catholic Colin P. Kelly, pilot of an army bomber, became the nation's first war hero when, after his plane was damaged by enemy fire, he ordered his crew to bail out, and then died in the crash of his airplane that destroyed a Japanese battleship on December 9, 1941. Nearly one of every four servicemen serving the United States were Roman Catholics. In the Pacific, the nation was stunned by the loss of the Sullivan brothers, all on the same ill-fated destroyer. Americans revered the memory of the four chaplains, from different faiths, who went down together, arms interlocked, when their ship, the *Dorchester,* was mortally hit by Japanese bombs. In Europe, as American soldiers of different faiths broke into the horrors of concentration camps where millions of Jews had been destroyed, they were incensed with a common revulsion against the inhumanity.

Back in America, old differences still showed. But some new differences grew sharper. In February of 1940, not long after the signing of the Russo-German nonaggression pact, Roosevelt said, "The Soviet Union as a matter of practical fact . . . is a dictatorship as absolute as any other dictatorship in the world."[12] Strong new sentiments appeared. Roosevelt faced a different nation when he reflected in his 1945 Inaugural, "We have learned that we cannot live alone at peace . . . we have learned to be . . . members of the human community [with] the spiritual strength of our people."[13] In 1943 three of every four persons asked said they would like to see the United States belong to a world organization after the war.[14]

With victory and its aftermath came the first formal international recognition of human rights, embodied in the United Nations Charter: "We the people of the United Nations . . . reaffirm faith in fundamental human rights, in the dignity and worth of the human person, in the equal rights of men and women and of nations large and small. . . ." Of these rights, religion was foremost in many minds, as written in Article XVIII of the Universal Declaration of Human Rights: "Everyone has the right to freedom of thought, conscience and religion; that right includes freedom to change his religion and belief, and freedom, either alone or in a community with others, and in public or in private, to manifest his religion or belief, in teaching, practice, worship and observance. . . ."

Now men and women came home once again to meet and make the future with their dear ones in an America preserved and conscious of its mission. The warning of a Catholic "conspiracy" in the 1928 campaign had either failed to take hold or had been forgotten or superseded by more pressing concerns in the thirties and forties. By September, 1945, barely one of every ten persons, when asked whether any one racial or religious group had too much power, expressed the feeling that Catholics did (9 per cent). The Jews had passed the Catholics in this respect (13 per cent).[15]

Many needs in the nation clamored for attention. And some of the men who had fought to preserve the country now devoted themselves and their careers to it in peacetime, carrying on for comrades fallen around the world who, in their sacrifice, mingled with that of millions of innocents, had added a solemn note of consecration to the bitterness and cynicism that also accompanied the strife.

Out of Alamogordo, on July 16, 1945, had come a new age. The moralists abdicated in the blinding light of its awful birth. The Uncertainty principle proved one thing certain: the awful fact of Uncertainty itself. Instead of philosopher-kings, it was now the physicists who were the philosophers of the age. With their myriad mysteries, they had fulfilled the ultimate test imposed by a pragmatic society. Their theories had worked, with terrifying force and unbelievable magnitude. The age they had launched was theirs by right. Or so it seemed in the deeply troubled and unspoken sense of the time.

At a small college town, Fulton, Missouri, in 1946, Winston Churchill drew a global picture that spread from its pastoral confines across oceans and countries, and delineated a new division in a world still reverberating from being split asunder. "From Stettin in the Baltic to Trieste in the Adriatic an iron curtain has descended across the Continent," he said.[16] In prostrated Europe, amid friends and foes alike, a new doctrine was penetrating the minds and lives of the people. The cold war had arrived to bank the fires of the grand alliance of wartime allies.

Among the returning servicemen going into politics in that same year was a young man who fought eleven other contenders for the Democratic nomination for Congress from the Eleventh District of Massachusetts, which included Charlestown, where once there had been a small Ursuline convent 112 years earlier. John F. Kennedy went on to fill the unexpired term of James Curley, and to be reelected to successive terms.

Meanwhile, the great encroachments of a totalitarian state were assuming entirely fresh proportions as a threat to freedom. The United States Government sought to bolster defenses against communism, while most of the people seemed heedless. The Truman Doctrine and then the Marshall Plan came out of State Department policy-planning sessions, and fell on a nation wary of large-scale commitments and peacetime governmental programs and spending. The plans sounded a sour note to millions of Americans who were slow in giving up isolationism and the concept of Fortress America even after the Second World War. Most Americans went about their business and took their liberties for granted—well, not quite for granted. After all, millions had fought and made the great sacrifices to preserve their liberties. In 1947 citizens around the country were asked to tell, after some reflection, what they would say was the greatest advantage of "our type of government." One of every four said "freedom in general." Freedom from what, and to do what? Well, said 7 per cent, "freedom of opportunity." About one in five said freedom of speech, and of the press. Nearly as many felt the greatest advantage was that "people have a voice in government." Fewer than one in ten said it was "freedom of worship."[17]

The world was still far away. But in other ways it wasn't. War brides came home with local boys who now had a new lease on belonging in their community. Individuals now found much in common with foreigners who once had been "strange and strangers." But the old nativism clung to the heartland. In Iowa in 1948, when asked whether Congress should allow displaced persons to enter local counties there at the rate of twenty per county per year for four years, a majority said it should not, twice as many as those who felt it should.[18]

While the rest of the world picked itself up slowly to build again, the United States gave it aid, and had much left over to enjoy herself. Americans enjoyed a boom. People were known by the things they owned: cars, new and gleaming . . . the new wonder of television . . . the marvels of home-making—refrigerators, electric mixers, toasters, washing machines. Identity was a matter of acquisition, not of reflection. And of place, not of spirit. Did you see Mr. and Mrs. Smith in church? Did you see the Browns at the P.T.A.? Did you see Baxter mowing his lawn? Live and let live. And acquire. Gather your riches while you may.

Then gradually new questions began to occupy the nation. It could not avoid them. Labor, aided by its crucial role in the war, had grown into a national force that could paralyze a country's commerce with its new power. And civil rights took on an urgent new note as millions of Americans stirred impatiently from second-class citizenship. They had fought in the war.

Now the Negro continued to be left behind, or pushed behind, as the country made a better life for itself. The relation between the federal government and the rights of the little man, as well as the vast, powerful paragovernments that ruled in concert with Washington, moved to the top of the agenda. In 1948 the Supreme Court ruled that the giving of religious instruction in public school classrooms after students were released for it was in violation of the First Amendment. In 1947 the Court had approved a law allowing the use of public funds for parochial-school bus transportation, but both the majority and dissenting opinions had strongly indicated their unwillingness to relax the precedents for separation of church and state.

A wave of antipathy followed between organized religious groups. There had been dissatisfaction on both sides with various elements in the situation and in the ruling. Some saw separation of church and state as a doctrine that had directed much of American life since the founding of the Republic and that was now being threatened. At the same time the Roman Catholic Church saw itself unduly and unlawfully penalized, and its freedom curtailed by government. The controversy raged sharply. Among its conflicts there was an exchange of letters between Francis Cardinal Spellman of New York and Mrs. Eleanor Roosevelt.

Mrs. Roosevelt wrote, "We do not want to see public education connected with religious control of the schools. . . . They should not receive federal funds; in fact, no tax funds of any kind." She apparently received many complaining letters, but the strongest was one from Cardinal Spellman himself, who wrote: "I am ignoring your personal attack (*sic*). . . . But why I wonder do you repeatedly plead causes that are anti-Catholic?" She replied: "I have no bias against the Roman Catholic Church. . . . If you carefully studied my record I think you would not find it one of anti-Catholicism or anti-any religious group."

Old charges were raised in anti-Catholic quarters to the point where the administrative board of the National Catholic Welfare Conference saw fit in January of 1948 to issue a statement of its position:

We deny absolutely and without any equivocation that the Catholic bishops of the United States are seeking a union of Church and State by any endeavors whatsoever, either proximate or remote. If tomorrow Catholics constituted a majority in our country, they would not seek a union of Church and State. . . . In complete accord with the Catholic doctrine we hold firmly that our own constitutional provisions are the best for our country. Even if we had the authority to do so we would not change one iota of them.[20]

The nation faced other questions relating directly to its internal structure and principles. In 1949 eleven communists, leaders of the American Communist party, were found guilty of conspiring to advocate the overthrow of the American government by force.

The conflict sharpened. The entire conduct of American society and the administration of its basic principles came under scrutiny. As the United Nations Headquarters was dedicated in New York, the Berlin airlift seemed to stand perilously between war and peace itself. Then in 1950 the gantlet was thrown down. North Korean and Chinese Communist troops streamed into the southern zones of Korea. Outright territorial aggrandizement had confronted the West with its most serious challenge to date. Doctrinal challenges had been translated into actual military strategy. But something new had been added. America noted with unnerving awe the subjection of American young men to subtle new onslaughts reaching into and undermining the very foundations of American identity that had been constructed out of the political principles and social experience of American society. Brainwashing attacked the very sources, the basic premises —if the individual was indeed conscious of any—that underlay the mind of the American. And in a disturbing number of instances, strong men as well as weak gave way under the combined strains.

It was no longer a time for vacillation. The Korean War and the McCarthy Era had jarred Americans awake to a host of dangers. One was the danger to their country's existence, the danger directly controlled by external forces. The other was the threat to the very heart of a free society that had for decades striven to maintain the rights and liberty and integrity and dignity of the individual as something almost—if not actually— sacred. Now it was again asked: Just where do we stand? What do we believe? What are we for? In 1954, three thousand government employees were dropped for "security reasons," which meant anything from moral turpitude to political conspiracy.

The strong ideological nature of the struggle was recognized on broad fronts. In January of 1950 a young congressman, in an address to the graduating class at Notre Dame University, noted the new focus on the ideological struggle. John F. Kennedy told his listeners:

You have been taught that each individual has an immortal soul, composed of an intellect which can know truth, and a will which is free. Because of this every Catholic must believe in the essential dignity of the human personality on which any democracy must rest. Believing this, Catholics can never adhere to any political theory which holds that the state is a separate distinct organization to which allegiance must be paid rather than a representative institution which derives its powers from the consent of the governed.[21]

Faced with the unparalleled prospect of mutual annihilation, the cold warriors entered a stage that gave way to smaller regional shooting hostilities coupled with massive programs of propaganda, economic warfare, and the subversive fomenting of divisive unrest in the political affairs of nations. It was an offensive no less earnest and no less deadly than, and in some ways just as encompassing as, total war. In it religion was singled out and opposed head-on with godless militancy. The world listened incredulously as Cardinal Mindzenty of Hungary confessed almost listlessly in open court to the charges of treason leveled against him. Scores of priests faced imprisonment on charges of plotting in concert with the West against the new "people's democracies."

In the new communist design of total warfare, the church itself was an object of infiltration. In the subtle dialectic of the Soviet, communism became virtually equivalent with the basic uncluttered premises of Christianity as interpreted and delivered to the war-weary, pious, wondering, yet skeptical workers of Europe. In Italy a wave of "Red priests" faced excommunication by their own church.*

In medieval times, hell had crowded close outside the limits of the small community of men where the church stood as a pillar and was a shelter in the center of the city. Now again it was an almost indisputable fact and condition of existence that those who controlled the government controlled the mind. In communist countries and in Western countries, the battle moved to the mind, and symbols took on renewed importance. The world beyond the individual citizen's small daily world of concerns was shaped by great instruments of mass communication. These created a picture of the world that was unverifiable. Instead, they promoted a kind of consensual picture of reality.

---

* And in America in 1953 a congressional investigation was threatened into communist infiltration of churches; in 1960 a furor was raised over an Air Force Reserve training manual that told of this alleged infiltration.

Increasingly, in foreign-policy pronouncements by the new American Secretary of State, John Foster Dulles, there was a sense of the traditional forces in Western civilization; of the Christian traditions that bound and underlay the community of Western nations. Dulles, whose father once spoke from the same pulpit, addressed an interdenominational community service in 1953 celebrating the 150th anniversary of the First Presbyterian Church in Watertown, New York:

Our institutions of freedom will not survive unless they are constantly replenished by the faith that gave them birth. The terrible things that are happening in some parts of the world are due to the fact that political and social practices have been separated from spiritual content. That separation is almost total in the Soviet communist world. . . . It denies that men are spiritual things. . . . Such conditions repel us . . . it is irreligion. If ever the political forces in this country became irreligious, our institutions would change.[22]

In 1954 the phrase "under God" was added to the Pledge of Allegiance of the United States. Open controversy flourished over the correctness of a nation lending an implicit moralistic aura to its conduct and aims in foreign policy. The West was finding an extragovernmental, almost supragovernmental, consensus. The memory of the great religious wars rose like a specter in the minds of the great debaters.

"Almost everywhere in the world," wrote one observer, "religion is on the retreat. It is on the defensive."[23] Controversy grew within religious circles much as it had in the transition of the late nineteenth century into the new age of the twentieth. It almost seemed that as the new underdeveloped "uncommitted" nations came into independence, and wide disorder and anarchy reigned, that it was not the American Revolution that provided the model, but the godless French Revolution. Within church and lay circles, the question was posed between "liberals" and "conservatives": Was the church to turn its back on the new wave of the modern world, or to attempt to "redeem the time"? Christianity was being placed in the position of being the reactionary force.

An American traveler returning from months of journeys through the villages and cities of Asia noted the complete absence of a Christian church. Upon his return he noted by contrast the presence of seven Christian churches for a population of 1,500 people in his home town. He expressed alarm and regret at the "sin of division" within the Christian church. "The manpower we use in at least four of our . . . churches should be sent to those villages in India," he wrote. "I've seen the face of tomorrow on five continents, and if you have such a look I don't think you can view your fellow Christians of other denominations as competitors."[24]

In 1958 the world witnessed the ascension of a new Pope to the throne. A Commission for the Promotion of Christian Unity was established in the Vatican soon afterward. Pope John XXIII had served as a papal diplomat close to communist borders in eastern Europe. He faced caution from conservatives within the Church hierarchy. But as the first Vatican Council since 1870 loomed, the Archbishop of Canterbury joined the Pope in Rome for an informal meeting in December, 1960. Not since before the Reformation had such a meeting taken place. It was by no means a sign of reunion, but it was interpreted as a sign of co-operation and even concordance. Adding to the aura of a solid front was the Archbishop's visit to Athenagoras, the Patriarch of the Eastern Orthodox Church in Istanbul, just before his meeting with the Pope. Occurring at about the same time was a little-publicized informal meeting of Jewish lay leaders with the Pope at the Vatican.[25]

Strikingly coinciding with the meetings was a great gathering of the eighty-one world-wide Communist party leaders in Moscow a month earlier. Sharp doctrinal differences had been aired and reportedly resolved between communist Chinese and Khrushchev's Moscow party, and had included Tito. A new pledge of solidarity had been shaped to smooth the ideological differences.

In France, the people had returned Charles de Gaulle, a man of fervent spiritual strength and national dedication, to office. In Germany, at the office of Chancellor Konrad Adenauer, three framed photographs stood in a row: Dwight D. Eisenhower, John Foster Dulles, Pope John XXIII.[26] A New York *Times* commentator noted:

Any move in the direction of uniting the spiritual forces of the world's various faiths—and not just those of Christianity but Judaism, Islam, Hinduism, Buddhism and other forms of acknowledging divinity—is welcomed not only by spiritual and lay leaders, but also by thoughtful statesmen.

President Eisenhower makes no secret of his hope that the projected ecumenical council may be but one of a series of moves seeking to ally those who believe in God more closely in their struggle against those who proclaim their disbelief in God.

The President is convinced that if all religions could direct their attention to a single main point—namely that of insisting upon supremacy of spiritual values and thus demonstrating clear kinship among themselves—there would develop a more unified and stronger purpose among free peoples to yield no single inch of advantage to atheistic communism.[27]

In November, 1959, a survey under UN auspices of its member nations "saw a more tolerant attitude in many areas, including predominantly Roman Catholic countries." The report stated, "Nearly all religions and beliefs display a similar trend towards a greater measure of tolerance."[28]

The Archbishop of Canterbury, the Most Reverend Geoffrey F. Fisher, shortly after returning to England from Rome, said he was confident that interchurch discussions with Roman Catholics would be frequent and useful. He went on to suggest that the words "Catholic" and "Protestant" as commonly used were "completely out of date" and "mean nothing at all." He said, "Each word means a different thing to each person," and he noted that the words "corporate" and "personal" almost exactly matched the words "Catholic" and "Protestant."[29]

As the year of these momentous events ended, the World Council of Churches said it saw "a relaxation of tensions within Christendom."[30] Earlier a plan to unite the four major Protestant bodies in the United States had been advanced by the Reverend Dr. Eugene Carson Blake, chief executive officer of the Presbyterian Church in the United States of America, and the Right Reverend James A. Pike, Bishop of the Episcopal Diocese of California. At the time of the council report, the Eastern Orthodox Patriarch Athenagoras issued a statement that called Christian unity "the greatest responsibility faced in our day by the church and all the faithful who bear the name of Christ."[31]

Meanwhile, opposition to the communist total offensive had stiffened. In Hungary, in 1956, thousands from among the millions of members of the Eastern Orthodox Church who now dwelt under communist domination through eastern Europe and in the Soviet Union had fought back heroically for several wild and bloody weeks against the Soviets in their nation's capital.

In Cuba, in 1960, after releasing his people from the yoke of a prior tyranny, Fidel Castro succumbed to communist influences in his closest circle of advisers. In an effort to stem the rebellion that now sprang up against his new domination, Castro struck at the churches of the great island. In response to repeated attacks in which Castro had proclaimed, "With our revolution or against it," the aging Archbishop Pérez Serrantes of Havana declared, "With Christ or against Christ!" He wrote: "It is certain that we fight communism. If it ever existed for us, at this time of life the hour of fear has passed. We fight because we know that today there exist in the world only two fronts face to face. . . . One is composed of those who are disposed to give their lives for Christ . . . the other of those who consciously or unconsciously are trying to eliminate God and erase him from human life."[32]

Commenting on the breaking off of diplomatic relations with Cuba's Castro government in retaliation for a series of calculated abuses, the New York *Herald Tribune* editorialized: "The moral victory is the victory that is likely to matter most in the long run, and we must resolve not to let it escape us."[33]

Meanwhile, what was happening to the people for whose allegiance these forces were vying? Had the American's awareness of his allegiance undergone changes since 1947 when freedom of worship had seemed such a secondary advantage to his type of government? Was there a contemporary "sense of the state" such as had emerged in the 1840's?

It seemed that a relapse into materialism had occurred. Looking back over the decade, one observer in viewing the question of national purpose said, "We have been living in an age of moral fatigue." A survey of business executives resulted in the conclusion that unfair business practices were on the increase in a steady upswing. The "operators" were snaring great profits. Public relations and concern for his "image" were new additions to the businessman's worries, and "the really sincere guy" became a commodity in trade. Misrepresentation of merchandise in advertising was noted, as price gouging and the demand for kickbacks zoomed. A little harmless cheating on expense accounts became the new substitute for the old prohibition game. After all, reasoned many, it was somewhat justified. The government was taking almost all of what a man earned, and the more you earned, the more it took. Top executives in some of the nation's largest corporations came under scrutiny for questionable practices, and in a severe reprimand some of them were sentenced to jail terms for conspiring to fix prices in one of the nation's most vital and dynamic industries. Upright men, pillars of their communities, joiners and leaders of reputable lay and community groups found themselves locked up with criminals.

Something was wrong. Where did the line of demarcation begin and end? In Washington, in successive administrations, the 4 per-centers raised their fee to 5 per cent as they peddled influence and favors. The murky wave reached into the highest councils of government and lapped at the foundations of the White House itself.

It was the age of the quick buck and the short cut. Get it on installments. Buy now and pay later, as easy as one, two, three. Live fast, die young, and have a good-looking corpse, heard the youth of the nation in movies and in magazines. It permeated their lives in a kind of crazy beat that meshed with the state of the world. *Beat the bomb before it beats you.*

Matching the hysteric mixture of complacency with awareness

was a kind of silent internal surrender. It was the age of anxiety, the age of analysis, the age of quiet desperation. The age of faith had passed out three hundred years ago. Everything was relative now. After all, hadn't the scientists said so themselves— at least those who understood it all, or professed to? What was this theory of relativity? From a theory of physics it extended to societies. Yet with it came the feeling that we *were* tops. After all, what did we lack? We had electric blankets, sun lamps, flashy convertibles, money in the bank or on wheels. The pursuit of excellence drew the frustrated wrath and secret envy, mixed with the loud derision and inner despair, of millions. No one was exempt. What makes you think you're better than I am, buddy?

In many instances, where the thirst for technical training had been quenched in affluence, there arose a deeper hunger. Tradition now was defined more in decades than in generations. Shorn of values and bereft of heritage, the inner man cried out, and sought diversion.

Even the entertainment was contrived. Over television, into the homes of millions, came the wonder of a personable young man's mind pitting itself against the awesome demands of questions on which were riding thousands of dollars. The "quiz" shows held millions spellbound. It was no longer the fun of the $64 Question. It was the drama of the $64,000 Question. But the fix was in—all over. A championship national collegiate basketball team was discovered shot through with bribe takers. What was the great harm in "fixing" the point spread? It wasn't as though you were throwing the game. But that came too, in time.

Did corporations and industries dare to do things that the individual did not dare to do, just as warfare and armies sanctioned what was mortally sinful for the individual? If, indeed, as it seemed, the private conscience was growing ineffective, where was the public conscience to replace it?

In his State of the Union Message in January, 1959, President Eisenhower stated his intention of setting up a National Commission on Goals "to explore the long-range aims of the nation and methods to achieve them."

The rate of growth in church membership in America from 1940 to 1956 was more than twice as great as it had been over the previous two decades. From 43 per cent of the population in 1920 it had grown to 63 per cent in 1960. And it continued to accelerate. But to whom and what were these citizens coming when they took membership?

After the initial aristocratic mien and origin of ministers in the early American Colonies, coinciding with the democratization of religion, more men of the cloth had begun to come from the lower echelons of society, economically and educationally. From humble families they made their way into the ministry, and through its formal preparation out into American society, continuing through the nineteenth century. Now many men who had been through the trying and soul-searching and awesome, harrowing experiences of combat had gone into the ministry. They were men profoundly given to earnest pursuit of the meaning of man's relation to self, his fellows, and to God. The brotherhood of man was accorded more priority on a greater scale than ever before. Rabbi Joshua Liebman's book *Peace of Mind* exemplified it, staying on best-seller lists across the country.

One study of four thousand members of twelve denominational churches indicated that religious membership among these people had increasingly become merely a popular and social activity, that "the largest number approached religion as an organizational activity rather than as an intellectual, creedal or devotional experience."[34]

There was skepticism and hard thinking. In some quarters, outright opposition sprang up to religious authority. When a Roman Catholic Church in New Jersey decided to impose tithes on its members rather than holding bingo games, culprits stole collection money and a number of religious items a few days later.[35]

In broader ways, religious authority was questioned when it took the initiative in social matters. In 1955 in New Orleans a fiery cross was burned on the grounds of the Catholic archbishop after desegregation became policy in some parochial schools. The leader in the anti-integration movement was a Catholic judge, active in the White Citizens Council. A Catholic laymen's group was threatened with excommunication. In St. Louis, Catholics began proceedings to halt desegregation plans. A direct appeal to the Pope was made to nullify the bishop's threat of excommunication, and asked that the Pope refute the statement that segregation was sinful. From Rome came a declaration that all men are "equal sons in the house of the Father."[36]

Certainly there was sincerity too in those thousands who joined congregations as a means of finding their place as a total personality in their communities. In the great pattern of the accelerated church-membership flow, it seemed that, faced with the great imponderables of the world's new age, they were experimenting with answers. And because of a tradition of answers from the church they returned to old psychological haunts, despite the overriding secular nature of society at large. They constituted a challenge to church and clergy to "deliver." And as was the case when sweeping social change marked colonial times and then the passing of the Old World in the late nineteenth century, thousands sought direct spiritual sustenance in the appeal of fundamentalist doctrine.

In 1941 the Council of Christian Churches had been founded "to represent true historic Christianity and to combat modernism." A year later the National Association of Evangelicals came into existence. A fundamentalist with the modern grain in his personality and approach, yet combined with unchanging hard fundamentalist doctrine, was Billy Graham, who rose to lead this march "back to Christ." Significantly, Graham did not limit his work to the continental United States, to the circumscribed society that had marked the boundaries of fundamentalism in the late nineteenth century. He traveled across the seas and met with interested receptions in foreign cities. His work was no longer the work of an itinerant preacher in the "Bible Belt" of the United States. It now found receptive responses in the higher councils of government. Graham employed modern tools of communications and of public relations.

How had America changed from the turn of the century, when

Henry Adams had observed that "my country in 1900 is something totally different from my own country of 1860" and that "the American boy of 1854 stood nearer the year 1 than to the year 1900"?[37] Had the social currents of the nation changed since the end of the great waves of immigration and the slow consolidation of the new arrivals?

For one thing, the Roman Catholic Church had made great strides since the early days of the 1900's, when Cardinal Gibbons had written that it would be difficult to arouse such anti-Catholic fanaticism as he had seen in Know-Nothing days.

In Pittsburgh, the Right Reverend Monsignor Michael J. Macken bequeathed $90,000 in government bonds and securities to the federal government when he died at the age of eighty-two in 1958. In his will he explained that he did so "in grateful acknowledgment of the opportunity to prosper both spiritually and materially which this great country has afforded me and members of my religion and nationality."[38]

By 1948, 37 per cent of the Catholic population in the United States was employed in professional, business, or white-collar capacities, the same percentage as among Protestants. Catholics no longer were the lower-class citizens that had been victimized a century earlier. Nearly half of the Catholic population in the United States was concentrated in cities of 100,000 or more. In contrast, three-fourths of the Protestants resided in communities of 100,000 or less, and on farms.[39] Dr. Donald N. Barrett, of the University of Notre Dame, took note of this in a report to the American Catholic Sociological Society. He said that from 1950 to 1959, 41 per cent of the total United States growth had been derived from Catholic growth. Dr. Barrett attributed it to higher birth rates, lower death rates, a rise in Puerto Ricans, Mexicans, and displaced persons, and an increase in adult baptisms.[40]

The Reverend Dr. Gardner C. Taylor, a leading Protestant churchman, asserted that the 62,500,000 citizens who listed themselves as Protestants had virtually become a minority influence in the United States, in their influence on the country's social and political life.[41] And tensions remained. This had been sharply shown in the reaction to the Supreme Court decision on religious instruction in public school classrooms in 1948. And in 1958, in the off-year elections for Congress, some observers noted "a growing tension between one religious group and another, and between the forces of religion and secularism."[42] With the resurgence in religious organizational membership and with the nativity plays and Bible reading in public schools, clearly differences had been somewhat heightened despite the suffusion of the religious spirit into an American community that was no longer essentially Protestant.

CHAPTER NINE

JOHN F. KENNEDY
From New Hampshire to Los Angeles
"I am not the Catholic candidate"

ONE GENERATION AFTER THE GREAT MIGRATIONS, THE CHANGES IN
the social currents of the nation were being shown in new ways.
The descendants of those who had come to America at the turn
of the century occupied positions of unquestioned influence in
the political affairs of the country. The carriers of old animosities had watched with increasing concern as the number of
Catholics in positions of responsibility and authority continued
to grow.* Even viewed as a natural, inevitable process, it remained vastly unsettling. Not least among the reasons for this was
that it was part of the growing Democratic tide that threatened
conservative strength throughout the country.

For years in the Midwest, for example, the demarcation between Republican and Democrat had closely followed religious
lines. Democrats had constituted almost a Catholic party in
states heavily rural and Protestant. But the magic of Roosevelt
and the crises of the time apparently broke this hide-bound tradition in the thirties as many Catholics and Protestants joined in a
new kind of coalition in which economic interests predominated.

---

* For example, Samuel Lubell observes that during the Republican reign
from 1920 to 1932 only one of every twenty-five appointments to the
Federal judiciary had gone to a Catholic. After 1932 this was increased to
one of every four. During the same period, according to the *Official
Catholic Directory*, the proportion of Catholics to the total population
climbed from approximately 10 per cent in 1928 to 24 per cent in 1959.[1]

122

To this change were added the urban minorities and the "solid South," providing a broad coalition for Democratic strength.

The number of Catholics who maintained allegiance to the Democratic party far outweighed those who consistently or gradually moved to the right. For all political purposes, and for conservative economic interests, it was a serious matter.

For six years following his election in 1946, one such Catholic, Congressman John Fitzgerald Kennedy, had represented the descendants of early Irish and other immigrants who continued the struggle for a living and a decent place in the new society after three and four generations. John F. Fitzgerald, Kennedy's maternal grandfather, had served as a congressman and much-loved mayor of Boston, but failed in a 1916 try for the Senate seat held by the redoubtable Yankee Brahmin Henry Cabot Lodge. Patrick Kennedy, too, had been a successful Boston politician, and his son Joseph—the younger Kennedy's father—had amassed a fortune in the ways of the new society, through high-keyed activities in banking, shipping, the movie industry, liquor, the stock market, and real estate.

On his road to Congress, Kennedy had faced almost no direct opposition stemming from his religion. He had been sent to Washington from a heavily Catholic area. Once in Washington, though, he began to experience the issue concerning Catholicism that had plagued the country throughout its history. Early in 1947, during a congressional hearing on federal aid to parochial schools, a witness testified that the Roman Catholic Church was intent on destroying American liberties and sought to "further expand their theocracy as a world government."[2]

Kennedy directly challenged the witness, testily asking: "Now, you don't mean the Catholics in America are legal subjects of the Pope? I am not a legal subject of the Pope." The witness persisted in his assertion of a dual allegiance among Catholics, and Kennedy finally replied, "There is an old saying in Boston that we get our religion from Rome and our politics at home, and that is the way most Catholics feel about it."[3]

In that same year Kennedy accepted an invitation to attend the dedication of a memorial chapel to the four chaplains who had died arm in arm in World War II. One of them was Lieutenant Clark V. Poling, son of Dr. Daniel Poling. Shortly before the event Kennedy learned that the chapel was in a Protestant church. He declined to attend, stating that the event would be against the precepts of the Catholic Church and that he was being invited not as a congressman but as a representative of that faith. Dr. Poling was offended by the rejection, and the entire incident was to arise thirteen years later to plague Kennedy.

Also in 1947 the young congressman demurred at signing a petition for clemency in the case of his predecessor from the Eleventh Congressional District, Irish-Catholic James Curley, who faced prison on charges of mail fraud. The break between the old school and the new was thus sharply underscored. The Kennedy family represented a force in frequent combat with the Curley elements in Boston politics.

In 1952, thirty-four-year-old Congressman Kennedy sought the Senate seat held by Henry Cabot Lodge, Jr. Many Irish Catholics in the state who for years had voted Yankee Republican as a measure of respectable assimilation now could feel they had a candidate of their own. He was polished, personable, educated in the best Yankee schools, on equal terms with the best of Yankee society, descended from a fine conjoining of Irish families, and possessing all the advantages that wealth and fine education could bring—the first of the Irish Brahmins.[4]

In a whirlwind campaign marked by thorough attention to detail, astute political planning, and ceaseless effort, capitalizing unremittingly on every disadvantage of his opponent's position, Kennedy came from behind to displace Lodge by 70,000 votes as Eisenhower swept Massachusetts by more than 200,000 and voters brought Republican Christian Herter into the governor's office. The power of the Kennedy personality and what it represented had been demonstrated on a large scale for the first time.

Early in his career in the Upper Chamber Kennedy increasingly showed broader concerns than those of regional interest.

In 1956 the great national schisms that had been manifested repeatedly in presidential elections were once again reflected in a move to revise the electoral college system. Under fire was the persistent support that had solidly backed Wilson, Roosevelt, and Truman—and was to figure crucially in the presidential race in four years.

There had been strong objections for several years in conservative quarters in the Senate to the bloc delivery of a state's electoral vote rather than proportionately dividing it, based on the state's popular vote. Under the system, it was argued, minority groups and ethnic blocs located in the largest states with the greatest number of electoral votes were exerting undue influence on the outcome of presidential elections. Six years earlier a constitutional amendment had been cosponsored by Henry Cabot Lodge, Jr., but then turned aside. Now a new bill to remedy the situation seemed to have the wide base of support for passage. Kennedy was among those opposing the measure.

Taking the floor over a two-day period, he defended the system "under which," he said, "we have on the whole obtained able Presidents capable of meeting the increased demands on our Executive." He warned against disposing of the method "for an unknown, untried but obviously precarious system which was abandoned in this country long ago, which previous Congresses have rejected and which has been thoroughly discredited in Europe."[5] The "urban" interests singled out by opponents of the system included Negroes, Catholics, and Jews, who would be deprived of political influence almost entirely if the new proposal were adopted. Any great influence of the larger, heavily urbanized states, Kennedy and others felt, actually served as a balance on what otherwise would be a continuing predominant influence held by smaller and rural regions in the Houses of Congress. Following his vigorous floor leadership against it, the measure failed. Among those opposing it now were eight of its original sponsors.

As the presidential nominating conventions approached, there was talk of a possible Stevenson-Kennedy ticket. And as the prospect was weighed, the religious question arose early. Draw-backs were pointed out. If the Republicans won again, with a Catholic on the Democratic side, much of the onus might be laid at his feet and constitute a mortal political blow. Times were not propitious for the national launching of a Catholic candidate. On the other hand (it was reasoned by Kennedy supporters), such a candidate stood to gain prominence nationally, and might even definitely add strength to the ticket. To document this assertion, Kennedy aides prepared a "memo" based on detailed and compre-hensive analysis of voting patterns. It suggested the definite exist-ence of a "Catholic vote" of substantial proportions strategically placed, which represented considerable potential support of any ticket that included a Catholic vice presidential candidate.

The study went back to 1940, presenting an analysis of results in fourteen states where, in the current election, the Catholic vote was viewed as possibly decisive. It noted Samuel Lubell's observation that "Catholic voting strength is currently at its peak, in view of the maturing of the offspring of the Italians, Poles, Czechs and other former immigrant elements."[6]

Not only were one of every four actual voters Catholic, the report maintained, but these voters were also concentrated in key states with large electoral votes. (It was in fact true that since 1940, Catholics eligible to vote who did so far outproportioned the number of Protestant qualified voters who actually cast ballots.)

The memo cited defections of normally Democratic Catholics to Eisenhower in 1952, and warned that the "immigrant base" of Democratic support that had begun to coalesce with Wilson and had moved together for Smith in 1928 was now "cracking." A nation-wide survey had shown that in 1948, 66 per cent of the Catholics voting for President had voted Democratic, while only 51 per cent did in 1952. If Stevenson were now able in 1956 to recapture only those Catholics who had voted for Truman and then switched to Eisenhower, it could mean enough additional electoral votes, when combined with the traditionally Democratic states of the South, to provide a necessary majority.[7]

The report said the "myth" that Smith had lost in 1928 because of his Catholicism was "one of the falsest . . . in politics." In fact, it asserted, Smith had actually "helped the Democratic party more than he hurt it." Citing the Ogburn report, on the power of the prohibition sentiment, Kennedy's aides opined that "1928 was a Republican year regardless of who was on either ticket," and went so far as to assert that had Smith run as a dry Republican even he too could have won. Moreover, said the memo, "The nation has changed since 1928." The political role of Catholics was now more frequent and accepted. And, they added, "the nation is considerably more tolerant on religious matters."[8]

The report concluded by asserting that "the Catholic vote" would add more strength to the Democratic ticket in 1956 than either the "southern vote" or the "farm vote," and suggested that a Catholic vice presidential candidate could "refashion" the political base established by Smith, concentrating his campaign in cities with heavy Catholic populations, for example, St. Louis, Gary, Albany, and Buffalo.

To back up its assertions, the report cited thirty-four specific instances across the country in which local Catholic candidates had run ahead of their ticket in 1952, winning in their areas while Stevenson lost. One notable instance was Kennedy's own victory in the senatorial race in Massachusetts. The report suggested that Catholic candidates for Congress, the Senate, and the governorship consistently ran ahead of their national ticket. Indeed, this had been the case in New York in 1924, after Smith had lost the Democratic presidential nomination.

The validity of the report's conclusions was immediately challenged in some quarters. Catholic organs joined in the criticism. The percentage of turnout among Catholic voters was unduly inflated, they held. And, it was pointed out, incumbent congressmen as a rule run better than the national ticket. Some non-Catholic congressmen ran even further ahead of their tickets than did Catholics. Moreover, it was pointed out, Kennedy himself in his 1952 victory did not run particularly strong in uniformly

Catholic areas.[9] Despite these objections, though, the report seemed to have some effect.

As the convention fought and maneuvered toward a decision, Kennedy was approached by Stevenson and his advisers to place the governor's name in nomination.[10] Kennedy put Stevenson's name before the delegates, and after a resounding first-ballot victory Stevenson expressed the desire that the selection of a vice presidential candidate should be made through the "free process" of the convention. President Eisenhower's incapacities in the previous year, it was held, made the selection of a vice presidential candidate a grave responsibility that should not be dictated by one man.

Supporters of Kennedy, Estes Kefauver, Hubert Humphrey, Robert Wagner, and others now moved helter-skelter to summon the necessary support for their man. A strong stop-Kefauver sentiment among eight southern delegations provided enough support for Kennedy to give him a lead on the second ballot, just sixty-eight votes short of nomination. Significantly, five of the southern states supporting him had moved into the Hoover column in 1928, away from normally Democratic allegiances.

The Kennedy drive lost ground, however, as Kefauver's strength held. Then other delegations switched into his column on the next ballot, and the Tennessee senator had the nomination.

Had Kennedy been chosen, his presidential aspirations might have ended with the party's defeat in the election that followed. But now he gained ground. Al Smith had always been keenly aware of his colorful parochialism and had almost stubbornly and deliberately accentuated it, even as he spoke of one America. Now it was a different American and a different Catholic in a different world who crisscrossed the country giving dozens of lectures, receiving a Pulitzer Prize in biography for his *Profiles in Courage,* being featured on the cover of *Time* magazine—all the while continuing to serve actively in the Senate and moving into a coveted seat on its Foreign Relations Committee.

The subject of 1960 loomed early. After a weekend visit to Georgia in 1957, the state's Democratic chairman said it was "highly likely that the state's next Democratic delegation will support Kennedy" for the presidential nomination.[11]

As the 1958 congressional elections approached, the junior senator's reelection seemed virtually assured. But Kennedy forces saw the chance of a boost in his national party prestige if he were to win a resounding victory in his home state. Kennedy waged a hard campaign, and also spent days stumping for fellow Democrats in a number of other eastern seaboard states and in the Midwest. When the ballots were in, he had been returned to the Upper Chamber by more than 870,000 votes, the greatest edge piled up by any senatorial candidate in the country.[12]

When the smoke of the year's elections across the nation had cleared, there were five new Catholic governors (raising the total to eight, including the major states of Pennsylvania and California), eight new Catholic senators (raising the total to twelve), and ninety-one Catholic representatives. The possibility of another "Catholic candidate" for President suddenly fell heavily on old sensibilities.

Within weeks, Baptists in Georgia and Alabama at year-end conventions issued resolutions reaffirming their fundamental and historic principles regarding the "separation of church and state," and "religious liberty" for all citizens.[13] In each instance the resolutions adopted had been different from those originally proposed, including the elimination of a direct reference to the Catholic Church in one. Nevertheless, it was plain that in noting "the election of an individual as President of the United States whose religion teaches him his church should be supported by the state and above the state" was a "matter of . . . serious religious concern," the historic call to arms had once again been sounded.[14]

The muted note on which the call had been sounded could hardly have been expected to last. Despite this, to some the signs were encouraging. It was true that in several elections there had been a clear resurgence of anti-Catholic sentiment. But in Minnesota, for example, a state with a heavily Lutheran population, Democrat Eugene McCarthy had been sent to the Senate. There now seemed comparatively little trace of the intense opposition that in earlier years had confronted Catholics running for office, at least on the state and local levels.

In an effort to anticipate and dampen the religious issue before it could flare up, Kennedy explicitly stated his views on a number of matters of traditional concern to non-Catholics in an article in *Look* magazine several months after his reelection. "Whatever one's religion in his private life may be," he wrote, "for the office-holder nothing takes precedence over his oath to uphold the Constitution and all its parts—including the First Amendment and the strict separation of church and state. . . ."[15]

This attempt to throw cold water on the religious issue resulted in Kennedy's getting into hot water with some of his own co-religionists. An editorial in the Catholic weekly *America* took him to task for his view: "No religious man, be he Catholic, Protestant or Jew, holds such an opinion. A man's conscience has a bearing on his public as well as his private life. . . ."[16]

It was the danger of Kennedy's statement being subject to mis-interpretation that had seemed most harmful. The implication that "his religion, which teaches him to know, love and serve God in all things," might conceivably be at variance with his oath to uphold the Constitution and its spirit was what worried many.

Earlier the candidate had said, "Public issues are certainly not divested of moral implication when they emerge in the political arena, but the responsibility of the office-holder is to make decisions on these questions on the basis of the general welfare as he sees it, even if such a decision is not in accord with the prevailing Catholic opinion."[17]

Dispositions now were growing ruffled. Within weeks after the publication of Kennedy's article, the National Association of Evangelicals gave its approval to the statement, "Any country the Roman Catholic Church dominates suppresses the right of Evangelicals. . . ." Without specific reference, the association and its officers agreed: "For that reason, thinking Americans view with alarm the possible election of a Roman Catholic as President of the United States. . . ."[18]

There was far from complete agreement on this point in the Protestant religious community, and this was made clear early. "Having seen Catholicism in thirty countries," said the Reverend Dr. Richard C. Raines, Methodist Bishop of Indianapolis, "I am convinced that Catholicism in the United States is the most spiritually wholesome and soundly alive in the world."[19] Alabama Methodists were less temperate in their attitude. Following public support of Kennedy by Governor John Patterson, they declared that "the people of Alabama whose attitudes are basically Protestant do not intend to jeopardize their democratic liberties by opening the doors of the White House to the political machinations of a determined, power-hungry Romanist hierarchy."[20]

The challenge that Kennedy had sought to meet before it could gain a commanding voice had been issued. Before the year ended, Oklahoma Baptists went on record as "opposing the election to any governmental office in state or nation of any person whose first allegiance is to any other power which would influence or lead him to fail to take a bold stand for our principles of separation of church and state."[21]

For the first time in a quarter of a century, a Catholic again stood in serious contention for nomination as a candidate for the Presidency. The historic opposition had voiced itself early, and as the nation entered its election year the chorus swelled.

Speaking in Boston, Glenn L. Archer of Protestants and Other Americans United for Separation of Church and State told his audience: "We see no reason why a man's religion should serve as a shield to protect him from embarrassing questions. If there is any possibility of a conflict of interest between church directives and duties connected with the Presidency, this should be known."[22]

Dr. Ramsey Pollard, president of the 9,000,000-member Southern Baptist Convention, emphatically declared he would not "stand by and keep my mouth shut when a man under control of the Roman Catholic Church runs for the Presidency of the United States."[23] Kennedy was not referred to specifically. By this time, however, there was little doubt as to the front runner in the minds of the opposition.

Permeating the tone of these early pronouncements was an unmistakable element that was striking in its newness. In place of the old emotionalism and militancy there was a measured rational quality and even a strange defensiveness. An unsigned editorial in *Christianity Today*, with a reported circulation of 200,000 among Protestant clergymen and including the Reverend Billy Graham as one of its contributing editors, stated: "Informed Protestants believe not at all irrationally that the interests of the nation are safer in the hands of one who does not confess to a foreign, earthly power."[24] It said that Protestants who opposed a Catholic candidate were not therefore guilty of "bigotry."

American society in 1960, it appeared, had moved a long way from the bitter rancor and personal vituperation of 1928, when there had hardly been what could be called defensiveness among most of Smith's critics.

Early in June, for example, the Augustana Lutheran Church, encompassing a synod of more than 600,000 members—the largest Lutheran synod in the nation—issued a resolution urging "conscientious and prayerful study" of the "ideological beliefs and affiliation or the lack of them" among presidential candidates. Excluded from the final draft, however, had been firmly worded suggestions that there were "grounds for reasonable doubt that a Roman Catholic President would be free from institutional control and from desire to promote in special ways the ends of the Roman Church," and that this would constitute a "potential threat to . . . traditional ideals and sense of justice of American society."[25]

Since 1928 there had been wide-scale efforts by interfaith groups to meet bigotry with educative contacts across group lines. Yet there remained a need to counter specific expressions of bigotry in political campaigns. Here the more removed and broader interfaith efforts had little neutralizing effect.

The Fair Campaign Practices Committee represented such an effort. A voluntary nonpartisan group, it was without precedent in American politics. Its formation had been urged by Anna Lord Strauss, Palmer Hoyt, Gardner Cowles and others in 1954, in the wake of indiscriminate smear tactics that had riddled the country's political affairs in the years just prior to that. Since then it had served as a clearinghouse for spotting and countering grievous abuses of fair play in political campaigning.

Under its executive director, Bruce Felknor, and chairman, Charles P. Taft, the committee initiated its efforts in the 1960 campaign several months before the party conventions. In March it joined with the National Conference of Christians and Jews in bringing together prominent religious leaders in a two-day conference in Washington. The group declared the need for "intelligent, honest and temperate discussion of the religious issue as it might arise in the campaign."[26]

The early expressions of anti-Catholicism, despite their scattered nature, were enough to confront Kennedy with a serious, and for the present, much more formidable problem. The leaders of his party were far from convinced that Kennedy was the best man in 1960. (As late as the eve of the convention, reports indicated that Lyndon Johnson of Texas was much the stronger choice among party stalwarts.) Kennedy's religion had been but one of several factors regarded *in toto* as virtually insurmountable obstacles to his nomination. But the early objections now made it the most prominent one.

A year earlier a Gallup poll had found that 57 per cent of those asked would like to see Kennedy win, running against Nixon, "if the election were held today." But fewer than half had expressed any awareness of Kennedy's religion. Now, in March of 1960, as the number of persons aware of his religion increased, the choice had leveled to an exactly even split.[27]

It was clear that Kennedy would have to carry his campaign for the nomination right into the final stretch, and with renewed intensity. The state primaries in the spring had to provide a decisive test of whether the young senator could demonstrate the vote-getting ability over diverse areas and among a multiplicity of groups that would mark him as a winner.

When confronted with the belief that a Catholic could not win the Presidency, based on the assumption that Smith's defeat in 1928 had been chiefly the result of his religion, Kennedy said that he hoped in the primaries and his drive for the Presidency "to demonstrate that it is not a valid conclusion." As he campaigned in Indiana in areas containing scores of ethnic groups, including many Catholics of Irish and Polish ancestry as well as Greek Orthodox groups from eastern Europe, he referred to the seven hundred years of "foreign oppression" in Ireland.

For a time, at least, it seemed as though the "religious issue" was again being viewed as it had been in 1884 and even down to 1928, when the "old country" still retained more salience for many than the new society. But it soon became clear that these were not at all the terms on which the issue was to be dealt with.

As Kennedy arrived in Indianapolis to file a petition, formally entering the Indiana primary, he was met by a group identifying themselves as representatives of the Indiana Bible Baptist Fellowship.[28] Fresh from an all-night prayer meeting at their church, the group challenged Kennedy to a debate: "Resolved that a Roman Catholic President cannot impartially defend the Constitution and advance the true welfare of the United States while remaining true to his religion." After filing his petition, Kennedy replied in a press conference: "Why didn't you issue this challenge when I joined the United States Navy?" The demonstrators were entitled to their views, he said. He believed in the Constitution and in freedom of speech. But, he added, "I also believe in the First Amendment which provides for the separation of the church and the state. I also believe in Article VI which says there shall be no religious test for qualification for public office." As the conference concluded and the candidate left, the demonstrators remained in the room. "We would have a safer and quieter country," said one, "if we were free from Vatican politics." Newsmen listened. "I like Kennedy better than Nixon but I will have to vote for someone else than Kennedy. Some of his statements sound more like a young Irish thug than like those of a statesman." A man in the audience jumped to his feet. "You are a rabble rouser!" he cried out. "You are arousing hate!" The old animosities had exploded with ugly suddenness.

Old antipathies, prompted by bitter frustration in the face of their expression, caused some to return to the image of earlier immigrant politicians and their henchmen and cronies. The antiquated images were reinforced by old themes. From Wisconsin came reports of the circulation of copies of *Maria Monk*, which could be had on order from a religious publishing house in Gainesville, Florida. "No book like this in print," promised a circular. It advertised "blood-curdling experiences" and a running account of "America's fair daughters . . . forced into involuntary servitude" and "every crime from seduction to murder." The advertisement editorialized, "Convents in America must be done away with—they are unlawful and uncalled for and un-natural, un-American and un-Scriptural." Also circulating were a "description" of the assassination of Lincoln, allegedly by Roman Catholics, and the old fraudulent Knights of Columbus "oath." It bound the "oath"-taker to "spare neither age, sex or condition" in the "relentless war" in which he was to "hang, burn, waste, boil, flay, strangle and bury alive these infamous heretics." He vowed further to "provide myself with arms and ammunition that I may be in readiness when the word is passed."[29]

And there were new themes, as befitted the age of the H-bomb. "When hydrogen and atomic-bomb-equipped bases are established in Italy," said one writer, "they will be under the direct personal control of the Pope, and he will use them to annihilate all those nations and individuals who refuse to worship, obey and enrich him."[30]

Amid the increasing amount of such material, little was personally directed at Kennedy. In Indiana, where years before the Klan had waged bitter campaigns of individual harassment, a minister lecturing on aspects of the issue took care to state, "This is in no wise a reflection on the integrity or the ability of the man John Kennedy."[31]

This early careful avoidance of what could possibly be interpreted as *personal* abuse or slander involving religion went hand in hand in fact with a tentative separation of Kennedy from his "church." From Union, New Jersey, Conde McGinley's *Common Sense,* advertising itself as "The Nation's Anti-Communist Newspaper," declared: "Senator Kennedy's religion is no problem unless his is not strong enough. He was vaccinated for a Catholic, but how strong did it take?" It noted: "Last year, Kennedy said in an interview that there had been no Catholic influence in his personal education. He could well say that for he never attended a Catholic school a day." Instead, the paper said, "It's not his religion—it's his record that should be examined." It went on: "No one can deny he has been soft on communism. . . . Kennedy's nomination or election can only be harmful to the well-being of our country and especially to Catholics who will be ashamed of him. He will open the gates to the Reds, equal only to F.D.R."[32]

This stratagem reached an extreme in New Hampshire's primary campaign. There was placed before voters the paradox of a Roman Catholic who was "soft" on communism. It was stated that Kennedy's nomination would be "extremely dangerous to the safety of the United States."[33]

The assertion that a loyal Catholic could not possibly give primary loyalty to the Constitution gained ground. Therefore, if Senator Kennedy were to be allowed the benefit of the doubt and to be believed, in his affirmation that "nothing takes precedence" over an oath to "uphold the Constitution and all its parts" (which had clearly caused a furor in Church circles), it was implied that he couldn't be a very good Catholic. Instead, he was a man who made his religion subservient to his political purposes, or worse.

And, as other candidates had learned earlier, it was a far greater political sin in America to appear an agnostic or irreligious or nonreligious than to be a member of a religious creed, however suspect that creed might be. Richard Nixon sounded this tradition, that reached back to the early nineteenth century, to Andrew Jackson's campaigns and his opposition among religionists. "There is only one way I can visualize religion being a legitimate issue in an American political campaign," Nixon stated in April. "That would be if one of the candidates for the Presidency had no religious belief."[34] A week later, on a television program, Nixon reiterated his view that the only important criterion was whether a candidate had a "basic belief in God."[35] He added that he was certain from his personal acquaintance with John Kennedy, dating back to 1946 when they both had come to the House, that Kennedy would "put his country and the Constitution above other considerations." Nixon stated that "since all the candidates recognize and cherish both in their personal and public lives the religious and moral principles which are the very foundation of our American ideals there is no excuse for continued discussion of a so-called religious issue."[36]

But by that time, as Nixon himself noted, the religious issue was "commanding major attention throughout the nation." It had been propelled into national prominence by the results of the Wisconsin primary in the first week of April.

Wisconsin had for years constituted a striking social laboratory in American society. Into it had come Germans, Norwegians, Poles, Irish, and Jews, with many other ethnic strains, to create a vivid mixture in the heartland of America. It boasted large cities, yet had a strong rural farm population. And fully 32 per cent of its population was Catholic (as against a national proportion of 24 per cent).

As the primary there neared, the religious factor increasingly preoccupied most observers. Voters leaving political gatherings were questioned as to their religious affiliation. Finally a major advertisement appeared in the state's newspapers, signed by a number of civic-minded persons, questioning whether Kennedy was truly independent or owed his allegiance to the Pope as Christ's vicar on earth, as had been asked repeatedly of Smith in 1928. As a counter to what the advertisement said was a Catholic vote building for Kennedy, it suggested an attempt to marshal a "Protestant vote," noting that many normally Republican Catholics were stating their intentions of "crossing over" to vote for Kennedy (permissible under Wisconsin law).

It became clear even before the primary that in the event of a victory for Kennedy it would be attributed largely to a "Catholic vote." The candidate would thus be forced into a damaging situation despite his victory. The primary in West Virginia five weeks hence loomed as even more crucial than had been the one in Wisconsin. Looking ahead, Kennedy observed, several days before the Wisconsin balloting, that West Virginia's 3 per cent Catholic population was "the smallest proportionate Catholic population of any state. If I thought there was a massive Catholic vote," he asked his listeners, "do you think I would be entered in West Virginia?"[37]

When the Wisconsin vote was in, it was clear that in certain districts a crossover vote for Kennedy among Catholic Republicans had in fact occurred. In normally Democratic areas with a high proportion of Roman Catholic voters, he scored a heavier margin than was usual for Democratic candidates. In several instances counties normally Republican but with substantial numbers of Catholics went for Kennedy.

A number of factors had combined to bring Catholics, as well as many Protestants, to Kennedy. Among conservatives—whether Catholic or Protestant—the Massachusetts senator's dispassionate moderate approach to issues seemed to be reinforced by his personal reserve and charm, his "nice" manner and his sincerity. By contrast, Humphrey had offered a crusading temperament and untrammeled, forthright liberalism. Kennedy represented, it seemed, the best virtues of the Midwest, embodied in a sophisticated cultured easterner; rather than regional, he was almost a national ideal type.

Confronted with such ". . . a Catholic . . . smart as hell, or a rabble-rousing Protestant . . . ,"[38] a considerable number of voters retired to the overriding safety of the conservative Midwest tradition, feeling reassured by the aura surrounding Kennedy. And, as had been the case in Massachusetts, a number of Catholics felt proudly that they finally had a candidate of their own, or that at the very least they were compelled to pay tribute to this dynamic and personable member of their faith.

There had been a light crossover vote reported on the part of Republican Protestants, for Humphrey. The fears of divisive voting along sectarian lines had been borne out in a limited degree. It was an ill omen for the national election. For whatever reason, Kennedy had "made his best showing in the three most heavily Catholic districts," while Humphrey "made his best showing in the two most strongly Protestant districts."[39] Any political advantage in Kennedy's Roman Catholicism was potentially offset by the stiffening of opposition to him on this basis.

From this standpoint, the Democrats faced another possible problem in the effect upon Catholic Democrats, who, it was reported, "make up over half of the registered Democratic voters in the large and decisive cities of the North,"[40] if Kennedy, following a succession of victories in the primaries, were by-passed for the nomination. Already there was sentiment behind an effort within the party to shunt him into the vice presidential spot on the ticket.

As James Reston noted, there was "no longer any chance of avoiding the issue after the evidence of Catholic bloc voting in Wisconsin." It was now "a national question, beyond the borders of one state or even the limits of this particular Presidential election." Concluded Reston, ". . . an unnecessary split in the country at this moment in history is intolerable."[41]

To many, the split was far from unnecessary or intolerable. Within days of the Wisconsin result, one thousand delegates to the annual meeting of the Missouri Baptist Women's Missionary Union gave a rousing amen to a prayer asking "the Lord's blessing and assistance" in electing a Protestant President of the United States.[42]

As Kennedy pushed his campaign in West Virginia, there was a strong current of anti-Catholic feeling in questions put to him at street corners, roadsides, meeting rooms, and college campuses —almost everywhere he went. He met it head-on. There was, in a sense, little else he could do. The religious test squarely confronted him, unconcealed, as it had not squarely confronted any candidate—including Smith—since perhaps the ordeal undergone by Frémont in 1856. And it was only the beginning.

Yet there continued to be a more subdued tone in the queries,

even in more instances than in 1928. The Reverend Dr. Ross Cul-
pepper, Methodist Superintendent of the Charleston District,
noted: "It isn't at all like it was in the Al Smith campaign, and
I was here then. There was so much grunt and growl then about
'we're going to lose our country to the Catholics' and so on." He
noted how he and others in his area had worked hard to build up
a feeling of cooperation among religious groups over the years
since the war. "I think we have a much broader feeling of tolerance today," he said.[43]

In an area suffering from extended and severe unemployment,
the people listened as it was charged by his opponents that millionaires and city machines were on the side of Kennedy. In the
rest of the nation, across its farm belts and great rural stretches,
this throwback to the Populist appeals of the late nineteenth
century no longer held the impact it once did. There, thousands
held stocks in what had once been regarded with hostility as the
very biggest of the "capitalist" enterprises. But in West Virginia
the people listened.

Into the state came Franklin Delano Roosevelt, Jr., to campaign for Kennedy. Kennedy moved through the southern parts
of the state, talking for hours with miners deep in the earth and
families in worn and crumbling communities.

Five miners, their faces still blackened, just up from their shift,
sat and talked with a stranger about the impending primary. "If
Kennedy is a good man I wouldn't let his religion stand in my
way," said one of them, a crew leader. The four others nodded
to show they agreed. "If he's religious, why then more power to
him," another man remarked.[44]

Along mountain roads and in local high school gymnasiums, in
an area containing a preponderance of Pentecostal groups, the
religious theme appeared and reappeared. He did not "take orders
from any Pope, any Cardinal, any Bishop or any priest," he told
coal miners, ". . . not that they would try to give me orders."[45]
He named Catholics who had occupied high offices without any
question of their having been subject to ecclesiastical influence,

and called attention to the Constitution and its spirit of separation of church and state.

In the same breath with which they raised the question of loyalty to papal policy and susceptibility to church pressures, Kennedy's challengers noted, as did one minister, "Now, Kennedy doesn't believe that, but the Pope does."[46] Once again, in effect, the candidate was damned if he did, and damned if he didn't, as had been implied at the very outset of his drive for the nomination.

As the West Virginia primary entered its final weeks, it appeared that there was more concern among Protestants about church pressures on a Catholic candidate in those areas in which there were almost no Catholics than there were in areas with substantial numbers of Catholics. It seemed that living and working among them as neighbors inclined people to be less attentive to such remote considerations. The phenomenon of assimilation throughout decades of American social history was being pointed up. No longer could the religious issue be couched in terms of alien strangers threatening "native" ways. All were natives now, indeed neighbors. Even where ethnic differences remained, contact bred no old frictions of the scale that had once been wrought by the Klan.

Now, in 1960, the Klan was resurrected in a different cause. A firm opponent of Kennedy, Virginia Senator Robert C. Byrd had been accused in his campaign two years earlier of having been a one-time Kleagle or founder of the Klan in that region.[47] The charges against Byrd, combined with the revered memory of F.D.R., brought large numbers of Negro voters toward the Massachusetts senator's side.

Despite these efforts, reviewing his position in the final days, Kennedy confided that his decision to enter the primary had been a mistake. He regarded himself as the underdog.[48]

Kennedy was scheduled to address the American Society of Newspaper Editors in Washington on "America's role in the underdeveloped world." He interrupted his West Virginia campaign to fly to Washington for a Senate vote on a bill affecting distressed coal miners, and then once again on April 21st broke from his exhausting pace to grapple with the issue that now seemed to be outweighing all other obstacles before him.

Confronting four hundred newspaper editors, Kennedy began by stating bluntly, "I want no votes solely on account of my religion."[49] He continued: "Neither do I want anyone to support my candidacy merely to prove that this nation is not bigoted—and that a Catholic can be elected President. I have never suggested that those opposed to me are thereby anti-Catholic. There are ample legitimate grounds for supporting other candidates," and Kennedy noted aside, "though I will not of course detail them here." A ripple of laughter ran through his audience. But it was soon to feel slightly uncomfortable, as Kennedy launched into the burden of his message: Although "the press did not create this religious issue" it had a responsibility to beware "of either magnifying or oversimplifying it." Kennedy enumerated examples of excessive prominence given to religion at the expense of what he regarded as many more relevant and dominant issues. He firmly voiced his opinion that the voters object to their being categorized as either Catholic or Protestant in examining their political choices.

"Is the religious issue a legitimate issue in this campaign?" Kennedy brought the focus back to himself. "There is only one legitimate question underlying all the rest: Would you as President of the United States be responsive in any way to ecclesiastical pressures or obligations of any kind that might in any fashion influence or interfere with your conduct of that office in the national interest? I have answered that question many times. My answer was—and is—'No.' "[50]

He went on to state his belief that federal assistance to parochial schools "is clearly unconstitutional." (Henry Cabot Lodge was to come out in favor of such aid later in the campaign.) Kennedy reiterated his opposition to an Ambassador to the Vatican ("last proposed by a Baptist President," Kennedy noted). He specified other questions that, he said, he would decide on the basis of "what I consider to be the public interest without regard to my private religious views. . . .

"Is there any justification for applying special religious tests to . . . the Presidency? The Presidency is not, after all, the British crown, serving a dual capacity in both church and state. . . . We are in no danger of a one-man constitutional upheaval. The President, however intent he may be on subverting our institutions, cannot ignore the Congress—or the voters—or the courts."

Now Kennedy warmed to the battle. "Some may say we treat the Presidency differently because we have had only one previous Catholic candidate for President. But I am growing weary of that term. I am not the Catholic candidate for President. I do not speak for the Catholic church on issues of public policy—and no one in that church speaks for me."

Taking note of the suggestions that he withdraw, and perhaps accept the vice presidential nomination, Kennedy said he found this "highly distasteful." After all, where was the logic, when he might still be but a "heart-beat away from the office"?

Finally, the broader implications of all this on the country's image were explored. "Are we to admit to the world—worse still, are we to admit to ourselves—that one-third of our population is forever barred from the White House?" Kennedy concluded: "If there is bigotry in the country so great as to prevent fair consideration of a Catholic who has made clear his complete independence and dedication to the separation of church and state, then we ought to know it. But I do not believe this is the case. I believe the American people are more concerned with a man's views and abilities than with the church to which he belongs. I believe that the founding fathers meant it when they provided in the Constitution that there should be no religious test for office. . . ."

When he had finished, the hall rang with vigorous applause for a full minute. Senator Humphrey, following Kennedy to the rostrum, prefaced his talk on disarmament by saying he would "not want to receive the vote of any American because my opponent or opponents worship in a particular church whatever that church may be." Later he said: "I am sick at heart over the whole thing. If this continues, it will result in a situation that will be disastrous for every person in public life."[51]

The ramifications of the issue were in fact beginning to evoke remonstrances in high places. Within a week, President Eisenhower at his news conference, in response to a request for his views on the religious issue, read Article VI of the Constitution and the First Amendment. He said the Constitution answered it better than any words he could think of.[52]

Of more immediate import, however, was the reaction of Dr. Robert E. Strider, former Episcopal Bishop of West Virginia for thirty-two years. Shortly after Kennedy's Washington talk it was reported he was "profoundly impressed with the forthright manner" in which Kennedy was handling the religious issue, and had told the candidate, "You have left no doubt in my mind concerning your loyalty to the Constitution of the United States."[53]

In the second week of May, the people of West Virginia went to the polls. The results appeared to vindicate Kennedy's faith. By a three-to-two margin they expressed their preference for him. Methodists, the largest single Protestant denomination (200,000) in the state, did not seem to have cast their weight heavily against him. Kennedy, with characteristic caution, appraised its effect on the issue: "If it hasn't eliminated it, I would think it had diminished it very substantially."[54]

But even as Kennedy spoke, millions of Americans were reading the views of Dr. Eugene Carson Blake, of the United Presbyterian Church, and Methodist Bishop G. Bromley Oxnam in *Look* magazine. The two stated that they felt "uneasy" about a Catholic candidate for President. They explained: "This uneasiness arises from a feeling widespread among American Protestants that the election of a Roman Catholic to the Presidency would both symbolize and strengthen the growing and direct political influence that the Roman Catholic Church exerts on our government and our society."[55]

Here, the new terms of the issue which had appeared quietly amid the 1928 protestations and warnings about "conspiracy" and "allegiance" took root in 1960. It was the broad social force of the church moving openly, unconcealed in American society, that constituted the danger. By comparison, the seeming diminution of Protestantism as an influence gave profound cause for concern. It was no longer a question of conspiracy. It was a question of philosophy, of doctrinal influences on personality. Nor was "bigotry" a fair label to give to the expression of such concerns. "When the religious issue is injected into politics in order to stir up prejudice and bigotry," noted the churchmen, "it is wrong. But when any citizens worry about how the religious affiliation of a candidate may affect his fulfillment of his official duties, they surely have the right to ask the candidate honest questions, and the right to expect candid answers from him.[56]

"We worry about how a Catholic President could square his political duties with the 'official' position of the church to which he owes allegiance, on questions that range from the use of public funds for parochial schools . . . to the conduct of foreign affairs." They enumerated several issues they considered vital.

The two Protestant leaders decried a charge that compared the POAU with which they were affiliated to the Know-Nothing party of the 1850's. "We recall with regret," they said, "those chapters in our history when religious prejudice ran amok in the Know-Nothing movement and the Ku Klux Klan." They praised Kennedy's "candid and fearless" answers to inquiries on his position regarding public money for parochial schools and the appointment of an Ambassador to the Vatican. But, they noted, "Senator Kennedy was vigorously attacked by many important Catholic journals in the United States, for just these views."

They would consider voting for a Roman Catholic for President, they concluded, but their votes would "be determined by the quality of the candidate himself, by his campaign, his political record, his platform—and, no matter what his faith, by his position on some of the matters . . ." discussed in their article.

The volume of discussion on the issue continued to swell. It was becoming apparent that, at least to date, most of the discussion by far was among the clergy. They appeared far more concerned than the mass of citizens. And with good cause. The campaign was coming at a time of major ferment within the churches themselves and in their relation to American society.

Dean Liston Pope of Yale's Divinity School and Dr. Donald O. Soper and the Reverend Gustave Weigel of the Catholic Woodstock College noted the possible effect of the religious issue on the ecumenical movement and feared the situation might be critical enough to necessitate a top-level conference of Protestant and Catholic leaders.[57] (Even as early as the 1930's the strongest opposition to such a movement had come from Baptist groups in the South and Mountain and Pacific regions, while sentiment for such a move—combining Protestant churches in the United States into one church—had appeared strongest in New England.)[58] Bishop Oxnam and Dr. Blake, even as they released their views in the *Look* article, had joined with the Reverend Dr. James E. Wagner, president of the Evangelical and Reformed Church; Dr. Edward Hughes Pruden, minister of the First Baptist Church in Washington; the Reverend Gaines M. Cook, executive secretary of the International Convention of Disciples of Christ, and eight other leading Protestant clergymen in signing a letter written by the Very Reverend Francis B. Sayre, Jr., dean of the Washington Cathedral (Episcopal).[59]

The letter termed "profoundly disturbing" the reports that in Wisconsin and West Virginia "unnamed Protestants have been drawing religious lines" and that "sometimes secretly, but more often openly," Kennedy was being attacked or even supported "merely because he is a Roman Catholic." Urging "moderation and reasoned balance of judgment," the letter decried anti-Catholicism as inconsistent with democracy or with our Constitution and its principle of no religious test.

As was apparent from the Sayre letter, in some sects the clergy seemed far more liberal in their views than the laity. In others there was uniform concern among both laity and leaders, while within still other groups opposition was stronger among clergymen.

In the midst of the campaign in West Virginia, a "substantial majority" of the delegates to the Methodist General Conference in Denver had rejected a resolution introduced by a minister from that state describing them as "uneasy" about a Catholic's running for the Presidency.[60] Meanwhile, by "overwhelming voice vote," a resolution before the General Assembly of the Southern Presbyterian Church officially opposing the election of a Roman Catholic to the Presidency was rejected as "bigotry." Instead, "the historic American position in regard to the separation of church and state" was "reaffirmed," and all Presbyterians were encouraged to focus responsibility on basic issues, "recognizing that the candidates' personal faith in God, their integrity, and their positions concerning public policies are more important than their denominational or party affiliations."[61]

Several things were happening that were to become increasingly discernible as the campaign progressed. Liberal and conservative divisions within individual churches were being pointed up. The debate was creating pressures for commitment among these divisions. At the same time, moves toward resolution of the differences became increasingly important. And gradually, amid the welter of words and exhortations, there was to arise a renewed sentiment of genuine religious and moral awareness.

With the appointment of James W. Wine, associate secretary for interpretation of the National Council of Churches, who left his position to head an "Office of Community Relations" for Kennedy, the consensus within the Protestant community was to be mobilized with increasing effectiveness later in the campaign.[62] Wine directed the efforts of committees aimed at combating religious prejudice in forty states, aided by the Reverend Arthur Lazell.

Another factor tended to promote and sustain the religious discussion. The presidential campaign of 1960 was coming at a time of major self-appraisal in America, not only in the religious community but also in the nation as a whole. As recently as February, President Eisenhower had announced the appointment of the Presidential Commission on National Goals, first proposed in his State of the Union address a year earlier.

Ultimate questions of our society and of the individual within it were being placed in the foreground, in the face of the ideological struggle with communism and its Eastern allies. Where such ultimate issues of our society were involved, it was inevitable that religion would be a major concern. (As late as 1952 the religious tradition had been stated by Justice William O. Douglas: "We are a religious people whose institutions presuppose a Supreme Being.") And where ultimate questions of the nature of the individual entered, there also entered questions of religion.

The men seeking the candidacy of their party indicated a strong sense of the full significance of the religious current beneath the political tides. Religion and politics were being merged in greater degree, it almost seemed, than at any time since the role of religion in government had been an issue in the campaigns of Jackson's time. Now, however, religion was tied to a new sense of "national concern" as it had never been in the 1840's and 1850's.

A new kind of nativism was in evidence. If not yet a manifest sentiment, it was a definite preoccupation. It was to be distinguished from its earlier counterpart, coming in a changed nation in a changed world. Into it were woven the strands of pluralism, toleration, and humanism that had emerged into genuine social practice since the middle of the nineteenth century. But its outline was yet to rise above the growing strident cacophony that grew in direct proportion to John F. Kennedy's approach to the goal immediately before him: the nomination.

By May 21st he had won his eighth primary,* defeating Wayne Morse in his home state of Oregon with 51 per cent of the vote. Meanwhile his extensive political spadework had continued among party politicians across the country. Some pointed out that the party could now ill afford to by-pass him and run the risk of alienating great numbers of Catholics. Others asserted that it made little difference now, that Kennedy had the nomination sewed up. This was the picture as Democrats began to gather in Los Angeles to choose their candidate.

---

* The eight: Indiana, Wisconsin, Massachusetts, Pennsylvania, West Virginia, Maryland, New Hampshire, Oregon.

CHAPTER TEN

JOHN F. KENNEDY
The Washington Manifesto

"Our American culture is at stake"

SEVERAL DAYS BEFORE THE DEMOCRATIC CONVENTION OPENED IN Los Angeles, former President Harry S. Truman declared his intention of staying away from the gathering. Charges had been circulating periodically for several months that the convention was being "rigged" in favor of the Kennedy drive. Said Truman: "I have no desire whatever to be a party to proceedings that are taking on the aspects of a pre-arranged affair."[1] Viewed in another light, it seemed to be simply a matter of adroit, thorough, and relentless political maneuvering paying off on the part of Kennedy's forces, after four years of ceaseless effort.

Reading a prepared statement, explaining his reasons for withdrawing formally as a delegate from Missouri, the titular head of the Democratic party referred to "the backers of Senator Joseph [*sic*] F. Kennedy . . ." Correcting himself and continuing, he directed a blunt question to his fellow Democrat: "Senator, are you certain that you're quite ready for the country or the country is ready for you in the role of President in January, 1961?"[2]

In the question was an implication that had been troubling many Catholics themselves. Beginning early, and for some time, there had been sensitivity, hesitancy, and even opposition to his candidacy among not a few of his co-worshipers. In one direct-mail poll of one thousand subscribers to *Jubilee*, a Roman Catho-

149

lic magazine for Catholic laymen across the country, "only one-third" said they thought Kennedy could win if nominated—or even thought he would be nominated.[3]

In March, weeks before Wisconsin, an astute observer of American society, Father R. L. Bruckberger, had offered his opinion that "American Catholics should not complain of never having had a Catholic President. They are fortunate," he said. "A President is exposed to many errors and arouses many hostilities. If he were Catholic, people would not fail to say that all his errors came from the fact that he is a Catholic."[4]

The Truman statement confronted Kennedy now with what to many appeared as an unexpected and most serious public challenge. Two days later, on the Fourth of July, he gave his reply to Truman. Standing before a battery of television cameras, klieg lights, microphones, newsmen, and spectators in the crowded ballroom of the Hotel Roosevelt in New York, he referred to Truman as "one of our most dedicated and courageous Presidents" and as one of "the three great Democratic Presidents in the twentieth century."[5] Kennedy noted his own eighteen years of experience and service to his country. "I do not undertake lightly to seek the Presidency," he said. "It is not a prize or a normal object of ambition. It is the greatest office in the world."

He replied tensely, in clipped, serious phrases, carefully but not without irony. "To exclude from positions of trust and command all those below the age of forty-four," he said, "would have kept Jefferson from writing the Declaration of Independence, Washington from commanding the Continental Army, Hamilton from serving as Secretary of the Treasury, Clay from being elected Speaker of the House, and"—Kennedy paused—"Christopher Columbus from even discovering America." Swiftly he moved to return the challenge. "This is still a young country founded by young men 184 years ago today and it is still young in heart, youthful in spirit and blessed with new young leaders in both parties. . . . The world is changing. The old ways will not do. It is time for a new generation of leadership to cope with new problems and new opportunities."

Nowhere had he met and answered Truman's question of whether the country was ready for him in the role of President. That question, it seemed, was still to be resolved. Instead, Kennedy closed by recalling the words of Abraham Lincoln, one hundred years earlier: "not yet President and under fire from veteran politicians. I see the storm coming and I know that His hand is in it. If He has a place and work for me, I believe that I am ready."[6]

It had been a masterful handling of a formidable maneuver. And once again the hand of Theodore C. Sorenson, Kennedy's close adviser, had been much in evidence in formulating the substance of the effort. (He had flown from the West Coast to Hyannis Port the day before to help in drafting the reply.) But Truman's open challenge had come late, too late, some felt, to have had any material effect on the outcome.

In his statement the former President mentioned Senator Lyndon B. Johnson of Texas as the foremost of a number of possible choices before the convention, suggesting that he "deserves serious consideration."[7] Several days earlier a poll of party opinion among 220 Congressmen had indicated Johnson as most favored, with Kennedy second.

But Kennedy strategists claimed to have virtually all the 761 votes needed for victory on the first ballot, as the combative legions within the Democratic party converged on Los Angeles: the power wielders of the great Northeast, the canny professionals of the South, the new entrepreneurs of the Near and Far West. Demonstrating, caucusing, carousing, the delegates swept into the city, as bands sang out a brassy booming welcome. The stops were out.

Favorite sons, mayors, bosses, and governors shifted, jockeyed, prepared, weighed deals, checked and rechecked, marshaled last-minute support, the candidates ceaselessly making the rounds of delegations: Kansas, Pennsylvania, Iowa, California, Minnesota, Illinois—several were reported ready to swing away from Kennedy after the first ballot. The support of the big cities across the North was crucial. Meeting on the eve of the balloting, Jacob

Arvey, national committeeman from Illinois; Chicago Mayor Richard J. Daley, Governor David Lawrence of Pennsylvania, Representative William Green (Democratic chairman in Philadelphia), former New York Governor Averell Harriman and New York Mayor Robert Wagner cast their lot with the phenomenal drive of the young senator from Massachusetts. Johnson, it was felt, could not draw so well in their vast and polyglot northern bailiwicks.

In mid-May there had been reports of "petitions, to be presented at the Republican and Democratic conventions, in July [*sic*], opposing the nomination of a Roman Catholic as President or Vice-President."[8] These had been quickly dissipated as major threats.

It was a time for the calling in of political debts, for the final roll of the political dice, from the points of Democratic power all across the country.

"*Al-a-bama!*" The calling of the roll began. As one speaker yielded to another, the floor of the convention shook with successive waves of pandemonium. Senator Eugene McCarthy, of Minnesota, speaking for Adlai Stevenson in ringing tones, implored the delegates: "Let this convention go to a second ballot." From the galleries came a tumultuous roar that swept down across the floor in a prolonged demonstration.

Injuries from placards were reported. One woman watching on television called Los Angeles police to ask if they couldn't restore order on the floor so that she could hear the proceedings better. Governor LeRoy Collins of Florida, the convention chairman, demanding, "I must have order," repeatedly banged his gavel so hard that it smashed.[9]

After twenty minutes, order finally restored, the Senate Clerk Emery Frazier, of Kentucky, continued with the canvass, "Illinois!" Of its sixty votes, 59½ pushed Kennedy above the 100 mark. On past Kansas, busy caucusing, to Pennsylvania and 64 of its 81 votes added to Kennedy's column. Meanwhile, from Alabama through ten states across the southern tier of the nation west to New Mexico and back to Virginia, Lyndon Johnson's total climbed above 400.

With West Virginia followed by Wisconsin, Kennedy reached 750. There was a mounting rustle of noise and activity through the great hall. "Wyoming!" On the floor with Wyoming's delegation, Robert Kennedy called to Tracy S. McCraken, its chairman: "Ten won't do it, but eleven will!" McCraken threw up his hands. "Let 'em all go."[10]

"Mister Chairman . . . " He had to move closer to the microphone to be heard. "Mister Chairman, Wyoming casts fifteen . . ."

Twelve miles away, Kennedy, sitting before a television set, rose from his chair. "This is it."[11] He called his wife, Jacqueline, at home in Hyannis Port. Then he started out for the convention arena behind a motorcycle escort, its sirens screaming in the warm Los Angeles night.

The strong backing given Johnson by the late Sam Rayburn and Truman had been to no avail, and the convention had passed by Stuart Symington and Adlai Stevenson. The mantle of leadership had been handed down across not one generation, but two.

It was a doubly noteworthy achievement. The nomination had been a far cry from the bruising contest that had raged across the floor of the 1924 Democratic convention and that had resulted in the rejection of Smith. In 1960 the real battle had gone on for months before: in the political wars of the primaries and the flexing and alignment of power among Democratic leaders for months before that.

The generation of which Kennedy was a member had come to maturity in a nation and a world removed by far more than the quarter-century that separated it from Al Smith. Yet the coalition that had jelled first among the electorate with Wilson, before being marshaled by Smith and consolidated by Roosevelt, still lived in the sixties.

Kennedy moved to fuse and summon into battle the coalitions that had been put into the service of his party since Wilson. Over the vigorous objection of many northern groups, he extended the vice presidential spot to Lyndon Johnson, the great

Senate tactician. Johnson was aware of the historic implications of its acceptance in terms of his own presidential aspirations. There was strong opposition to his accepting it from many southern conservative elements whose support he had enjoyed. Yet even as Truman had boosted him for the top position, the Texan had responded to a question about his availability for the Vice Presidency by saying, "I wouldn't want it even thought that I would refuse to serve my country in any capacity . . . if I felt that my services were needed and my experience and my qualifications . . . could be helpful."[12] Now, with Johnson's acceptance, the coalition that F.D.R. had repeatedly put to supreme political advantage would once again rise on the distant horizon of November.

By Friday the Kennedy–Johnson ticket was a reality, as thousands of delegates filled the vast reaches of the Coliseum to hear their two candidates acknowledge the tribute and the responsibility. Kennedy noted, as he addressed the throng grown quiet and waiting in the warm dusk: "I stand here tonight facing west on what was once the last frontier. Some would say that . . . there is no longer an American frontier." But, Kennedy declared, the fact is, "We stand today on the edge of a new frontier . . . [that] is here whether we seek it or not."[13]

He continued: "Woodrow Wilson's New Freedom promised our nation a new political and economic framework. Franklin Roosevelt's New Deal promised security and succor to those in need. But the New Frontier of which I speak is not a set of promises—it is a set of challenges."[14] Thus Kennedy was setting the theme of his campaign's political issues. But even before that, in the opening moments of his address, he had paid heed to what had been a most troublesome issue in his drive for the nomination, supplanting all others in the out-and-out wars of the primaries: "I am fully aware of the fact that the Democratic party by nominating someone of my faith has taken on what many regard as a new and hazardous risk—new, at least, since 1928." (A bow and a tribute to Al Smith's trail-blazing efforts.)

But in so doing, Kennedy observed, the party had not only placed its confidence in the American people "to render a free and fair judgment" but also in his own ability to do so: "to uphold the Constitution, and my oath of office—to reject any kind of religious pressure or obligation that might directly or indirectly interfere with my conduct of the Presidency in the national interest."

Kennedy again reaffirmed his record of fourteen years in "supporting complete separation of church and state—and resisting pressure from sources of any kind." He declared finally, regarding the matter of his religion: "I hope that no American, . . . considering the really critical issues facing this country, will waste his franchise and throw away his vote by voting either for or against me solely on account of my religious affiliation. It is not relevant. I am telling you now what you are entitled to know; that my decisions on every public policy will be my own— as an American, a Democrat and a free man."

In an unprecedented manner, a presidential candidate had touched on the religious issue in the very opening words of his official campaign, in an effort to remove it from that campaign. To some, it seemed hardly the manner in which to do so. (That sentiment was to grow.) Kennedy continued: "My call is to the young in heart, regardless of age; to the stout in spirit, regardless of party; to all who respond to the scriptural call: 'Be strong and of good courage: be ye not afraid, neither be dismayed.' "

Declaring that "courage—not complacency," and "leadership— not salesmanship" were the nation's greatest needs in the face of a choice between "public interest and private comfort—between national greatness and national decline," Kennedy sounded a final note of mission and of pilgrimage: "It has been a long road from the first snowy day in New Hampshire many months ago to this crowded convention city. Now begins another long journey taking me into your cities and homes across the United States. Give me your help and your hand and your voice. Recall with me the words of Isaiah: 'They that wait upon the Lord . . .

shall mount up with wings as eagles; they shall run, and not be weary . . .'* Then we shall prevail."

The pervasive sense of dedication and mission, and the scriptural allusions generously sprinkled throughout with stirring cumulative effect, surely offset the vague whispers about irreligiousness. But this being so, the question of his religiousness remained. Nevertheless, a sharp precedent had been set. The religious issue was out in the open, and it was a fighting issue as it never had been.

The campaign surrounding the issue was not about to begin. It had already begun, in the first of what were to be three separate drives in the course of the campaign.

Who was this man Kennedy? He himself had indeed "mounted up with wings" during the primaries, and he continued to do so in the early weeks of the campaign. Traversing the continent several times within a fortnight, from Maine to Alaska to Michigan, then Washington, then Idaho, then California, he seemed to be conquering space, telescoping time, implanting almost subconsciously an aura of omnipresence. Through it the central factor of personality had emerged as early as January of the election year in Gallup polls and other private surveys. These indicated that Kennedy received highest recognition among the public in terms of "personality," while Nixon was identified with "experience and accomplishment."[15]

The full force of the Kennedy personality, of the "aura," had begun to come through in the primaries, particularly in Wisconsin and then in West Virginia. It moved only as rapidly, or perhaps a little ahead of, Kennedy's own increasing sense of sureness and rapport with the people. An accomplished campaigner in New England, he seemed at first on less firm footing in initially facing the vast hinterland. But in Wisconsin his aristocratic mien mixed with warmth, sincerity, and reserve had become the dominant impression. Then, under pressure in West Virginia, he had begun to open again into the fighter, while being profoundly

---

* The quotation is from the King James (Protestant) Version of the Bible, Is. 40:31.

moved by what he encountered there in terms of human personal hardship and the quiet dignity, deeply ingrained religious faith, and resoluteness of those who suffered.

He continued to convince listeners of his sincerity not by bombast, but quietly, eagerly, and with a singleness of purpose. His "demanding conscience" was noted, combined with "a capacity to act,"[16] only after thorough, cool, methodical deliberation, sometimes rapidly, but sometimes with what almost seemed indecision. In his presence one felt restive energy, a charged alertness. Yet there was a final silent reserve, a discipline and self-control modulating the contact. For the first time since perhaps before Jackson, a young aristocrat of the new American vintage was seeking the Presidency. To some he was almost a Hollywood prototype of an active, rising young professor or executive.

Here, then, was a new kind of candidate—as indeed there had been in 1928. But the newness no longer strictly came from his religion or his antecedents. It did reside in his significance as the symbol of a new American society and one that was no longer essentially Protestant. The controversy surrounding these characteristics was no longer merely a religious one. The religious test now was to be integrally linked to the greater test confronting a society once again in search of itself.

At their encounter in Chicago, some Republicans, possibly thinking in terms of a Catholic bloc vote, had boomed a Catholic for a place on the GOP ticket with Nixon. The first move was made by Governor Christopher Del Sesto of Rhode Island on behalf of Secretary of Labor James P. Mitchell; Del Sesto called the Kennedy–Johnson selection a "marriage of convenience" and "hypocrisy," and said that the selection of Mitchell to run with Nixon could mean the difference between victory and defeat for the Republicans.

Reporters thought they knew what Del Sesto meant when he said "convenience" and "hypocrisy." When the governor pushed Mitchell, they concluded that he wanted the Catholic labor secretary to balance the GOP ticket, and offset what Catholic bloc votes Kennedy might draw. In his response, Del Sesto denied the balance theory by saying he regretted the subject was raised in that context. He had been supporting Mitchell for more than a year, he said, and he himself was a Catholic.

Henry Cabot Lodge was Nixon's personal choice for Vice President. At the last moment, the New Jersey delegation had voted to urge Nixon to choose Mitchell for his running mate, but observers said the move had come too late, that Lodge had been picked.

Former President Herbert Hoover was cheered lustily as he mounted the platform at Chicago. But Hoover was not in an all-is-well mood, as the somber tone of his words indicated. "America is in the midst of a frightening moral slump," he said. "[Since] . . . the end of the second world war, . . . major crimes . . . have increased . . . we witness . . . state and municipal corruption. . . . This nation needs a rebirth of a great spiritual force. . . ."[17]

Governor Mark O. Hatfield of Oregon, one of seven governors who had urged an open contest for the vice presidential nomination, nominated Nixon in a flurry of alliteration, calling him the man who knew "the titanic tensions that test our times," the man who had demonstrated "courage in crisis from Caracas to the Kremlin," a "fighter for freedom and a pilgrim for peace." As if in response, two spectators in an upper gallery held up a sign saying, "Kennedy Kan't Kome Klose."

Nixon, who had predicted that the election would be "the closest . . . in this century," was quickly asked to comment on the religious issue. Since religion was to be involved in the campaign, said a reporter, would Nixon consider naming evangelist Billy Graham to his staff? There was a visible annoyance on the Vice President's face as he answered: "Religion will be in this campaign to the extent that the candidates of either side talk about it. I shall never talk about it and will start right now."

The failure of the first manifestation of the religious issue to achieve its initial objective only served to point up in some quarters the genuine seriousness of the threat. From Honolulu, Mrs. Margaret Sanger, renowned leader in the world movement for birth control, announced she would "find another place to live" than America if Kennedy became President.[18] Even as the convention had rolled to a climax, Dr. W. A. Criswell, of the First Baptist Church in Dallas, Texas, had warned that Kennedy's selection would "spell the death of a free church in a free state and our hopes of continuance of full religious liberty in America." "Roman Catholicism is not only a religion," he said in a broadcast sermon, "it is a political tyranny . . . that covers the entire world."[19]

After the convention, Criswell stated that Senator Johnson had "let us down by taking the vice presidential nomination. I no longer support him."[20] Johnson received a letter from a Fort Worth constituent: "I have always voted Democratic as my father did before me," it said, "but I plan to use the considerable facilities at my disposal to defeat the Democratic ticket in November."[21] The constituent was Paul M. Stevens of the Southern Baptist Convention's Radio and Television Commission.

Carr P. Collins, Sr., organizer of Texans for Nixon, was a member of Criswell's church. Democrats demanded "equal time" to counter what was interpreted as a clearly political statement. A week later Methodist minister F. Braxton Bryant expressed two principal sentiments in reply to the assertions made by Criswell and others in the state. "American Catholics," he told a reporter, "are part of our democratic heritage—they believe in separation, despite what their church might have said in the past." Said Bryant, "Even though Jack Kennedy has a reputation for telling the truth, we are asked to believe he is a liar."[22]

Here again was proof of American pluralism as a social reality that had withstood the assaults of the 1928 campaign and come to grow and flourish through a series of national crises. It was being illustrated again as it had been weeks earlier in West Virginia. And here again, too, was the unique factor of the importance of the candidate's personal qualities, his characteristics, and appeal. They seemed to be almost a living refutation of the charges against him. "I believe," said the Reverend Dr. E. S. James, editor of the Texas *Baptist Standard*, "that Senator Kennedy is a clean, intelligent young man. His utterances show he believes in keeping church and state separate. If the Roman Catholic Church itself would declare for separation I would be for a man who is a Catholic. But the church hasn't done it; the issue remains."[23]

The issue not only remained; it grew. After a relatively quiet interlude following the Republican convention, there was a rash of resolutions on the matter from widely scattered localities around the country. In the first week of August groups in Michigan and Kentucky announced their opposition to the election of a Roman Catholic.[24]

The second swell of the wave had begun. Throughout the succeeding weeks into early September it ran silently spreading. In Danville, Virginia, twenty-five ministers, including Baptists, Methodists, Disciples of God, and Pentecostal Holiness sects, pledged to "oppose with all the powers at our command the election of a Catholic to the Presidency of the United States." Their statement declared, "We do not believe a man can be a loyal Catholic and fill the office. . . ." Another local minister said he considered the meeting "repulsive."[25] The Minnesota Baptist Convention declared that Roman Catholicism posed "as serious a threat to America as atheistic communism."[26]

It reflected again the concern with the individual in an age when the differences between Catholicism and Protestantism were being boiled down, in the words of one leading churchman, to "corporate" and "personal." For the Minnesota Baptists in this sense the corporate tyranny of the individual under Catholicism was no better than the subjugation of his soul under communism. The broader questions of the age, freedom *from* what and *for* what, were thus clearly noted again in the significance and meaning of the religious issue as it developed anew in 1960. This significance, this validity of the issue, was to remain as a fact even after revelations had clearly illustrated its use as a calculated political device in much the same way as in the middle of the nineteenth century, apart from honest convictions and differences.

It was not simply a matter of labels, of bigotry, or prejudice. It involved a view of the world and of the individual's place in that world. But where there existed a legitimate basis for discourse surrounding differences in this sense, there was also a clear, unreasoning persistence on another level. And as was soon to be dramatically exhibited, the two levels were not always easily distinguishable in degree or kind, especially in the heat of a presidential campaign. Meanwhile, the rising chorus moved from regional toward national volume.

The North Bend Baptist Association, representing approximately 17,500 Baptists in thirty-three churches across northern Kentucky, joined in the opposition. And the General Presbytery of the Assemblies of God, meeting in Springfield, Missouri, added the voice of its one million members across the country, while disclaiming religious bias as a label for its action. Instead, it charged, it was the Roman Catholic Church that was guilty of bigotry "as reflected in its position of infallibility of its leadership."[27]

The increasingly outspoken opposition made it begin to appear as though the sentiments of 1928 were again being equaled. There had been changes, however. A new South, for example, had begun to impinge on the South of 1928. For one thing, the law had become a more active instrument.

The religious issue, in a broader way, had moved into the courts just prior to the 1928 campaign. There the attempt had been made to have declared illegal the parochial school system in Oregon. Now in 1960 the law again began to be used in combating bigotry. (Its use or the threat of its use was to increase as the campaign progressed.) The fraudulent Knights of Columbus "oath" was withdrawn from widespread use when the Knights threatened libel suits against users. In Pittsburgh, after a preliminary injunction against printing and circulating copies of the false oath, one minister from a nearby Bible Church was indicted by a grand jury in a criminal libel suit brought by several Knights for the minister's refusal to retract his assertions.[28] Klansmen now picketed instead of night-riding. The bulk of the attack had shifted to communal pressures.

In Arkansas, the Baptist State Convention gave its approval to

a letter sent to the state's eight Democratic electors, signed by
the Reverend Dr. W. O. Vaught, a vice president of the Southern Baptist Convention and pastor of the Immanuel Baptist
Church in Little Rock. The letter said in part, "We cannot
turn our government over to a Catholic President who could be
influenced by the Pope and by the power of the Catholic hierarchy."[29] The group announced plans for a series of rallies for
"religious freedom"—the first one to be held in Little Rock.

There was another element in the South of 1960—indeed in
the nation—that had not been prominent in 1928. The Baltimore
Afro-American observed: "From now until the election we shall
be listening to the Bible Belt's hate-Catholic campaign. We are
used to it. It's a common thing whenever we have colored candidates. . . . If religion is made a serious issue in this campaign
then all of us shall have to elect Kennedy, first because we cannot admit to the nations we would like to influence that religion
as well as racial intolerance is decisive in our thinking. If we hate
Catholics that much, neither Mohammedans, Buddhists, Coptics
or Hindus will believe a word we say about freedom or tolerance
or the boasted American way of life. Communism seeks to rule
the world by repressing religious faiths. We claim freedom of
religion. How free? That is what this election is about."[30]

Roy Wilkins, executive secretary of the National Association
for the Advancement of Colored People, addressing the National
Urban League, maintained that "most of the Protestant churches
that pictured the Negro as virtually a chimpanzee now picture
the Roman Catholic Church as an evil octopus."[31] (He did not
specify which Protestant churches.)

Aside from its presence as a legitimate issue in 1928, the matter
of prohibition or "wetness" had served as a screen in many instances for anti-Catholic sentiment. Now there was no such
screen. Anti-Catholic sentiment stood by itself in the open.
And when one took his stand openly, the tone was not nearly
so astringent as it had been. It was more often moderate or
rational. It wasn't the candidate; it was his church.

Baptist opposition, said Dr. Ramsey Pollard, must be based on historical facts about Catholic attitudes and actions, "and not on absurd statements that cannot be proved."[32] Baptists objected to being called bigots when their views were based on principles in support of religious liberty. Baptists were cautioned against using, for example, a piece entitled "America Is a Catholic Country." Mailed anonymously in large quantities as a reputedly pro-Catholic circular, it was designed to incite anti-Catholic reactions. "Ever since the tragedy of the Reformation," stated this pamphlet, "western history has been a conspiracy against the Catholic Church." It said, "There is fairly good reason to believe that the [American] Revolution had been largely financed by wealthy Catholics, and that Washington was converted to Catholicism on his death-bed, but that would never be admitted by any pagan historian." The pamphlet, distributed by the "Catholic Committee for Historical Truth, J. J. O'Connor Chairman," contained no other identification. After pursuing "historical" themes, it concluded: "Ideally, we should have Catholic political parties in all the free countries, but because of the predominance of non-Catholics in this country, it has been impossible to establish a party completely dedicated to Christian principles of government." Moreover, the pamphlet said, "We now have more than 100 Catholics in Congress, 18 or 20 Catholic governors and thousands of Catholics in our state legislatures.

"If these Catholics would forget the by now meaningless designation of 'Republican' and 'Democrat' and work together, keeping in mind the social and economic doctrines set out through the generations by the Church since at least the days of St. Thomas Aquinas, and if we elect a Catholic as president to take his place at the head of the Army of God, we can not only march triumphant against the scourge of communism, but we can bring a true and lasting peace to the entire world and make the United States a Catholic country in a real sense, and the greatest nation of all time."

Here was a "rational" and "historical" approach cleverly combining half-truths, distortion, and exaggeration of fact with appeals to latent prejudices as well as legitimate patriotic and religious sentiments. The most skilled communist propagandist could not have done better in precipitating divisive animosity.

And there was no longer any question that such divisive animosities had become a fact in the campaign. By the first week in September, Robert Kennedy, managing his brother's campaign, told a reporter: "Right now, religion is the biggest issue in the South, and in the country."[33] Its existence as an issue was still made up of a sum of regional and local outbursts. Yet it had rapidly become a matter of legitimate concern nationally.

Bruce Felknor, executive director of the Fair Campaign Practices Committee, called attention to "the circulation of rabidly anti-Catholic material," in reportedly immense quantities, and warned of "a substantial danger that the campaign will be dirtier on the religious issue than it was in 1928."[34] Noting the spread of this type of campaign literature, Senator Estes Kefauver declared, "Not only will a smear campaign damage the image of our country; it will also damage the soul and conscience of our nation."[35]

It was the manner of presenting the issue that was being condemned in virtually all quarters. Yet those who were concerned with the political aspects of Roman Catholicism feared that in the face of such widespread condemnation, the issue itself, which they saw as a crucial one, might be discounted.

Plans were announced for a meeting of members of the Protestant clergy and laity organized as the National Conference of Citizens for Religious Freedom. In Belfast, Ireland, on the eve of his return to the United States, Dr. Norman Vincent Peale, the designated chairman of the meeting, responded to questions about its purpose by stating: "You've got an issue here which everyone is talking about. We can't minimize it; it must be dealt with. I am concerned that the so-called religious issue be handled in a truly dignified and American manner."[36] His concern was soon to be heeded. The issue had grown steadily into one of national proportions. It was now to reach a crest.

On the morning of September 7th, at President Eisenhower's news conference in the old State Department Indian Treaty room adjoining the White House, he once again was questioned on the religious issue. A reporter noted its continuance in the campaign. Said the President: "Mr. Nixon and I agreed long ago that one thing we would never raise, and never mention, is the religious issue in this coming campaign. I not only don't believe in voicing prejudice, I want to assure you I feel none. And I am sure that Mr. Nixon feels exactly the same." He expressed the hope "that it could be one of those subjects that could be laid on the shelf and forgotten until the election is over."[37]

As the President's news conference continued, a few blocks away at Washington's Mayflower Hotel, Dr. Glenn L. Archer was addressing a meeting presided over by Dr. Norman Vincent Peale. Known to millions around the country as an author, columnist, and lecturer (his book, *The Power of Positive Thinking*, had been a great best seller), Peale had joined with the Reverend Harold J. Ockenga, a former president of the National Association of Evangelicals, and others "frankly concerned about the political aspects of Roman Catholicism," in an attempt to provide "an intelligent approach to the religious issue on a high philosophical level."[38] These others included most prominently Dr. Daniel A. Poling, editor of the *Christian Herald*, and Dr. L. Nelson Bell, an editor of *Christianity Today* (and the father-in-law of Dr. Billy Graham). The meeting was attended by many laymen, including Lieutenant General (retired) William Kelly Harrison, Jr., a former chief negotiator at the Korean War armistice talks, and William C. Jones, of Los Angeles, a member of the board of the Dr. Billy Graham Foundation.

An Arkansas man, William R. Smith, who had been a delegate to the Democratic convention, was chairman "during a major part of the conference."[39] In the meeting, closed to members of the press and public, Dr. Bell warned of the growth of "pseudo-tolerance," equating it with a kind of naïve ignorance that tended to abet the "Romish" attitude which, he asserted, sought "to eventually conquer as an ecclesiastical organization."[40] Dr. Peale then expressed his view: "It's a good thing to have this crisis forced upon us; it will bring us together, and we've got to stay together," he said. "Our American culture is at stake. . . . I don't say it won't survive, but it won't be what it was."[41]

The "American culture," however, already had changed. It was no longer the culture it had once been. The transformation had permeated nearly every corner of American society. Protestantism once again was faced with the task of interpreting itself as a vital, forceful, and relevant guide for twentieth century man. To do so responsibly and most effectively was not to express itself chiefly in terms of a reaction to Catholicism (itself faced with serious challenges). This belied the spiritual initiative of the faith. Moreover, and perhaps more seriously, it was to misjudge the direction from which the most imminent threat to Protestant survival was coming. The threat was being drawn on a larger canvas than contrasts within Christianity.

The meeting closed on a note of enthusiasm and dedication. Dr. Peale noted "this wonderful spirit of brotherhood" which had brought together diverse sects. Jokingly he advised his colleagues to "pray for us while we are talking to those reporters." Warned one: "Say one wrong word and the press will murder us; by next week we'll be out of business."[42]

Late that afternoon Dr. Peale and the Reverend Mr. Ockenga met with reporters to issue a statement. Dr. Peale described the meeting as "more or less representative of the evangelical, conservative, Protestants."[43] The group, consisting of "ministers and laymen in Protestant churches of thirty-seven denominations," expressed the feeling that the religious issue "should be discussed only in a spirit of truth, tolerance and fairness, and that no persons should engage in hate-mongering, bigotry, prejudice or unfounded charges." They believed "that persons who are of the Roman Catholic faith can be just as honest, patriotic and public-spirited as those of any other faith," but they questioned "whether it is in the best interests of our society for any church organization to attempt to exercise control over its members in political and civic affairs." Noting that the Vatican maintained diplomatic relations with the governments of forty-two countries, the statement said: "The Roman Catholic Church is a political as well as a religious organization." They maintained: "It is inconceivable that a Roman Catholic President would not be under extreme pressure by the hierarchy of his church to accede to its policies with respect to foreign relations in matters, including representation to the Vatican."

And there was another point: "Under the canon law of the Roman Catholic Church, a President of this faith would not be allowed to participate in interfaith meetings; he could not worship in a Protestant church without securing the permission of an ecclesiastic; would not a Roman Catholic President," the statement asked, "thus be gravely handicapped in offering to the American people and to the world an example of the religious liberty our people cherish?" It declared, "Brotherhood in a pluralistic society like ours depends on a firm wall of separation between church and state."

The statement concluded: "That there is a 'religious issue' in the present political campaign is not the fault of any candidate. It is created by the nature of the Roman Catholic Church which is, in a very real sense, both a church and a temporal state."

The group, numbering 150 members, announced its intentions of encouraging other meetings of Protestant ministers and laymen across the country to grapple with the issues posed by Kennedy's candidacy. Although Glenn L. Archer had addressed the meeting, he had not signed the statement. The organization of which he was executive director, the POAU, issued its own statement, in which it criticized "literature expressing religious bigotry and scandal," calling it "trash." It enumerated "world-wide" policies of the church regarding birth control, and public school attendance, and pronouncements on "partial union" of church and state.[44]

Of Kennedy, the POAU said: "To the extent that he repudiates these policies and demonstrates his independence of clerical control, he is entitled to our praise and encouragement." But, it added, "When a candidate belongs to an organization which champions such a policy [partial union of church and state], it is not bigotry or prejudice to examine his credentials with the utmost care and frankness and to ask how far his commitment goes."[45]

Both statements fell simultaneously on the public. The statement by the so-called Peale group precipitated the most intense criticism. It "misrepresents the breadth of Protestant interests, the intelligence of Protestant concerns, the charity of Protestant attitudes," wrote Dr. Harold E. Fey in the *Christian Century*.[46] A Protestant Episcopal rector in New York City told his congregation that the statement does "not speak for all of us. Even as Dr. Peale and his friends, I differ radically with the Church of Rome on many counts . . . but perhaps we ought to remember sometimes that both Protestants and Catholics agree much more than they disagree. So far as the deep underlying convictions of Christian men about God and man, life and death, are concerned, we share a common faith."[47]

Although it was not illegitimate to raise questions about church and state, the Methodist Church Board of Missions' *World Outlook* pointed out, "It is not legitimate to refuse to listen to the answers and to declare that a candidate must be voted for or against not because of his stated position, but simply because of his membership in a certain group."[48] The American Jewish Congress concurred. The issue of separation of church and state was a legitimate one for discussion, it held, but the views of the candidate, and not the views of the organization to which he belongs, should be the basis for judging him.[49]

One lone voice added to the objections belonged to the Reverend George H. Spriggs, assistant pastor of the Second Presbyterian Church in St. Louis. Writing in a ministers' journal, *Monday Morning*, he said, "Which Roman Catholic are we talking about? Peter II of Aragon? Pope Innocent III? Ximenes de Cisneros? Jacques Maritain? Al Smith? Or Senator Kennedy? And which Protestant is going to oppose him? John Calvin? Norman Vincent Peale? Karl Barth? Or Richard Nixon? It makes a big difference, and that is the reason I'm ringing the bell to get off this bandwagon of generalities. . . . I may be a cynic, but I have trouble believing that the church to which a candidate does or doesn't belong is the primary issue at stake in a country where church membership is fashionable and many times sterile. . . . I do not see a single candidate . . . whose flaming faith in his God or his church is the motivating force of his actions. . . . Those who are on the bandwagon are not so bigoted as they are naïve. . . . Do we really suppose that 39,500,000 American Roman Catholics are working for the overthrow of democracy? Do we reject them as brothers in Christ? . . . I will not be bullied, and that's why I want off."

"I note," wrote Rabbi Arthur Gilbert, "that although Senator Kennedy has answered . . . questions clearly and forthrightly, they continue to be asked of him as though the hearer refused to believe he means it."[50] Another observer, Wayne H. Cowan, the editor of *Christianity and Crisis*, had a name for it: "Bigotry arises when the questioner is discovered to be not at all interested in the answer. . . ."[51]

From one who had attended the meeting came strong exception to the tenor of the reactions. Dr. George M. Doherty objected to the labeling as "undemocratic" of any "criticism" of the Roman Catholic Church. "Most of it," he said, "is a deep-seated concern for the maintenance of those human freedoms . . . which are basic to the American way of life."[52]

In some quarters the intentions of the groups were seen as no less culpable, when one looked at the entire canvas, than had been the intentions of Dr. Lyman Beecher when, in 1834, he had indirectly legitimized the baser sentiments of citizens bent on trouble in Charlestown. Among the first to speak out in opposition to the Washington conference had been Dr. Reinhold Niebuhr and Dean John C. Bennett of Union Theological Seminary. Besides not being representative of Protestant opinion, they asserted, the group was guilty of "blind prejudice." They said, "Most of those Protestants who have been in the forefront of this effort would oppose any liberal Democrat regardless of his religion."[53] By way of reply it was pointed out that Drs. Bennett and Niebuhr were vice chairmen of the Liberal party in New

York, which in the course of the campaign was to endorse the Democratic candidate.

In Catholic circles the reaction was sharp but controlled. From the Reverend John Courtney Murray, Jesuit professor at Woodstock College in Maryland: "The 'oldest American prejudice' is as poisonously alive today as it was in 1928, or in the 1890's, or even the 1840's." There was a difference, however. "Today even religious prejudice feels the need somehow to contrive for itself a semblance of rationality. [It is] embellished by a . . . set of footnotes," he observed, which "merely serve to cloak the prejudice that long ago wrote the text." Father Murray's chief hope was that "old Catholic angers will not rise. . . ."[54]

The Jesuit weekly *America* chided: "This is a time . . . for the keeping on of shirts. Dr. Peale and Dr. Poling would look a lot more dignified if they hadn't taken theirs off." It went on: "The tragedy is that they appear to have dishonored themselves [by] the new alliances they seem to have contracted with elements . . . for whom it would seem they could have no conceivable feeling of kinship."[55]

What of Dr. Peale himself? As the controversy raged about his head he had left for a retreat scheduled long before the Washington conference. At least one major newspaper canceled its handling of his column. He sent the Citizens for Religious Freedom a telegram indicating that he could "not participate in any further activities of the group." Because of the widespread adverse publicity, he offered his resignation to the elders and deacons of his church. They rejected the offer. The following Sunday his congregation, expressing their support and continued confidence, rose in silent greeting as he entered the sanctuary. Dr. Peale issued a statement in which he reiterated that he had not called the Washington meeting. Nor had he had anything to do with setting it up. "I was merely present as an invited guest," he stated. "I did not take part in the preparation of its conclusions. . . . The unwarranted implications which have been drawn from my attendance at that meeting contradict my record of thirty years of ardent interfaith activity of which I am justly proud. . . . The people have a right to elect a Catholic, a Jew, a Protestant or even someone of no religious affiliation as President, and he has a right to serve.

"The election should be on the basis of the man best qualified. Each of us must vote according to the dictates of his conscience. This I believe, and regret that my position had ever been presented as anything else," Dr. Peale declared.[56]

To some, it all appeared to represent a retreat from his position on the day he had faced reporters to issue the statement. This impression was quickly countered by Dr. Poling: "Neither Dr. Peale nor I repudiate the Washington resolutions," he said, but he did wish to "repudiate the manner in which these resolutions have been attributed to Dr. Peale."[57]

What had originally no doubt seemed an advantage to the Conference planners—the prominence and newsworthiness of Dr. Peale—had proved to be a factor compounding the unfavorable reception they received in many quarters, and a disservice to the man himself. One had to go back to 1884 to find a similar cataclysm befalling an earnest member of the ministry honestly expressing his attitudes in the midst of a heated presidential campaign. Unlike 1884, the effect of the incident on the course of the campaign was not sudden and dramatic. But events had been set in motion that were to reinforce and hasten changes in the handling of the issue for the remainder of the campaign.

The statements of the Washington Conference and of the POAU had, both in their timing and in their reception, failed to reckon with the candidate himself.

CHAPTER ELEVEN

JOHN F. KENNEDY

Houston and the Public Conscience

"The whole nation . . . will be the loser"

As HE STEADILY WHISTLE-STOPPED HIS WAY DOWN THE DRY AND
sunny San Joaquin Valley in California, John Kennedy was far
away from the East and from the furor created by the so-called
Peale group's Washington pronouncements—but not for long.
Learning of the statements, he said he would not respond directly
to the group's challenge. He did have a statement for a press
conference in Burbank, California, however: "The Constitution is
very clear on the separation of church and state. I have been
clear and concise in my commitments to that Constitution not
merely because I take the oath which is taken to God, but also
because I believe that it represents the happiest arrangement for
the organization of a society. Therefore I believe in that theory
. . . just as strongly as Dr. Peale or anyone else."[1]

The next day a heckler in Modesto, California, confronted him
with the question of whether he thought all Protestants were
heretics, an official view that had been ascribed to his church in
the Peale statement. "No," said Kennedy, "and I hope you don't
believe all Catholics are." He continued, more seriously: "May
I say that it seems that the great struggle today is between those
who believe in no God and those who believe in God. I really
don't see why we should engage in close debate over what you
may believe or what I may believe. That is my privilege and your
privilege."[2]

172

His campaign schedule called for him to swing into southern California and then across the Southwest into Texas. From there he would move into the heartland to St. Louis, then eastward to New York. As he was being driven to the Los Angeles airport to fly to San Diego, Kennedy listened on the car radio to Nixon's replies on "Meet the Press" to questions about the religious issue. Emphasizing again that he had "no doubt whatever about Senator Kennedy's loyalty to his country and about the fact that if he were elected President that he would put the Constitution . . . above any other consideration," Nixon said that "if the two candidates refrain from raising the issue—refrain from discussing it— that means that at least to that extent it won't be in the news." He had a suggestion: "I feel that we ought to have a cutoff date on its discussion."[3]

The question of whether it would remain as a silent issue, or evolve into a whispering campaign, as it had in 1928, was not answered. Smith had referred to the issue in major addresses only twice, meeting with little success in curbing it.

As Hurricane Donna swept up the Atlantic coast, Kennedy headed straight into the eye of another storm in the Southwest. Strong opposition to him continued in the home state of his running mate, Senator Lyndon B. Johnson of Texas. (The rancor was heightened in intensity as the campaign progressed.) Responding to suggestions that Baylor University was a center of the opposition, Mrs. Lyndon Johnson scoffed graciously. She noted that the senator had "plenty of Baptist forebears in his blood line. . . . Lyndon's great-grandfather . . . was the second president of Baylor. . . . He converted Sam Houston—and we still have the letter from Sam Houston to him saying so. It is framed and hanging on the wall. . . . If my house was on fire I'd grab that letter on the way out."[4] Under such circumstances, it seemed, it was hard to imagine bitterness among one's own brethren.

Prior to the POAU and the so-called Peale group's conferences, the Ministerial Association of Greater Houston had extended a general invitation to the candidates to give their views on a range of topics. When Kennedy arrived at the Rice Hotel in Houston to address the association, he was met with standing applause as he entered the ballroom. He had just come from addressing a rally of 12,000 at the Sam Houston Coliseum in downtown Houston. Scuffles had occurred there, among groups outside the hall, before and after his speech. Now his audience consisted of several hundred ministers and about an equal number of laymen. Thousands more across Texas would view the evening's events on television. Far from all who were present, among laity and clergy alike, could be counted as supporters. In the lobby of the hotel, anti-Catholic material had been circulated. Kennedy had agreed to face questions following his address. They were to be from a number of ministers seeking "clarification" of his views.

The meeting opened with a prayer. Shortly thereafter, the candidate rose to face his audience. Not since West Virginia had the issue confronted Kennedy so squarely and so crucially. "I am grateful for your generous invitation to state my views," he began. "While the so-called religious issue is necessarily and properly the chief topic here tonight, I want to emphasize from the outset that I believe that we have far more critical issues in the 1960 election. . . ." Then he came directly to grips with the opposition. "But," he continued, "because I am a Catholic, and no Catholic has ever been elected President, the real issues in this campaign have been obscured—perhaps deliberately—in some quarters less responsible than this. So it is apparently necessary for me to state once again not what kind of . . . church I believe in, for that should be important only to me, but what kind of America I believe in."[5] The audience, alert and still, awaited his commitment.

"I believe in an America where the separation of church and state is absolute—where no Catholic prelate would tell the President (should he be a Catholic) how to act and no Protestant minister would tell his parishioners for whom to vote—where no church or church school is granted any public funds or political preference—and where no man is denied public office merely because his religion differs from the President who might appoint him or the people who might elect him.[6]

"I believe in an America that is officially neither Catholic, Protestant nor Jewish—where no public official either requests or accepts instructions on public policy from the Pope, the National Council of Churches or any other ecclesiastical source—where no religious body seeks to impose its will directly or indirectly upon the general populace or the public acts of its officials—and where religious liberty is so indivisible that an act against one church is treated as an act against all.

"For while this year it may be a Catholic against whom the finger of suspicion is pointed," Kennedy reminded his audience, "in other years it has been, and may someday be again, a Jew—or a Quaker—or a Unitarian—or a Baptist." The battle had been joined. Now the candidate moved to issue a terse counterchallenge.

"I would not look with favor upon a President working to subvert the First Amendment's guarantees of religious liberty (nor would our system of checks and balances permit him to do so). And neither do I look with favor upon those who would work to subvert Article VI of the Constitution by requiring a religious test—even by indirection—for if they disagree with that safeguard, they should be openly working to repeal it."

The Committee for Constitutional Government, an organization concerned with the interpretation of traditional American principles, numbered Dr. Peale and others opposed to Kennedy among its leading members. Kennedy met the charges of his opponents: "I want a chief executive whose public acts are responsible to all and obligated to none, who can attend any ceremony, service or dinner his office may appropriately require him to fulfill, and whose fulfillment of his Presidential office is not limited or conditioned by any religious oath, ritual or obligation."

Across the electorate, above the thousands of localities and out of the disjointed words and moments of the 1960 campaign, Kennedy was conducting a dialogue of timeless proportions.

"This is the kind of America I believe in—and this is the kind of America I fought for in the South Pacific and the kind my brother died for in Europe. No one suggested then that we might have a 'divided loyalty,' that we did 'not believe in liberty' or that we belonged to a disloyal group that threatened 'the freedom for which our forefathers died.'

"And in fact this is the kind of America for which our forefathers did die when they fled here to escape religious test oaths, that denied office to members of less favored churches, when they fought for the Constitution, the Bill of Rights, the Virginia Statute of Religious Freedom, and when they fought at the shrine I visited today—the Alamo. For side by side with Bowie and Crockett died Fuentes and McCafferty and Baily and Bedillo and Carey—but no one knows whether they were Catholics or not. For there was no religious test there."

Once again across a century the conscious spirit of America was being asked to recall the deeds of its sons. But now it was not Winfield Scott fondly recalling "that brogue . . . I am always happy to hear" as he had heard it in the Mexican War. It was not Sam Houston rallying his countrymen in the face of alien tides from foreign shores, in the interests of the responsible and independent democracy he had fought to defend. Out of their time had come a new nation to fit the American tradition. "I ask you tonight to follow in that tradition," said Kennedy, "to judge me on the basis of my fourteen years in the Congress. . . ." He continued, ". . . do not judge me on the basis of these pamphlets and publications we have all seen that carefully select quotations out of context from the statements of Catholic Church leaders, usually in other countries, frequently in other centuries, and rarely relevant to any situation here. . . .

"I do not consider these other quotations binding upon my public acts; why should you? But let me say, with respect to other countries, that I am wholly opposed to the state being used by any religious group, Catholic or Protestant, to compel, prohibit or persecute the free exercise of any other religion. And that goes for any persecution at any time, by anyone, in any country."

Then he repeated with emphasis what he had said at the height of the West Virginia primary: ". . . let me stress again that these are my views—for, contrary to common newspaper usage, I am not the Catholic candidate for President. I am the Democratic party's candidate for President who happens also to be a Catholic. I do not speak for my church on public matters—and the church does not speak for me."

Now he issued a pledge to his listeners. "Whatever issue may come before me as President, if I should be elected,—on birth control, divorce, censorship, gambling or any other subject—I will make my decision in accordance with these views, in accordance with what my conscience tells me to be in the national interest, and without regard to outside religious pressure or dictate. And no power or threat of punishment could cause me to do otherwise. But if the time should ever come—and I do not concede any conflict to be remotely possible—when my office would require me to either violate my conscience, or violate the national interest, then I would resign the office, and I hope any other conscientious public servant would do likewise.

"I do not intend . . . to disavow either my views or my church in order to win this election. If I should lose on the real issues, I shall return to my seat in the Senate satisfied that I tried my best and was fairly judged."

But, he warned, "if this election is decided on the basis that 40,000,000 Americans lost their chance of being President on the day they were baptized, then it is the whole nation that will be the loser in the eyes of Catholics and non-Catholics around the world, in the eyes of history, and in the eyes of our own people."

Finally Kennedy affirmed that, if elected, he would "devote every effort of mind and spirit to fulfilling the oath of the Presidency. . . . For without reservation, I can, and I quote, 'solemnly swear that I will faithfully execute the office of President of the United States and will to the best of my ability preserve, protect and defend the Constitution, so help me God.'"

With his closing words "something approaching an ovation" broke from the audience.[7] But there was clear reserve among many. The senator's remarks in places had seemed almost personally directed at themselves. Now the candidate was about to engage directly many of the men who perceived his church as their almost mortal enemy. As the questioning opened, one minister turned attention to something he considered "more important than the religious issue." Citing the Democratic platform, he questioned whether in effect it did not amount to "abolishing the open shop." In doing so, he asserted, "you are taking away the freedom of the individual worker."[8] Kennedy replied to his assertion, but to some the question seemed out of place. It significantly reflected a situation in which opposition to Kennedy among some clergymen and laymen on the basis of his religion was tied closely to a general conservative opposition to him because of his "liberal economic policies."

The next questioner declared he "appreciated very much" Kennedy's "very clearly stated" position on propagation of the Gospel "by all religious groups in other countries," and then asked: ". . . if you are elected President will you use your influence to get the Roman Catholic countries of South America and Spain to stop persecuting Protestant missionaries . . . ?" Throughout the campaign the issue had been injected by those who claimed that to do so was made justifiable by the worldwide nature of the Catholic Church. Once again, foreign religious controversies were entering an American presidential campaign, as they had at the turn of the century, and before.

Kennedy had declared his position minutes earlier. Now he placed it in a broader and nonsectarian context. He would, he replied, use his influence as President to encourage the development of freedom all over the world.

A Baptist minister followed. He read a petition that was to be submitted to Kennedy on his arrival in St. Louis: "With deep sincerity and in Christian grace," said the resolution, "we plead with Senator John F. Kennedy . . ." to apppeal to Richard Cardinal Cushing of Boston, in his home diocese, "to present to the Vatican Mr. Kennedy's sincere statement relative to the separation of church and state and religious freedom as represented in the Constitution of the United States in order that the Vatican may officially authorize such a belief for all Roman Catholics in the United States."[9]

Kennedy gave his answer without hesitation, an answer that again emphasized the spirit of separation in his approach. ". . . as I do not accept the right of, as I said, any ecclesiastical official to tell me what I should do in the sphere of my public responsibility as an elected official, I do not propose also to ask Cardinal Cushing to ask the Vatican to take some action. I do not propose to interfere with their free right to do exactly what they want. . . ."

For the first time in the questioning, applause burst from the audience. A minister arose to make clear his "great admiration" for Kennedy and for his "courageous" statements, "but until we know this is the position of your church," he said, there could be no ignoring of the issues. The candidate replied with impatient sincerity, almost imploringly, "Why do you possibly doubt that I represent a viewpoint which is hostile to the Catholic Church of the United States? I believe I'm stating the viewpoint the Catholics in this country hold toward the happy relationship which exists between Church and State."

"Let me ask you, sir, do you state it with the approval of the Vatican?"

"I don't have to have approval in that sense," retorted Kennedy.

Reflecting afterward, one minister wrote, "The meeting had many of the earmarks of an inquisition, and we always thought we were against inquisitions."[10]

Now a clergyman rose to report a telephone conversation a day earlier with Dr. Daniel A. Poling. He read a telegram from Poling, again raising the matter of the 1947 interfaith dinner and dedication of a chapel to commemorate the four chaplains who died on the *Dorchester*. (The veiled reference to this in the Washington statement of the Citizens for Religious Freedom had been met indirectly by Kennedy in his speech earlier in the evening.) Now he said again that he never had discussed "in his life" with the late Dennis Cardinal Dougherty of Philadelphia the propriety of attending the dinner. (This had been alleged in the

Poling account of the incident.) Instead, said Kennedy, he had learned of the circumstances characterizing his proposed attendance through his administrative assistant who had been in touch with a member of the Catholic Welfare Conference in that city. The drive had not enjoyed the full backing of the Catholic archdiocese.

Noting that the speakers were to have been Charles P. Taft, Herbert Lehman, and himself, Kennedy said he didn't think he had misinterpreted when he'd assumed that each was supposed to be implicitly representing a faith.

"I don't mean to be disrespectful to Reverend Poling. I have high regard for his son. I have high regard for Dr. Poling." But, admitting it was imprudent of him to have accepted the invitation without more information, Kennedy said, "I don't really feel it demonstrated unfitness to hold a public office." Noting he'd voted in fourteen years on hundreds, probably thousands of matters, "some involving questions which border on the relationship between church and state," he reminded his audience: "This took place in 1946. Is this the only incident that can be shown?"

Again applause came, mostly from the lay members in the audience. Then the questioning moved into the historical issues. A minister quoted a series of statements on mental reservation and on the permissibility of lying, from the *Catholic Encyclopedia.* Then he cited a Vatican newspaper statement regarding the "right and duty" of the Roman Catholic hierarchy "to intervene in the political field to guide its flock." Finally, he recited a statement by Pope John XXIII concerning the role of the hierarchy in guiding Catholics. Someone in the audience shouted, "I object to this!"

"Well, let me say in the first place, I've not read the *Catholic Encyclopedia,*" began Kennedy. In any case, however, he did not agree with the sentiments in the passage and he found "no difficulty" in saying so.

He did think he could comment better, however, if he had the entire quotation before him. ". . . If the quotation is meant to imply that when you take an oath you don't mean it, or that it's proper for you to take oaths and then break them, it's proper for you to lie, if that is what this states—and I don't know whether that's what it states unless I read it all in context—then of course I would not agree with it."[11]

He asked to have the Pope's statement reread. When it had been, he asked, ". . . guiding them in what area? If you're talking about in the area of faith and morals, in the instructions of the Church, I would think any Baptist minister or Congregational minister has the right and duty to try to guide his flock. If you mean by that statement that the Pope or anyone else could bind me in the fulfillment . . . of my public duties, I say 'no.' "

Replied his questioner curtly: "Thank you, sir. Then you do not agree with the Pope on that statement." A stir ran through the audience. Murmurs ceased.

"Gentlemen," said Kennedy imploringly, "now that's why I wanted to be careful because that statement it seems to me is taken out of context that you just made to me. I could not tell you what the Pope meant unless I had the entire article. I would be glad to state to you that no one can direct me in the fulfillment of my duties as a public official under the United States Constitution."

After the tension and thinly veiled hostility, there now seemed an apologetic note, even embarrassment, as the questioning moved on. The next clergyman congratulated Kennedy on his "laudably" clear statement regarding separation of church and state; but on the matter of resigning office, that Kennedy had briefly noted, if it should be "in conflict with your church—"

"No, I said with my conscience," Kennedy quickly corrected him.

"Was it really the young Senator from Massachusetts who was on trial, or was it we?" wrote a minister afterward. "It became increasingly clear that he was equal both intellectually and personally to whatever questions were asked of him . . . we were not sure that the same could be said of ourselves."[12]

The next question, regarding the syllabus of errors of the church, was prefaced with a defensive acknowledgment that it was from several centuries in the past, but that it nevertheless still remained a part of church doctrine. Time was running out. Kennedy answered all three parts of the inquiry, and now there were a number of things he wished to make clear.

Hurriedly he began: "I don't want anyone to think because they interrogate me on this very important question that I regard that as unfair . . . or unreasonable, or that . . . somebody who is concerned about the matter is prejudiced or bigoted. I think this fight for religious freedom is basic in the establishment of the American system and therefore any candidate for the office, I think, should submit himself to the questions of any reasonable man.

"My only objection would be—" He was interrupted by applause. Hardly pausing he continued, "—if somebody said 'Regardless of Senator Kennedy's position, regardless of how much evidence he's given, that if what he says he means, I still wouldn't vote for him because he's a member of that Church' I would consider that unreasonable."

What *was* reasonable, said Kennedy, was attention to the stating of a candidate's views, the investigating of his record, and then a rational, independent judgment as to whether he could be entrusted with this highly important position.

He was grateful for the invitation, he told his audience once again. "I'm sure that I have made no converts to my Church, but I do hope that at least my view, . . . may be of some value in at least assisting you to make a careful judgment."

It had been a grueling test. Regardless of what one saw as the issue, Kennedy had considerably enhanced his personal stature and respect in the eyes of many, including some of those who had heretofore been hesitant about the man and his position. Kennedy himself called his appearance "satisfactory."[13] Dr. Poling, in New York, termed the performance and the address "magnificent." However, he maintained, the issue continued as a valid one.[14]

The Houston *Chronicle* observed, "There is something in the sight of an American having to defend his religious beliefs that repels Americans." The late Sam Rayburn was more direct. "He ate 'em raw," he said.[15] Others, however, did not share that view. In Washington, the Citizens for Religious Freedom, "after careful study," termed Kennedy's remarks "the most complete, unequivocal and reassuring statement which could be expected of any person in his position."[16]

They called for acceptable acknowledgments and statements from "the American bishops" on birth control, interfaith marriage ceremonies, freedom of worship and of missionary activity everywhere, and freedom for those public officials who are Catholic to fulfill their responsibilities "without interference from their church."

It had not been the intention of the National Conference of Citizens for Religious Freedom to stir animosities, they said, "but rather to clarify certain of these problems which had become apparent in the current national situation." Kennedy, they noted, had not only touched on these, but had shed light on others not yet fully examined.

His personal affirmation on the separation of church and state was "made sincerely and commends itself to the attention of the American people. The only remaining question is whether his statement is acceptable to his church. . . ."[17]

Whether they counted on it or not, they were soon to receive their hoped-for response. In 1928 and in earlier campaigns, the Catholic Church had remained largely silent while its lay organizations and publications were content to handle the matter more by ridicule than by serious discussion of the accusations leveled against it. Even during the early days of the 1960 campaign the church remained silent while it was continually being provoked and involved in debate; calls for an official pronouncement from the church clarifying its position on church and state in the United States had been made both to Rome and to the American hierarchy.

In mid-May, in an editorial described as "authoritative," the Vatican newspaper *l'Osservatore Romano* had declared that "the unalterable antithesis between the Marxist system and Christian doctrine is self-evident," and that Roman Catholicism "commits and guides the entire existence of man."[18] It termed it "the right and duty" of the Roman Catholic hierarchy "to intervene" in the political arena. The editorial had been prompted by a very specific political situation in Italy. Certain elements in Premier Fanfani's Vatican-backed Christian Democratic party were advocating working with left-wing socialists. The church took strong exception to this proposal.

The editorial had been given to the paper for publication by the Vatican Secretary of State. A reported statement by "a high Vatican source" that "the Vatican newspaper certainly did not have in mind the United States Presidential campaign" was called inaccurate.[19] On the other hand, no explicit mention of the United States had been made. It was quickly pointed out, however, that the editorial's condemnation of "the absurd split of conscience between the believer and the citizen" had been reportedly described by churchmen as binding on Roman Catholics throughout the world.

In July, an American Catholic prelate had finally made a clear statement. In Cincinnati, Archbishop Karl J. Alter stated, "We seek no privileged status; we proclaim our full adherence to the provisions of the Constitution as of now as well as for the future."[20] But his declaration went largely unheard in the heat of the July conventions.

The day after the first national TV debate between Nixon and Kennedy, a lecture was delivered at the Shrine of the Most Blessed Sacrament in Washington by the Reverend Gustave Weigel, S.J., professor of ecclesiology at Woodstock College, the Jesuit theological seminary outside Baltimore. It was entitled, with appropriate calm, "A Theological Consideration of the Relations Between Church and State."[21]

After an exposition on the "two sources of human allegiance"— the sacral, or "inviolability of conscience," and the secular, or the state and its laws—Father Weigel noted the Catholic principle of "greatest possible concord between the sacral and the secular." When viewed in concert with political action by individual Catholics, he observed, this caused the non-Catholic in some instances to see "a threat to his own freedom and existence." By way of reply, he termed the doctrine of the First Amendment "not a theological statement, but a legal principle," and one that had been "enthusiastically accepted" by Catholics as "a good law, to be preserved now and in the future." He said: "Officially and really, American Catholics do not want now or in the future a law which would make Catholicism the favored religion of this land. They do not want the religious freedom of American non-Catholics to be curtailed in any way. They sincerely want the present First Amendment to be retained and become more effective. With a note of desperation, I ask, what more can we say?"22

He moved to answer critics of the church on another level, and one that actually possessed far more cause for concern. It was expressed in the emphasis on Catholicism as a broad intellectual and social force influencing American life. "Some non-Catholic Americans feel quite assured," Father Weigel said, "that American Catholics do not want to, and what is more important cannot change, our American freedom of religion. They are afraid of something else. A Catholic lawmaker or a Catholic executive might deviously push Catholic moral precepts into our laws and in consequence non-Catholics would be hampered. . . ."

The making of a Roman Catholic state out of America, it had been maintained, "did not mean a State in which all citizens accept Roman Catholic theology, morals and ecclesiasticism as binding." Instead, it would simply be one in which the church's "social polity would approximate closely to a complete legislative expression and effectiveness."23 Protestantism would simply become a minority influence in this regard. This concern had been raised again just prior to the 1960 campaign by Bishop Oxnam and Dr. Blake and others. Some had raised the question in regard to future appointments to the Supreme Court that might be made by a Catholic President. The law of the land, they held, would thus be subject to interpretation by Catholic consciences. They were "uneasy" about the election of a Catholic, Bishop Oxnam and Dr. Blake had said, because it would "both symbolize and strengthen the growing and direct political influence that the Roman Catholic Church exerts on our government and our society."[24] Father Weigel now considered this point. "That a Catholic statesman comes to his task with a Catholic conscience is as true as the fact that a Protestant statesman comes with a Protestant conscience."

But, he continued, "for both of these men the task is exclusively the making of good laws. . . . I do not say that law can prescind from morality but I do say that the attempt to impose one's moral theory on another is not the function of the statesman." Instead, "he takes his lead from the consensus of the community. In America, any elected official is a citizen designated by the people for some temporary function of state. This man has a double life. He has his own and that of civil servant. . . . In his public role he is a man of the law which is framed for practical purposes and canonizes no philosophy or theology."[25]

Father Weigel did not specifically address himself to the fears of the vitiation of American Protestantism as a social and intellectual force. Here, apparently, Protestantism was left to put its own house in order.

"As for the interference of the Bishops of the Pope," he continued, "it can be said without hesitation that there would be none of it." Moreover, "The Catholic President's comportment with the clergy of his church would be exactly like the comportment of a Protestant President with the clergy of his church. Both would give the clergy the same social deference which the community at large grants them—no more and no less."

The Roman Catholic Church in America had been heard from on the issues at a time when many had been waiting to catch its voice amid the controversy. To what degree Father Weigel's exposition had cleared the air was problematical.

Three weeks after the lecture, Methodist Bishop John Wesley Lord directed a suggestion to the Roman Catholic Church that responsible sources within it declare that a Roman Catholic President would not be subjected to pressures by his church. The bishop noted, in doing so, that Kennedy's own statements on separation of church and state were "completely satisfactory."[26]

Differences would not be reconciled, in the campaign or by the election; that was becoming clear. The church, however, was to be heard from again in another connection shortly before the end of the campaign.

Meanwhile, another element contributed to the catalytic events surrounding the manifesto by the so-called Peale group. The controversy as it related to the campaign and the candidate was fanned by preexisting internal divisions within the Protestant community itself. (Nor was the Catholic Church immune from its own internal differences.) The differences within the religious community were to continue into the last days of the campaign and lead to calls for serious efforts toward "church amity" following the election. The effect of the internal feuds on the campaign emotions was precisely what the Founding Fathers had sought to avoid in separating established religion from formal processes of government.

Beyond sharply revealing several factors already at work, the events in Washington and Houston directly promoted fresh influences. The candidate's identity apart from his church was accentuated. He was not the "Catholic candidate" for President. He was Senator John F. Kennedy. He had views of his own. These views were not objectionable to his church. Moreover, they were inspiringly in harmony with the laws of the land and the traditions of American society.

The sharp sectarianism that had marked the clashes in Washington and Houston were disturbing and unsettling to many Americans. The unwritten rule of contemporary American pluralism—a rule that favored the blunting of sectarianism in a general merging of religiosity—had been abruptly violated. The hard side of pluralism was revealed, beneath the "American way of life" of Christmas trees, charity, Thanksgiving turkey, and church attendance.

Kennedy began to appropriate the advantages of earnest religiosity without any of the disadvantages of sectarian zeal—zeal particularly associated, by many, with his church. And in so doing he had affirmed, rather than denied, his allegiance to its moral precepts. "If he's religious, why, more power to him," echoed the words of the West Virginia miner.

The American public was still becoming acquainted with Kennedy. As the campaign progressed and he made vital and direct contact with his audiences, the earlier charges of being a playboy, too young, too aloof lost substance. They were replaced by images of competence, maturity, sincerity, and vitality. With television and the Great Debates, this process was to be accelerated and reinforced many-fold. (Said one highly placed Kennedy strategist after Election Day: "Without the debates it wouldn't even have been close.)[27] Meanwhile, despite the thousands of miles traveled, and the thousands of people they had met, the candidates had come face-to-face with only a fraction of the electorate. On September 21st Kennedy made his first nation-wide television address. An almost religious aura of rebirth and deliverance and dedication once again came through his words and imagery.

If Americans met their public and private responsibilities and obligations, he said, "then future historians will be able to say 'These were the great years of the American Republic. These were the years when America began to move again.' "[28] Concluding, he cited a sudden progressive darkening of the heavens over Hartford, Connecticut, one afternoon in the closing decades of the eighteenth century, and the words of the Speaker of the House, as "in that religious age" he rose in the State House of Representatives amid the trepidation and the clamor: "The day of judgment is either approaching or it is not. If it is not, there is no cause for adjournment. If it is, I choose to be found doing my duty. . . ."

Several days before that, Kennedy had taken the initiative as a kind of national spokesman to issue a reminder to Nikita Khrushchev, who was arriving in the United States in the midst of the campaign, in order to attend the United Nations General Assembly convening in New York: "Perhaps you have been misled into believing that we are a divided country. . . . Nothing could be further from the truth," Kennedy said. Nor was the country deceived by his deportment, Kennedy told him. "The Bible, one book with which you may not be familiar, Mr. Khrushchev, warns us . . . 'The words of his mouth were smoother than butter, but war was in his heart.' "[29]

Amid the rancor surrounding the religious issue in the campaign, something else had occurred. There had begun to emerge a clearer drawing of lines, and the marshaling of a consensus. Several days after the Washington manifesto, and almost simultaneous with the Houston exchange, Protestantism's voice was heard in fuller range.

A small group of laymen, including Francis S. Harmon, a New York attorney, had drafted and circulated a statement on religious liberty in regard to the 1960 campaign even prior to the meeting of the so-called Peale group in Washington.[30] Accompanying the statement had been a letter signed by Dr. F. Ernest Johnson, professor emeritus at Teachers College; Dean Liston Pope of Yale Divinity School; the Reverend John LaFarge, S.J., and Rabbi William F. Rosenblum. In response, fifty-five Protestant, twenty-nine Roman Catholic, fifteen Jewish, and one Greek Orthodox laymen and clergy in fifteen states from New Hampshire to California declared themselves as signatories. Among them were the Right Reverend Arthur Lichtenberger, presiding bishop of the Protestant Episcopal Church, and the Right Reverend Henry Knox Sherrill, his predecessor.*

The statement represented an attempt, "without reference to any political party or party philosophy," to "bring basic American principles of religious liberty in a democracy into a dispassionate focus."[31] Reaffirming their loyalty to the Constitution and its provisions regarding religion, the signatories declared, "The bearing of the religious views of any candidate of any party

---

* Among the others were the Rt. Rev. Angus Dun of Washington; Rabbi Wolfe Kelman of New York; Archbishop Iakovos of New York; Rev. James H. Robinson, and Dr. Jesse R. Wilson of Wells, Texas. Other signers included: Dr. Harry J. Carman, Millicent McIntosh, Mrs. Eugene Meyer, Hon. Carlton J. H. Hayes, Prof. William Ernest Hocking, Dr. Channing H. Tobias, Dr. Lewis Webster Jones.

upon his decisions in public office is a public matter. Inquiry regarding this relevancy is an exercise of responsible citizenship, if conducted in such a way as not to violate the constitutional prohibition against any religious test for public office." The signatories were not questioning the propriety of religion's presence in the political arena to this extent.

But, the statement continued: "We believe that it is the responsibility of the members of our various religious organizations to oppose vigorously all attempts to make religious affiliation the basis of the voter's choice of candidates for public office. It is a vicious practice and repugnant to all honorable Americans to set class against class, race against race, and religion against religion."

The statement sought to lend perspective to the religious issue. "The judgment of God," it continued, "finds us at a particular moment in history, confronted by its unique challenges and dilemma, and it is there that our testing is. In the circumstances that now confront us, we must act according to our principles, or be found wanting."

Said the declaration: "A candidate's faith, and his affirmations of it, as they bear upon his responsibilities in public office, should be viewed in their best light rather than their worst, and the response and expectation of the nation should be such as will encourage him to attain the highest spiritual and moral realization which his own faith can inspire."

The signatories concluded with a recommendation and even a word of advice: "Every public official who is a member of a religious group should, of course, take into consideration the spiritual and moral principles of his faith in confronting the decisions he must make. But in our pluralistic society he will recognize that the values in historic faiths other than his own must be brought to bear upon the problems of the day. He alone, under the judgment of God, can fully appraise the force and applicability of all such values and advice for his situation, and he should seek to apply all in such a way as to enhance and undergird the best interests of the nation."

The relevance of this expression of Protestant, Jewish, and

Catholic thought for the questions comprising the religious issue in the campaign was clear. The circulation of the fifteen-hundred-word statement itself was limited. But it represented most significantly a major crystallization of opinion among influential elements in the mainstream of America's life. As an unforeseen sum result, and unintended effect of the controversy surrounding the religious issue, the candidate—regardless of party—was being reminded in unprecedented degree of the high place of religious belief in a nation of many beliefs, and of the bearing of this on him in his role as its responsible leader. No presidential election in at least a century had carried with it an equivalent degree and kind of active religious sentiment. The conscience of the nation was being articulated.

Now, other groups launched sustained programs of opposition to what they considered to be bigotry in the campaign. Prior to 1928, the widespread activities of the Klan had led several members of the Federal Council of Churches and B'nai B'rith to join in promoting an organization that would "analyze, moderate and finally eliminate prejudice which disfigures and distorts business, social and political relations" among Americans.[32] The 1928 campaign had dramatically made evident the need for such a national force. Under Everett Ross Clinchy, the new undertaking, the National Conference of Christians and Jews, grew from a one-man operation with a $10,000 budget in 1929 to a national network of more than sixty regional offices staffed by several hundred persons under a budget of almost $3,000,000 by 1960.[33] Although having "no direct business in the area of doctrinal differences," the Conference emphasized that "human interests and . . . civil obligations" made "anti-Semitism, anti-Catholicism, anti-Protestantism . . ." the concern of all citizens.[34]

In October, in the midst of the campaign, the Conference held a New York meeting to map opposition to any final outcropping of bigotry in the campaign. It was attended by representatives of seventy-five religious, social, and political welfare organizations with a membership of 60 million.[35]

The public consensus was being articulated to a great extent around the law, both in a broad and in a very specific sense. In the broad sense it transcended party lines. Repeated references had been made to the Constitution as the supreme law of the land. The Republican candidate for Vice President, Henry Cabot Lodge, fresh from representing the United States in the community of nations, said in mid-September in Columbus, Ohio, "I absolutely refuse to admit my three Roman Catholic grandsons will be debarred from the Presidency" on religious grounds, "or for that matter my two Episcopal grandsons."[36] Pluralism had become an established fact in very personal ways since Lodge's illustrious grandfather had defeated John F. Fitzgerald for a Senate seat in 1916. Henry Cabot Lodge added: "Even to raise the question is against the Constitution which prohibits discrimination on grounds of religion."

On the same day, in the heart of the Peale controversy, former President Harry S. Truman had pinpointed the issue when he said he didn't think Kennedy "would do anything but protect the Constitution of the United States, and he certainly wouldn't yield to any pressures any more than I did."[37]

The Constitution, a distant symbol studied in school and then forgotten by most Americans, was being invoked as a forceful, living document of the American tradition. The law was being invoked, too, on a very concrete and specific basis. The indictment returned in Pittsburgh in the wake of circulation of the fraudulent Knights of Columbus oath had been a beginning. Simultaneously, the Justice Department and the FBI began looking into widespread circulation of anti-Catholic material in other areas. Involved was the possible violation of a federal law that prohibited the interstate mailing of material that had a tendency to affect election results, if the source was not given.

The United States code provided for a maximum penalty of $1,000 fine and a year in prison for persons guilty of knowingly contributing in any way to the publication or distribution of political statements that did not identify their source.[38]

Other aspects of federal law were involved. A 1954 amendment to the Internal Revenue Code prohibited the use of tax-exempt gifts to finance literature that advocates political action. The chairman of the Fair Campaign Practices Committee, Charles P. Taft, suggested that churches and religious groups might face loss of their tax-exempt status as a result of distributing anti-Catholic literature.[39] Moreover, others called attention to a section of the Corrupt Practices Act that required the filing of a report with the Clerk of the House of Representatives by anyone spending fifty dollars or more within one year "for the purpose of influencing in two or more states the election of candidates."[40] Clearly, the breaking of this regulation was necessary to avoid the effects of breaking the other.

Despite these laws, however, there was no explicit legal prohibition of adverse comment directed at a religious or minority group. It was pointed out by the general counsel of the Post Office Department that such a law would stand a strong chance of being declared unconstitutional under that document's guarantees of free speech.[41]

The character of religion in politics as a tool rather than as an autonomous force became increasingly evident as it was revealed that anti-Catholicism was being employed as a device by interests that opposed the candidate on grounds other than religious doctrine or affiliation.

The Justice Department was joined by the Senate Subcommittee on Privileges and Elections, headed by Senator Theodore Francis Green, of Rhode Island, in looking into the printing and mailing of the sermon by Dr. W. A. Criswell some time earlier in the campaign. It had been widely distributed, sometimes anonymously, but in violation of federal law. Investigation revealed that 102,000 copies, costing approximately $10,000, had allegedly been ordered for printing and mailing by an assistant to H. L. Hunt, Texas oil man and sponsor of "Facts Forum," a public affairs discussion program.[42] The publishing house from which the copies had been ordered said it had been assured that no violation of the law was involved. Hunt, denying any anti-Catholicism, said that he had heard the sermon by Criswell and had had it mailed as a warning that bitter religious controversy would ensue if the Democratic nominee were a Catholic.[43] The literature had originally been sent out just prior to the Demo-

cratic convention. (Hunt said he had been supporting Senator
Johnson for the nomination. Now he offered a substantial con-
tribution to the Democratic campaign fund, but it was reportedly
rejected.)

Meanwhile, another effect was occurring among certain seg-
ments of the electorate at large. In late August a report had been
given to Kennedy strategists confirming their earlier views about
the advantages of meeting the religious issue squarely. The report
was based on more than 100,000 interviews with "eligible voters"
across the country, all carried out since 1952 in the course of
dozens of intermittent national public opinion polls.[44]

The report said: ". . . Kennedy today has lost the bulk of the
votes he would lose if the election campaign were to be embittered by the issue of anti-Catholicism. The net worst has been
done. If the campaign becomes embittered, he will lose a few
more reluctant Protestant votes to Nixon, but will gain Catholic
and minority group votes. Bitter anti-Catholicism in the campaign would bring about a reaction against prejudice and for
Kennedy from Catholics and others who would resent overt
prejudice. . . . On balance he would not lose further from forthright and persistent attention to the religious issue and could
gain."[45]

The phenomenon forecast by the report now appeared to be
taking place. It had already been reflected in the reactions of certain portions of the Negro press and among Jewish groups. In
New York, shortly following the Peale and Houston episodes, an
advertising man who was also "an active Catholic layman" bluntly
told a reporter: "I want to vote for Nixon, but if the Protestants
keep on kicking my church around, I may change. . . ."[46] Many
Catholics had been cool to the Democrats. In 1952 and 1956 there
had been substantial switching to Eisenhower. The Kennedy
memo at the 1956 convention had even suggested that the coalition that had supported Roosevelt, and had comprised many
Catholics, might be cracking. Changes in Catholic voting allegiance were accompanying the move up through the social scale
over the years. Combined with this were adverse reactions to

several Democratic leaders. And Henry Cabot Lodge, stanch fighter against communism day after day in the arena of the UN, was appealing to many Catholics.

But now the traditional lines of the Democratic coalition that had begun to form with Wilson, that had been promoted by Smith and had solidified with Roosevelt, were coalescing once again, although it was far from assured. In New York, after a Kennedy visit in late October, Police Commissioner Stephen Kennedy estimated the crowds as "the largest since . . . Lindbergh."[47] In the South, Lyndon Johnson campaigned hard against stubborn opposition, and sought to win over recalcitrant Democrats.

Because of its many-sided nature in substantial areas of the body politic, the "religious issue" remained alive. Now, however, Kennedy's opponents contented themselves chiefly with propagandizing those portions of the population most in sympathy with their views or prone to be convinced by them. The religious issue took the form of a kind of shadow opposition working through local familiar personal networks, and even boasting a kind of civility.

Anti-Catholic sentiment was not altogether absent among many individuals who were otherwise "liberal" in their religion and their politics. Sophisticated and enlightened "anti-Catholics" saw the church, rather than its members, as a frequent if not perennial enemy of "liberal" or "progressive" doctrines. The threatened net result of their sentiments, however, was no different from that based on other degrees of variations of anti-Catholicism: the loss of votes for the candidate.

But something had happened. Those stanchly holding to sectarian concerns and doctrinaire secularism had been forced into self-examination even as had the bigoted. The issue was to flare again bitterly on the eve of voting. But its early inoculation into the national blood stream had allowed time for a reaction. By the time fevers rose again, a fixed and active resistance was able to curtail its spread.

CHAPTER TWELVE

JOHN F. KENNEDY
The Ultimate Test

"The heritage for which others have died"

THE RELIGIOUS ISSUE HAD "GONE UNDERGROUND" FOLLOWING THE repercussions of the Peale controversy and the Houston speech, but it continued to add no less heat to the steadily intensified campaign.

The ministers in Danville, Virginia, who had formed a Citizens Association for Religious Liberty in order to fight with all the powers at their command the election of a Roman Catholic President, reported that "the men seem to be stronger in their determination to carry on the campaign than before."[1] In San Antonio, Texas, that same night, former President Harry S. Truman was addressing four hundred spirited Democrats at a fund-raising dinner. "I wish I had time to tell you all the things that you are for—that Democrats are for—that Nixon has voted against," stormed the old give-'em-hell campaigner of 1948. Departing from his prepared speech, in hearty exasperation, he declared, "If you vote for Nixon you ought to go to hell!"*[2]

Republicans immediately cried out angrily. Senator Thruston B. Morton, Republican national chairman, complained to the Fair Campaign Practices Committee, and called on Kennedy to disown Truman's attack. The leader of the Republican "truth

---

* The statement immediately inspired button manufacturers, who quickly produced a large campaign button that read: "I'm voting for Nixon, but *I'm not* going to h—."

squad," Senator Hugh Scott, of Pennsylvania, called the remark "mudsmanship."[3]

Truman, meanwhile, had moved ahead without taking one step back. The injection of religious prejudice into the campaign "makes me want to fight and that is what I'm doing," he said the next day in Waco. "It makes me sick." Those behind it, he said, "don't really object to Jack Kennedy's election because he is a Catholic. They object to his election because he is a Democrat."[4]

Meanwhile, seventy-two Baptist ministers meeting in another part of the city were adopting a resolution that looked with disfavor upon "his manner of speech."[5] Weeks later, Dr. Ramsey Pollard, in Texas for the Baptist General Convention, speaking as "an individual," reportedly declared that Truman ought to be turned out of the church because of his remarks. Pollard also took the occasion to warn that if Kennedy were elected "there would be a decided influence from Rome in our government,"[6] thus maintaining his rational and judicious mode of appeal to the very end of the campaign.

Nixon himself was properly aloof in his response. Squarely eyeing a national television audience, he said with a solemn mien: "We all have tempers. I have one. I'm sure Senator Kennedy has one. But when a man is President of the United States or a former President, he has an obligation not to lose his temper in public."[7] He noted that as he traveled around the country there were a "tremendous number of children who come out to see the Presidential candidates. I see mothers holding their babies up so that they can see a man who might be President of the United States. . . . It makes you realize that whoever is President is going to be a man that all the children of America will either look up to or will look down to."[8]

Nixon closed his statement on the matter by telling the millions watching: "I can only say that I'm very proud that President Eisenhower restored dignity and decency and, frankly, good language, to the conduct of the President of the United States. . . ." He expressed the hope that if elected he could approach Eisenhower in maintaining the dignity of the office.

Truman's charges were matched by Republicans who asserted that his party was "playing up Kennedy's religion in ways they think will get him votes."[9] Democrats seemed to have contributed little to efforts at keeping the issue alive. Anti-Catholic literature urging voters to reject him already covered a four-by-ten-foot bulletin board in Kennedy's Office of Community Relations headed by James W. Wine. One of these pamphleteers, the Reverend Bob Schuler of Los Angeles, had issued the call to Americans in 1928 not to elect a "Bowery-produced, Tammany-trained, Roman-owned, liquor-dominated champion to the Presidency . . ." Now in 1960 he continued his efforts. He seemed, however, to have mellowed somewhat. A year before the Democratic convention he wrote of Kennedy: "While this young millionaire might lose a few votes over the Roman Catholic issue, he will more than make up for the loss by the bought and paid for labor vote. . . . I would rather have Kennedy, loyal Roman Catholic that he is, than to have Stevenson."[10]

At the other end of the nation, in New Jersey, the Reverend Carl McIntire, president of a branch of the Council of Christian Churches that had been formed in 1941 to combat "modernism," added his voice. In a letter appealing for funds to carry on his group's fight, McIntire asserted: "Nikita Khrushchev has put on a show at the United Nations, the import of which is horrifying. Yet the very things that he advocated we have heard from the leadership of the World Council of Churches and the National Council of Churches." He wrote that a major effort had "been made by men who are our chief opponents in the ecumenical movement to discredit and smear leaders of the International Council of Christian Churches in the public mind."[11]

Another member of the Council of Christian Churches joined in. In Englewood, Colorado, the Reverend Harvey Springer, the "Cowboy Evangelist," reported he'd delivered 270 speeches in twenty-five states in thirteen weeks. His publication *Western Voice* had served as a vehicle for continuous warnings against Catholicism. In one earlier issue cash prizes had been offered for the four best original sermons on "Why We Must Stop Rome's

March on Washington." He was the author of a pamphlet entitled "The Roman Octopus." All this didn't make him a hate- or rabble-rouser, he declared. "America is a Protestant nation," he said, adding that he simply wanted to keep it that way. "I would oppose any Roman Catholic for President—the name doesn't make any difference."[12] Asked Springer: "How many Catholics came over on the *Mayflower?* Not one." Moreover, "None of our Presidents was a Roman Catholic and I'm against setting a new precedent now." Springer revealed his plans to New York *Times* reporter John Wicklein: "Five days before the election, I'm releasing 1,500,000 volunteer workers to call on voters and give them our literature on Kennedy." For this final drive he was adding "a secret little letter." It accused Kennedy of "getting ready to socialize the country."[13]

About this time an anti-Catholic ballad called "I'm Just an Old Cowpoke" began to gain limited circulation. One stanza went: "No carpetbagger man/From any Popish clan/Can spur my horse to my remorse/By order, Vatican."

Another letter, mailed by the National Association of Evangelicals, was aimed at galvanizing local pastors around the country into action on Reformation Sunday: "If a Roman Catholic is elected President—what then? The Church of Rome will have a great new advantage, and the United States will no longer be recognized as a Protestant nation in the eyes of the world." The letter asked: "Don't you agree that it is time for the Protestants of America to stand up and be counted?"[14] Then the pastor was admonished: "We dare not sit idly by—voiceless and voteless— and lose the heritage for which others have died."[15] Pastors were urged to follow those who long ago "broke off the shackles of a dead, legalistic, hypocritical church" when Martin Luther nailed his Ninety-five Theses to the door of Wittenberg Castle Church in 1517.

The National Association of Evangelicals had taken on the effort that had been planned through the ill-starred National Conference of Citizens for Religious Freedom. Plans were revealed for prayer meetings, special services, and special offerings by other conservative Protestant groups during the last two Sundays in October. Buttons to be worn "on the street and on the job" as a "simple and unobtrusive Protestant identification" carried the words "Stand up and be counted" with the numerals "1517." Orders for literature had come from more than 6,000 churches, most of them smaller ones in scattered parts of the country.

The threat did not consist only of Catholicism, said the N.A.E. There was also concern expressed over growing communist infiltration, and the breakdown of morality in the nation. The group emphasized prayer as a major part of its efforts. "We are asking God to have His own way in the national election," a spokesman reported.[16]

A note of resignation had begun to be heard more frequently. It was pointed out that while it might be the time to stand up and be counted, the conflict was not at all one that would be decided in November. In Texas, Dr. Blake Smith, a widely revered Baptist clergyman, warned that the campaign threatened to "degenerate into a hassle over a religious controversy that has been with us since the beginning and shall remain unchanged no matter who is elected. This fear to which we are giving way is unworthy of the church," he cautioned.[17]

The warnings of other ministers, in the face of Kennedy's repeated reiterations of his position, had begun to shift. His election, it was now reasoned, might open the door to a later Catholic who would not be so independent of the church's discipline. From the candidate, and then the church, the emphasis had withdrawn to a more remote arena, the future. As preparations for Reformation Sunday proceeded amid talk of a reported "boomerang" effect among Catholic voters, other Protestants speculated on a more immediate danger.

Somewhat earlier in the campaign, 165 prominent Catholic laymen had sought to make their position in the church-state controversy clear, declaring that "efforts which tend to undermine the principle of separation . . . should be resisted no matter how well intentioned each such effort may be."[18]

Now it was feared by some Protestant churchmen that continued attention to the issue might work against the "growing practice" among Catholics "of using private judgment in widening fields of political and personal decision."[19] The laymen's declaration had been interpreted by some as an example of this. But then, almost as if to lend weight to the warnings of the more conservative Protestants as the religious issue gathered new force, three Roman Catholic bishops in Puerto Rico during the third week in October issued a pastoral letter severely cautioning voters there against supporting Governor Luis Muñoz Marin in his bid for reelection. The governor, a divorced Catholic, had in the past endorsed measures for birth control and sterilization. The island's public school pupils had not been granted time off for religious instructions. Now the church saw in some of his party's campaign pledges morality being "dictated by majority vote" rather than by religion. To vote for Marin was characterized by Bishop James E. McManus as a "sin of disobedience."[20] But when asked whether penalties would be imposed, if voters revealed they had voted for him, Archbishop James P. Davis replied it was "a matter between a Catholic and his conscience."[21] The prelate added, "If democracy in Puerto Rico had achieved the maturity of democracy in the United States, the letter would not have been made necessary."

Several days later, two churchmen spoke out to clarify the relevance of the episode for the United States political scene. Archbishop Egidio Vagnozzi, Apostolic Delegate to the United States, was in Mobile, Alabama, for ceremonies marking the fiftieth anniversary of the ordination of Archbishop Thomas J. Toolen.

In response to questions, he declared he was "confident the Roman Catholic hierarchy in the United States would never take political action similar to that of the Puerto Rican Bishops."[22] In Boston, Richard Cardinal Cushing said he was pleased to add his voice to that of the Apostolic Delegate "in declaring that it is totally out of step with the American tradition for ecclesiastical authority here to dictate the political voting of citizens. This has never been a part of our history and I pray God that it never will be."[23]

To some conservative Protestants, however, the episode had provided ample proof for what they had been contending all along. "If there has ever been any question in the minds of Americans whether the Roman Catholic Church would interfere in the internal affairs of a country when it felt the time was opportune," said Dr. George L. Ford, the N.A.E.'s executive director, "there certainly cannot be now."[24] The Catholic magazine *Commonweal* saw the episode in an entirely different light, as evidence *against* Protestant fears. "If any doubts existed" (about a hierarchical plot to help Kennedy's election), "the pastoral letter by the Bishops of Puerto Rico . . . should demolish those doubts once and for all," it said.

But to some, the "country" referred to by Dr. Ford was not most notably Puerto Rico, but the United States itself. It was rumored that internal power struggles within the American hierarchy were behind the timing and pronouncement of the Puerto Rican action. Church politics, it was charged, had dictated interference in American politics.[25]

Reactions in this country to the Puerto Rican episode seemed more to reinforce previously held positions on all sides than to change any intentions. Several days after the exchanges, the Reverend Dr. Robert J. McCracken, of New York's Riverside Church, reiterated what had been noted before the bishops had acted. "Among Roman Catholics, clerical and lay, in the United States, there is a growing practice of exercising the right of private judgment in political as well as private life," he maintained.[26] Secretary of Labor James P. Mitchell, who had been boomed by some in his party for Vice President, presumably to balance the Democrats' possible appeal to Catholics, used the occasion to direct a broad hint at them. Roman Catholic voters were "too intelligent to vote as a bloc," he said at a Republican rally in heavily Catholic Rhode Island.[27]

There was some fear in the Democratic camp, however, that any salutary effect stemming from Father Weigel's statement and other declarations earlier in the campaign might be seriously and perhaps crucially offset by what had happened. It might be particularly damaging, they felt, among voters in some of the more closely contested states. Shortly thereafter Kennedy left his text in the course of a nationally televised address from Philadelphia, while describing the kind of America he believed in, to reemphasize his position: "I believe in an America . . . where every citizen is free to vote as he pleases without instructions from anyone," he repeated, "—his employer, his union leader or his clergyman."[28]

The comment was doubtlessly prompted in part by the Puerto Rican occurrence, yet it reflected a more striking characteristic of the campaign. It had become evident weeks earlier in the announced purposes of the Citizens for Religious Freedom in Washington and the ensuing reactions. Almost all the parties involved had identified one another heavily in terms of political partisanship. There had been an open alignment of attitudes in both a political and a religious framework, liberals and conservatives. The intention of the Washington group, that of encouraging discussion at the grass-roots level around the country, further emphasized the steadily increasing conjoining of religion with politics. There had been an alliance of political attitudes with theological dogma. A major postelection study of voting behavior later revealed "a striking correlation between Protestant Democratic defections to Mr. Nixon and frequency of church attendance." For example, "outside the South, the defection among those who said they never attended church was 6 per cent . . . and among those who attended 'regularly' more than 35 per cent."[29]

It seemed to reflect a change in the United States since De Tocqueville had noted that religion in America "takes no direct part in the government of society, but . . . must be regarded as the first of their political institutions." He had observed that "religion exercises but little influence upon the laws and upon the details of public opinion; but . . . directs the customs of the community, and by regulating domestic life . . . regulates the state."[30] Now, it seemed, much the reverse was true. As religion ceased to regulate the domestic life, it appeared, religionists pressed their direct attention on matters through the political sphere.

In Jackson's time the religious issue had been symptomatic of a lessening impact of religion and clergy on public affairs. With the rise of the social gospel in the last decades of the nineteenth century, activity by religionists and churches in public affairs had almost become imperative as the individual conscience lessened in effectiveness. The 1960 campaign was revealing to what extent the churches regarded their renewed role as a legitimate and imperative one.

The General Council of the 3,000,000-member United Presbyterian Church took exception to what it regarded as attempts to make churches appear irrelevant in American life. At the same time it expressed "outrage and concern" at "exploitation of the religious issue in the campaign."[31] In Peoria, a group of evangelical ministers strongly defended their right of political action in distributing leaflets opposing Kennedy's election.

Estimates were that hundreds and possibly thousands of ministers across the country helped to guide their congregations to what was "right" in the course of Reformation Sunday sermons. What was "right" differed from sect to sect and even within sects. The divisions which had been made apparent earlier in the campaign remained. Religious intolerance was assailed. The designs of the Roman Catholic hierarchy were attacked. Other ministers made no reference to the campaign. (One of these was the Reverend W. A. Criswell in Dallas.) In New York, the Reverend Dr. Daniel A. Poling in a final word told his congregation that the candidates "are both Christian in faith" and "have a generous regard for the religious belief of all their fellow Americans."[32]

The wave of propaganda that had started with preparations for Reformation Sunday, however, did not end with it. A sermon on "The Central Issue Concerning a Catholic for President," preached in California, was distributed in thousands by an evangelist publishing house in Missouri, and received by ministers in upstate New York and other parts of the country.³³ Across the land, from California to New York, from Texas to Minnesota, other appeals, amounting to "tens of millions of pieces" at costs of "hundreds of thousands of dollars," found their way into circulation.³⁴ Most of it reached persons already convinced of the need to oppose warily Roman Catholic moves. But the number of such persons ran high in several areas: Their numbers were to be demonstrated at the ballot box. In a race as close as this one, no one was prepared to discount their effect.

Throughout the nation in 1928, Al Smith had been labeled a "Tammany" man. That had meant but one thing. Behind the rule of the man by the machine was the fact that Tammany had long been controlled by politicians who were Roman Catholic. In 1960 this was not true of the candidate. Yet that did not prevent some from drawing what they regarded as a valid comparison. Said one, in New York: "Many of us have decried the militant tactics of the Tammany machine. Events have shown that the Kennedy machine is no less militant. Both machines are dominated and controlled by members of the Roman Catholic faith."

Senator Lyndon Johnson, returning from a final swing through crucial states in which he again condemned the religious issue as a blot on America's national harmony and image, was greeted by a jeering group as the Senator and Mrs. Johnson made their way through a hotel lobby to a luncheon in Dallas. "It makes me sad to know that people could be so bitter and frustrated and so discourteous and desperate," Johnson said of the campaign's closing days.³⁵

A United Auto Workers publication in Michigan depicted the Statue of Liberty, and a hooded Klan figure with a torch and club in hand. Above were the words: "Which do you choose? Liberty or bigotry?" It was charged that this was raising the religious issue with a "reverse twist."³⁶ The charge reflected a scramble throughout the campaign to preempt the words, "freedom," "religious liberty," and "tolerance" for use in all quarters. Everyone, it seemed, was against "bigotry" and "bigots."

In Washington, the Reverend Harrison Parker preferred to shift the emphasis. "We are not anti-Catholic, we are pro-American," he said. He was working to prevent the Catholic Church from gaining "control of the guns."[37] Parker was not alone in his view. In Philadelphia 116 years earlier, on the eve of another presidential election, rioters aroused by reports of caches of arms in Catholic churches had left scores injured and several dead in their wake.

The *Patriot Press*, a four-page tract mailed anonymously, took a more direct attitude toward the meaning of the words "bigotry" and "bigot." *"Who are the real bigots?"* it asked. "The Roman Catholic clergy are supreme bigots. . . . They are such bigots because they refuse to worship with other sects. John F. Kennedy is a *proved* bigot . . . ," it proclaimed. To others, the meaning of the words remained clear. The clarity was sometimes maintained with a notable degree of courage. In Tennessee, the Reverend Batsell Barrett Baxter had directed a sermon on Roman Catholicism entitled "A Dangerous Doctrine," to his congregation during a Sunday service, in which he said, "If the Roman Catholic Church should ever become large enough and strong enough to dominate the United States, the rest of us would lose our religious freedom."[38] Representative Joseph L. Evins then arose to urge that all those present actively practice religious tolerance. Three weeks later a Church of Christ publication said his action "will have religious and political implications for many a day."[39] Not heard from in the matter was another member of the Church of Christ. Senator Lyndon Johnson was busy campaigning against religious bigotry.

If there were any doubts about one part of the Democratic coalition, there were signs that another segment was returning to the important position it had occupied before showing signs of "cracking" in 1952 and 1956. After years of being predominantly Democratic, Catholics in 1952 had gone for Eisenhower in a proportion of from 44 to 47 per cent.[40] The shift remained in 1956 when approximately 49 per cent of Catholics interviewed indicated they had voted Republican. In the 1958 elections there had been a tremendous return among Catholics to Democratic ranks. In 1956 only 51 per cent of these voters had done so.[41]

Republican Catholics were not seen as switching in such substantial proportions. As early as late September, President Eisenhower had received a warm response from his audience while addressing the Golden Jubilee dinner of the National Conference of Catholic Charities in New York. The Republican vice presidential candidate, Henry Cabot Lodge, and Secretary of Labor James P. Mitchell had continued to court Catholic voters throughout the campaign. In the late stages of the campaign, newspaper ads inserted by Catholics in Texas and Michigan cities accused Democrats of "trying to create a Catholic bloc vote," and declared their opposition to Kennedy because of "two-edged bigotry" on the part of his supporters.[42]

In its closing days, all restraint was removed in the final flurry of crossfire. Nine different versions of the Knights of Columbus "oath" were reported in circulation. In Minnesota, sheets urged Catholics to vote against the Masons who had allegedly opposed them vigorously throughout the campaign, "*namely* . . ." Senator Hubert Humphrey and Governor Orville Freeman (both Democrats). In New Jersey, a town of 13,000, of whose population more than 60 per cent were Catholic, was treated to a spurious "anti-Catholic" pamphlet. Sent through the mails, the single sheet listed a series of questions and answers intended to arouse their ire.

In its volume the literature exceeded 1928 or any other campaign in history, it was estimated by the Fair Campaign Practices Committee. Henry R. Tyler, Jr., head of the Civil Rights Division in the Department of Justice, told of "tracts in New York against Vice President Nixon. They say he's a secret Catholic, and when he gets elected he'll turn the country over to the Pope!"[43]

Nixon, meanwhile, inadvertently turned some other things over to another "Pope." Telephone calls to a last-minute Nixon telethon in Detroit were reaching John Pope's awning shop in Alexandria, Virginia. Viewers, thinking the program was originating from Washington, bombarded Pope with calls from six states from Massachusetts to Florida. His number was identical with the Detroit number. After a time, in exasperation, Pope let several callers think they were talking to the candidate. "They are happy as hell at my answers," he reported.[44] He did not indicate whether he himself might enter politics following the election.

On the last day of the campaign, as Kennedy answered viewers' questions while appearing on television from a New Hampshire station, he was asked once again about his views on church and state. He pointed out that he could be impeached if he permitted interference in the conduct of his office, by "the Pope or anyone else in my church." Religion remained an active but imponderable element to the last as citizens carried their decisions into the voting booth.

Elmo Roper called the election a "forecasting nightmare," and concluded, "The only ringing forthright honest declaration that any honest pollster can make . . . is that it looks like a close election, but either candidate could win in a landslide."[45] Despite this, major pollsters were within 2 per cent of accurately predicting the outcome of what was the closest election of the century.

In 1928 it had been prohibition that had contributed heavily to the defeat of Al Smith. Now, in 1960, Baptist minister Dr. Rutherford L. Decker, pastor of the Temple Baptist Church in Kansas City, Missouri, the Prohibitionist candidate for President, had scarcely caused a ripple among the electorate. The country had changed. To what extent remained in doubt for hour after hour as the returns now mounted in unprecedented numbers. The East provided Kennedy with a heartening lead. The Midwest checked what started out to have the makings of a landslide. The returns began to whittle his margin as the Midwest became the West. In the early hours of the next morning, the Far West returns continued to narrow the Democratic edge. Certainty did not come until weeks later, but Kennedy clearly had rolled up a decisive victory in the electoral vote while holding a narrow lead in the popular vote. Few people in the United States or elsewhere questioned the evidence.

In the closest presidential campaign since Cleveland had edged Blaine in 1884, the Democratic candidate held a margin of just under 113,000 votes. He was assured of 300 electoral votes, 31 more than the necessary 269. Nearly 69,000,000 votes had been cast, the largest total in the nation's history.[46]

George Washington's hope that American Catholics would in the future "enjoy every temporal and spiritual felicity" had come to pass. The nation awoke on the morning of November 9, 1960, with a Roman Catholic President-elect.

The outcome had been determined by the people. All had been a party to a test in which history played no favorites. In the framework of their institutions they had reaffirmed their heritage. Its voice carried strong above the discord.

The heritage could not have been affirmed in the nation's early years when isolated lives and convictions had been bound in prejudicial as well as illustrious fibers. It could not have been proclaimed before the country, at great civil cost in lives and good will, had wrenched itself out of slavish and constrictive attitudes born of medieval times to affirm and release the currents of its future.

Occupied for generations with the shaping and securing of its power, national vigor had often sufficed as national purpose. The heritage could not have triumphed before it had been given massive rebirth in the energies and travails of new millions. As the nation grew, the distance between its faiths had lessened. With the cataclysmic events of a new century, the sense of national community had been accelerated, and its ideals given new relevance. Increasingly, in modern America, religious differences had been balanced by harmonious expressions of religious principles as sources of its strength and identity.

The truth of this had not been obscured by the indulgences of one generation, or of two. It had arisen anew when confronted with far-reaching challenges to its existence. The nation returned to its ideals, the keepers of its greatness.

The old passions, the old prejudices, and the old fears—all had continued to exist. But in 1960 it had been made clear that a democratic system that permitted differences was not to be tragically ravaged by them. Great forces had moved out of the past, yet the triumph had been one of principle rather than of tradition. The time indeed had been "ripe for a reassertion of idealism."[47] Principle gave meaning to the triumph. Circumstances had given it force.

In the seacoast town of New Ross, Ireland, amid the breeze-whipped bunting of a rejoicing village, a quiet elderly man observed, "It is a great thing for a man whose great-grandfather came out of an Irish cottage to be elected President of the United States."[48]

And in Arizona, Mrs. Margaret Sanger said she would wait and see what happened in the first year of Kennedy's administration before deciding whether to move out of the country.[49]

CHAPTER THIRTEEN

JOHN F. KENNEDY
A Catholic Becomes President

"Let us go forth to lead the land we love"

WHEN THE RETURNS WERE OFFICIALLY COMPLETE, FIVE STATES which had gone Republican in every election after 1912, except during the Roosevelt years, had returned to the Democratic coalition. Two of them, Connecticut and Michigan, had even gone Republican once against Roosevelt. They, along with the other three, Pennsylvania, New York, and Maryland, all contained great urban industrial complexes with large concentrations of Negroes, Catholics, and other so-called minority ethnic groups. New Jersey, also similar in this respect, returned to the Democrats after having been won only by Roosevelt since 1928, when it had gone for Al Smith.[1]

Kennedy's religion appeared to have caused his defeat, or almost so, in other states. Kentucky, which had gone Republican in only one election, for Eisenhower, since the Roosevelt years, went to Nixon, as did Tennessee, which had given Eisenhower slim pluralities in 1952 and 1956. Oklahoma and Idaho, both of which had gone for Truman and Roosevelt, remained in the Republican camp. Each of these states gave a larger plurality to Nixon than they had given to Eisenhower four years earlier.

In Missouri, which had gone Republican only once since Roosevelt, Kennedy won by only .6 of the vote. Here, the city of St. Louis, which had gone for Eisenhower, gave Kennedy a solid plurality. By contrast, the surrounding county went Demo-

cratic by less than one-seventh the margin it had given to Stevenson. The lessened Democratic vote there was repeated in rural
counties across the state.

Illinois went to Kennedy by only a .2 plurality. In New
Mexico, which went Democratic by only a .8 edge, one county in
the eastern portion went for Nixon by almost four to one despite
a heavy Democratic trend in early years. Another nearby county,
after a strong vote for Stevenson, remained Democratic in 1960
by the slimmest of margins. In these three states, Missouri, Illinois,
and New Mexico, as well as in Minnesota and others, opposition to
Kennedy had included vehement anti-Catholicism. A heavy urban
Democratic vote wiped out the lead that Republicans had enjoyed
outside the cities.

By contrast, several other states had given Kennedy somewhat
heavier winning margins than Truman had received, among them
Massachusetts and Rhode Island. In a number of states that he
lost, Kennedy received substantial gains in certain areas over the
Democratic total in 1956. Wisconsin was one of these. In one
county (Outagamie) the Republican vote dropped 8 per cent
while the Democratic vote more than doubled (Kennedy still
lost the county). There, as in Milwaukee, there were large numbers of Catholic voters. The plurality received by Kennedy in
Milwaukee was approximately 70,000—more than reversing the
margin Eisenhower had received.

The patterns in these eighteen states were repeated in rural and
urban areas throughout the country. It seemed that much of
Kennedy's support, as in his Massachusetts senatorial victories,
had come from large numbers of Catholics in all economic
groups. Yet substantial exceptions to this conclusion existed in
1960 as they had then.

In Massachusetts in 1952 it had been noted that "Kennedy obtained his largest margin over Stevenson, . . . in the county
with the smallest percentage of Catholics."[2] This reflected the
absence of support for Stevenson that had in fact existed in 1952
and 1956 among many Catholic Democrats. But it also reflected
another factor in the patterns of Catholic voters that showed it-

self in 1960. The percentage of Catholics in business and professional occupations who had supported Nixon (approximately one in three) was about twice as great as his support among lower-income Catholics.[3] Economic and other factors apparently superseded religion as a determinant in many instances.

The Republican National Committee noted that in Philadelphia, among Negro, Polish, Jewish, and Irish voters, the largest proportion of the vote going to Nixon had been among the Irish. Most support for Kennedy, among the four groups named, had come from Negroes.[4] Nationally, Senator Thruston Morton observed, only 11 per cent of Negro voters had supported Nixon. More than twice this number had voted for Eisenhower four years earlier.

The combination of organized labor's efforts and the interests of ethnic minorities had combined with religion in many areas to make it hazardous to point to religion as the predominant element in the mixture. In Texas, for example, El Paso—containing many Catholic workers of Mexican extraction—had given Eisenhower a winning margin of 3,400. There were 15,000 additional votes cast in 1960. Kennedy received a plurality of 4,500. (Metropolitan Houston, Dallas, and San Antonio also went to Kennedy.)

In other areas of the country, Kennedy's religion was not offset by other factors, and he lost much because of it. The expected "farm vote" against the policies of the Republican administration did not materialize to the degree expected, despite a notable increase in Democratic strength in those states.

Despite this, it was apparent that a bloc vote against Kennedy had not generally occurred among the greater proportion of Protestant voters. Party loyalty prevailed over prejudice in many instances. In McLennan County, Texas, for example, where Waco is located, Kennedy received more than four times the winning margin that Stevenson had received four years earlier.

There is strong evidence for concluding that the "religious issue" was the primary factor in the votes of many thousands, and maybe even millions, who voted against Kennedy in 1960 and who might otherwise not have. There is not sufficient evidence for concluding that in 1960 a "Catholic vote" was responsible for putting Kennedy in the White House. But it did share crucial importance with a number of other factors.

In 1948 the University of Michigan Survey Research Center accurately predicted a Truman victory within a very few percentage points of the actual totals. The researchers noted afterward that 25 per cent of the Catholics questioned had voted Republican.[5] In the weeks following the 1960 election, polls taken among Catholics across the country by the Gallup organization indicated that approximately 22 per cent of them had voted Republican.[6] The Michigan group which had performed the 1948 study reported that the percentage of Catholics who voted Republican had been 19 per cent.[7]

These studies suggest a 3 to 6 per cent drop in 1960 from the proportion of Catholics who voted Republican in 1948. The swing back to the Democrats among Catholics in 1960 was part of a general return among substantial numbers of Democratic voters who had gone for Eisenhower.

The Republican National Committee's research department cited drops of from 7 to 44 per cent in the Republican vote compared to 1956 in various "Negro wards and counties."[8] Gallup estimated the decline in the Republican vote among Negroes at 7 per cent. The Michigan group indicated a 9 per cent drop. The decline in the Republican vote among union members was estimated at 8 per cent under 1956, by both the Republican study and the Michigan researchers.[9]

The definitive answer to the question of how important religiously motivated voting was in shaping the outcome of the 1960 election may never be adequately assessed. The existence of a widespread and traditional Catholic bloc vote, however, appears doubtful. In many thousands of cases, particularly among older Catholic voters, pride was no doubt a major factor in the decision to vote for Kennedy. To the extent that this reflected a long-held sense of injustice, there may be little in the decision to find fault with.

Among younger Catholic voting families, Kennedy's appeal

cannot be said to have stemmed primarily from his religion. He espoused ideas and values that these Catholics shared as Americans with many millions of their countrymen. The Republican National Committee's report noted, "The young voters, who had given Eisenhower 57 per cent of their vote in 1956, switched back to the Democratic party as they had throughout the Roosevelt and Truman years and in the 1952 election."[10]

Among other Catholic voters, religion was at best a partial and not at all sufficient basis for their voting decision. A vote for Kennedy was more a gesture of social identity than an act of allegiance to his church. The vote of Polish or Italian Catholics, for example, involved far more than religion. The cultural and ethnic ground out of which Kennedy's Catholicism had sprung was not their own. The unity they shared in the church was equaled if not superseded by other things they responded to in the candidate. One of these social or political bonds was the candidate's repeated and impassioned defense of the common interest that members of all immigrant groups shared in America, itself a nation of immigrants—the right of the individual to the good life, the American dream.

In the suburbs as well as in the cities, the attitudes of a culture long imbued with Protestant values continued to have strong influence on Catholics as well as on Americans of every other religious or ethnic group.

Social justice and individual advancement were not Catholic innovations in America. They were adopted as broad policy by a church many of whose children stood in urgent need of measures aimed at removing hideous social conditions. Such conditions did not undermine the welfare and integrity of the Catholics only. The same changing conditions of a complex industrial society confronted Protestants, Jews, and others. This was true in 1960 as it had been in Wilson's time and before, when Protestantism, too, had recognized the demands being placed upon it.

The "religious issue" has always actually consisted in large measure of a number of social issues brought together under one label. In 1960, for example, it was linked to the struggle for racial supremacy and the fight against economic liberalism. The "issue" was related to broad social changes in the country rather than to any conspiratorial takeover, although this charge too, remained from the campaigns of the nineteenth century. Catholicism was equated with these changes as though in some way responsible or causatively linked.

Because it has its roots not strictly in religious doctrinal schisms but in social cultural and economic differences, religion will no doubt remain an "issue" in future campaigns. Much of its validity, however, and a good part of its effectiveness evaporated in the 1960 campaign.

The religious issue has never been wholly a function of immediate circumstances or supposed dangers, and their manipulation by politicians. The issue has been involved in campaigns for the Presidency in almost every decade of our history because it has always been not solely religious but related to broader conflicts that have remained dynamic components of American society and the relations between its institutions.

The election of a President of Catholic faith in 1960 gave a ringing stamp of recognition to pluralism as an indelible fact of national political and social life. The issue of religion revived for individuals sources of identity that resided in a sense of community and that were more spiritual than material or acquisitive in status. It spurred attention to national principles and their wellsprings and promoted vital and vigorous commitment.

Business and the mercantile community have long been a major paragovernmental mediating force in American society, providing halfway values in social affairs. The casting away of sectarian anchors, a peculiar kind of noble laxity in America, has led to a kind of spiritual barbarism, and a rise in materialism. The 1960 campaign reflected a rise in the strength of the religious community as a mediating influence on the public conscience.

There was a renewal of the relevance and power of law, and of the founding laws of the land, as a force in regulating American life. Americans expressed widespread distrust of extremist positions and demagoguery, despite a great response to personalities.

In Scarsdale, a wealthy New York suburb, shortly after the election Father George French Kempsell, Jr., a Protestant Episcopal rector, provided a notable example of this ongoing resurgence. Anyone who had acquiesced in word, thought, or deed with the actions of parishioners who had recently sanctioned the barring of a convert from Judaism from a country-club Christmas dance, said Father Kempsell, would no longer be welcome to receive holy communion "until such time as he has worked out his own peace with God in his own way."[11] The Right Reverend Horace W. B. Donegan, Episcopal Bishop of New York, backed Father Kempsell's action with forceful words: "It is the duty of religious leaders to condemn religious, racial and social prejudices that embitter life and separate mankind. Discrimination, in whatever form it expresses itself, should be repugnant to all of us as children of God and as citizens of a democratic society."[12] The 1960 campaign indirectly may have further spurred a resurgence of religious authority leading the way in moral "oughts" derived directly from both Catholic and Protestant theology.

The religious issue generated healthy discussion regarding the separation of church and state, and also raised questions as to the proper degree and the character of influence exercised by churches in the country's political affairs. The church can never be viewed as irrelevant in American life. It is the church that carries a major share of responsibility for providing a broad moral base on which a citizen can build *his* responsibility. The Higher Law—articulated by the church and implemented by the citizen— then becomes effective on the mundane level; a church's central social position therefore produces an involved citizenry.

The campaign, however, called attention to doctrinal disagreements within and among the churches. It revealed disturbing gaps between the clergy and laity. Events underscored the responsibility of the churches to resolve these differences in such a way as to promote, rather than detract from, an effective American consensus, no less their own vitality.

With the resurgence of sectarianism in the conflicts of the 1960 campaign, there was an equally heartening and unprecedented degree of censure directed at those who presented the religious issue, not as a constructive dialogue, but with irresponsible extremism. The Reverend Dr. Billy Graham, following a meeting with the President-elect, expressed the view that Kennedy's election had helped relations between the churches. Certainly "a better understanding between the Protestant and the Catholic Churches in the United States has emerged,"[13] said Graham.

Shortly thereafter, a bid to end the aloofness between liberal and conservative elements within Protestantism was made by the Reverend Dr. James E. Wagner, president of the Evangelical and Reformed Church, at a meeting of the general board of the National Council of Churches. He urged a series of "quiet, unpublicized" meetings between liberal and conservative theologians to restore communication and confidence. In taking positions on social problems and issues, said Dr. Wagner, liberal Protestants should make it "crystal clear" that such actions are rooted in biblical faith and that "we in the National Council family are no less committed to the Scriptures as our ultimate authority in faith and practice than our brothers and sisters who claim that they and they alone are 'true to the Bible.' "[14]

The question of Protestant unity remains an issue, in the face of controversies that promise no rapid solution. But the president of the National Conference of Christians and Jews, Dr. Lewis Webster Jones, reflecting on the "horrible and destructive things" uttered in the internecine warfare waged among religious groups during the campaign, noted that with "better interreligious communication" the "considerable religious illiteracy" that was a partial cause of such misunderstandings could be lessened.[15]

In 1960 the "American tradition" was an appeal to which voters were again emotionally responsive. Surrounded by cynicism and despair amid affluence, they heeded a call to their past and to their greatness, a greatness that seemed to be slipping away. The religious issue in the campaign was resolved as it had not been in previous years; in degree, if not in kind. It was met by a nonsectarian sense of national purpose. A common ground was found in national social and political principles. Religion entered this blend not as sectarianism, but as a general religiosity.

But there had been frequent sectarian assertions of America as a Protestant nation. A new nativism was evident in 1960. Americans had increasingly been troubled and frustrated by Soviet harassment, subversion, and propaganda. With this, many had sensed the resentment of poverty-stricken, illiterate, and jealous millions in other lands—toward Americans, if not toward the ideals of America. National concern was once again a genuine element. Americans responded sharply to warnings and denials surrounding the question of national "prestige." The decline of apathy cannot be wholly attributed to the alarums of an election year. The campaign reinforced an aspect of the public climate that had existed for some time before it.

There was a vigorous revival of conservatism, accompanying such expressions of Americanism as the John Birch Society, named after a fundamentalist Bible student who had lost his life at the hands of Chinese communists shortly after the Second World War. Other groups with a strong aura of evangelical conservatism militantly sought to arouse Americans to the dangers of communist influence and infiltration. In their misdirected fervor they hurled threats and accusations, suspicion and anger, at many institutions and groups in the nation that are no less American but somewhat less conservative than they.

In the face of the massive and complex challenges that are an integral part of the world of the sixties, these persons in their passion for reduction of the conflict to uncomplicated essentials indiscriminately attack not only all that seems part of the new world, but the liberal and idealistic heart that has always been close to Americanism. The need continues for Americans to be led by responsible and temperate men no less sensitive to the threat of communism, but sharply sensitive to the dangers of a barbaric chauvinism that once passed for Americanism.

Americanism emerges today in a pluralistic society possessed of power and responsibility in the international community of nations, and coming to realize the truly towering and inspiring uniqueness of its character and its aims.

All of this took place within the context of larger trends in recent history. The resurgence in this country of a religious spirit that is fused with a national consciousness bears the seeds of a nationalism that could itself become a kind of secular religion. The line between the religious and the political sentiment wavers. There is a religification of secular institutions. In the emotional responses of people, patriotism replaced religious patriarchy. The religious spirit is transmuted and the state becomes the supreme end and law, the arbiter and interpreter of what is "moral," and the standard for absolute allegiance. Its leaders become the deities.

Here the religious community has a vital role in helping to maintain the proper balance between God and Caesar. In 1960 perhaps far more had operated to vitiate the scurrilous aspects of the religious issue than had at any previous time in American history. Yet the issue retained enough strength—whether seen as a doctrinal concern or as a political device—to nearly swing the balance in the election.

The force of the issue, as well as its form, raised the question of whether, in a "society of incompatible faiths," to use Father John Courtney Murray's term, there was not an imperative consensus to be affirmed around the rights and responsibilities of the individual as a creature of God. Whether the religious issue is seen in a doctrinal, social, economic, or political light, this remains the paramount focus.

Samuel Adams wrote, as the American Republic was being formed: "I have long been convinced that our Enemies have made it an object to eradicate from the Minds of the People in general a Sense of true Religion and Virtue, in hopes thereby the more easily to carry their point of enslaving them. Indeed my Friend, this is a Subject so important to my Mind that I know not how to leave it. . . . The diminution of publick Virtue is usually attended with that of publick Happiness, and the publick Liberty will not long survive the total Extinction of Morals."[16]

At a Washington interfaith prayer meeting shortly after the

election, President Kennedy observed that "the guiding principle of America is now, has always been and shall ever be 'In God We Trust.' "

Religion is not a weapon in the struggle between West and East, he pointed out. It does represent, however, the essence of the differences between the two systems. This difference, and the heart of the American consensus, was expressed with further clarity by President Kennedy in his Inaugural Address:

"We observe today not a victory of party but a celebration of freedom, symbolizing an end as well as a beginning, signifying renewal as well as change. For I have sworn before you and Almighty God the same solemn oath our forebears prescribed nearly a century and three-quarters ago.

"The world is very different now. For man now holds in his mortal hands the power to abolish all forms of human poverty and all forms of human life. And yet the same revolutionary beliefs for which our forebears fought are still at issue around the globe—the belief that the rights of man come not from the generosity of the state, but from the Hand of God.

"We dare not forget today that we are the heirs of that first revolution. Let the word go forth from this time and this place, to friend and foe alike, that the torch of liberty has been passed to a new generation of Americans—born in this century, tempered by war, disciplined by a hard and bitter peace, proud of our ancient heritage, and unwilling to witness or permit the slow undoing of those human rights to which this nation has always been committed, and to which we are committed today at home and around the world."

Concluded the President:

"With a good conscience our only sure reward, with history the final judge of our deeds, let us go forth to lead the land we love, asking His blessing and His help, but knowing that here on earth God's work must truly be our own."[17]

BIBLIOGRAPHY

No attempt is made to list the great number of materials and publications examined but not actually cited. Our major sources consisted of published and unpublished campaign materials, general biographical and historical works, official records, newspapers, periodicals and journals, and personal discussions.

Included were the *Annals of the American Academy of Political and Social Science*, the *Political Science Quarterly*, *Public Opinion Quarterly*, the *American Catholic Historical Society Record*; also, the *American Mercury*, *North American Review*, *Atlantic Monthly*, *Harper's Magazine*, *New Republic*, the *Reporter*, *Newsweek*, *U.S. News & World Report*, *Look*; also *America, Commonweal, Catholic World, Christian Century, Christian Herald*; also the *Congressional Record, Congressional Globe*, United States Bureau of the Census, *Historical Statistics of the United States: Colonial Times to 1957*; also, the New York *Times*, New York *Herald Tribune*, *Christian Science Monitor*, Philadelphia *Bulletin*, Houston *Chronicle*, New York *World-Telegram and Sun, Newsday*, New York *Journal-American*.

The following works are cited in the text:

Abell, Aaron A., *American Catholicism and Social Action*, Garden City, 1960.

Billington, Ray Allen, *The Protestant Crusade, 1800–1860*, New York, 1938.

Binkley, Wilfred E., and Malcolm C. Moos, *A Grammar of American Politics*, New York, 1958.

Bowers, Claude G., *Party Battles of the Jackson Period*, Boston, 1922.

Brownson, Orestes W., *Essays and Reviews*, New York, 1852.

Burnham, W. Dean, *Presidential Ballots, 1836–1932*, Baltimore, 1955.

Burns, James M., Jr., *John F. Kennedy: A Political Profile*, New York, 1960.

———, *Roosevelt: The Lion and the Fox*, New York, 1956.

Caldwell, R. G., *James A. Garfield: Party Chieftain*, New York, 1931.

Calvert, Bruce T., *Al Smith and the Presidency*, Mountain View, New Jersey, 1928.

Crèvecœur, Hector St. John, *Letters from an American Farmer*, New York, 1951.

Ebersole, Luke, *Church Lobbying in the Nation's Capital*, New York, 1951.

Elliot, Jonathan, *Debates on the Federal Constitution*, Philadelphia, 1859.

Ellis, Msgr. John Tracy (ed.), *Documents of American Catholic History*, Milwaukee, 1956.

Farrand, Max (ed.), *Records of the Federal Convention of 1787*, New Haven, 1937.

Fremantle, Anne (ed.), *The Papal Encyclicals in Their Historical Context*, New York, 1956.

Fusfeld, D. R., *The Economic Thought of Franklin Delano Roosevelt and the Origins of the New Deal*, New York, 1956.

Handlin, Oscar, *Al Smith and His America*, Boston, 1958.

———, *Boston's Immigrants*, Cambridge, 1959.

Josephson, Matthew, *The President-Makers*, New York, 1940.

King, James M., *Facing the Twentieth Century*, New York, 1899.

Konvitz, Milton R., *Fundamental Liberties of a Free People*, Ithaca, 1957.

Lecky, William E. H., *History of the Rise and Influence of Rationalism in Europe*, New York, 1873.

Leech, Margaret, *In the Days of McKinley*, New York, 1959.

Lorant, Stefan, *The Presidency: A Pictorial History*, New York, 1951.

Lubell, Samuel, *The Future of American Politics*, New York, 1952.

Mabee, Carlton, *The American Leonardo*, New York, 1943.

McCormac, Eugene I., *James K. Polk: A Political Biography*, Berkeley, 1922.

Minor, Henry, *The Story of the Democratic Party*, New York, 1928.

Morison, Samuel Eliot, and Henry Steele Commager, *The Growth of the American Republic*, New York, 1956.

Morse, E. L. (ed.), *Samuel F. B. Morse: His Letters and Journals*, Boston and New York, 1914.

Muzzey, David S., *James G. Blaine*, New York, 1934.

Myers, Gustavus, *History of Bigotry in the United States*, New York, 1943.

———, *History of Tammany Hall*, New York, 1917.

Myers, James, and H. W. Laidler, *What Do You Know About Labor?* New York, 1956.

Nevins, Allan, *Grover Cleveland*, New York, 1932.

Nichols, Roy F., *Franklin Pierce*, Philadelphia, 1931.

Niebuhr, H. Richard, and D. D. Williams (eds.), *The Ministry in Historical Perspectives*, New York, 1956.

Orth, Samuel P., and H. J. Ford, *The Age of Reform*, in *Chronicles of America*, XX, New Haven, 1919.

Overdyke, W. Darrell, *The Know-Nothing Party in the South*, Louisiana State University, 1950.

Robinson, Edgar E., *The New United States*, Stanford, 1946.

———, *The Presidential Vote 1896–1932*, Stanford, 1934.

Roseboom, Eugene A., *A History of Presidential Elections*, New York, 1957.

Schlesinger, Arthur M., *Critical Period in American Religion, 1875–1900*, Boston, 1932.

Schlesinger, Arthur M., Jr., *The Age of Jackson*, New York, 1945.

———, *The Crisis of the Old Order, 1919–1933*, Boston, 1957.

Scisco, Louis D., "Political Nativism in New York State," *Studies in History, Economics, and Public Law*, New York, 1901.

Sherman, S. P. (ed.), *Essays and Poems of Emerson*, New York, 1921.

Smith, Alfred E., *Campaign Addresses of Alfred E. Smith*, Washington, D.C., 1929.

Smith, Bernard (ed.), *The Democratic Spirit*, New York, 1941.

Smith, H. S., R. T. Handy, and L. A. Loetscher, *American Christianity*, New York, 1960.

Stokes, Anson Phelps, *Church and State in the United States*, New York, 1950, 3 vols.

Stone, Irving, *They Also Ran*, New York, 1943.

Thaman, Sister Mary Patrice, C.PP.S., *Manners and Morals of the Nineteen Twenties*, New York, 1954.

Thomas, H. C., *Return of the Democratic Party to Power in 1884*, New York, 1919.

Tocqueville, Alexis de, *Democracy in America*, New York, 1956.

Van Dusen, Henry P. (ed.), *The Spiritual Legacy of John Foster Dulles*, Philadelphia, 1960.

Weston, Florence, *The Presidential Campaign of 1828*, Washington, 1938.

Wibberly, Leonard, *The Coming of the Green*, New York, 1958.

Wittke, Carl, *The Irish in America*, Baton Rouge, 1950.

NOTES AND REFERENCES

Chapter One: The Founding Fathers

1. For compilation in the "Whig Almanac" of the period, see Gustavus Myers, *History of Bigotry in the United States,* copyright 1943 by Random House, Inc. Used by permission.

2. See Chapter One, "The Churchly Tradition," in H. S. Smith, R. T. Handy, and L. A. Loetscher, *American Christianity,* New York, 1960.

3. For a thorough discussion see W. E. H. Lecky's "The Secularisation of Politics" in Volume Two of his *History of the Rise and Influence of Rationalism in Europe,* New York, 1873, 2 vols.

4. Smith, Handy, and Loetscher, *op. cit.,* p. 144.

5. Hector St. John Crèvecœur, "What Is an American?" in his *Letters from an American Farmer,* New York, 1951, pp. 49ff.

6. W. W. Hening (ed.), *The Statutes at Large, Being a Collection of All the Laws of Virginia,* New York, 1823, Vol. 7, pp. 84–86, cited in M. Konvitz, *Fundamental Liberties of a Free People,* Ithaca, 1958.

7. *Ibid.*

8. *Ibid.*

9. Smith, Handy, and Loetscher, *op. cit.,* p. 144.

10. *Ibid.*

11. *Ibid.*

12. *Ibid.*

13. Jonathan Elliot, *Debates on the Federal Constitution,* Philadelphia, 1859, Vol. 5, pp. 446, 498. See also, Max Farrand (ed.), *Records of the Federal Convention of 1787,* New Haven, 1937, Vol. 2, pp. 342, 468, 579.

14. Anson Phelps Stokes, *Church and State in the United States,* New York, 1950, I, 351. Other aspects of Pinckney's life and career are presented in Dumas Malone (ed.), *Dictionary of American Biography,* New York, 1934, Vol. 14, p. 611.

15. Farrand, *op. cit.*

16. Elliot, *op. cit.,* p. 498.

17. Stokes, *op. cit.,* I, 534.

18. *Ibid.,* p. 540.

19. *Ibid.*

20. *Ibid.*

21. *Ibid.,* p. 543.

22. *Ibid.,* p. 338.

23. J. T. Ellis (ed.), *Documents of American Catholic History,* Milwaukee, 1956, p. 175.

24. Henry Minor, *The Story of the Democratic Party,* New York, 1928, pp. 20, 27.

25. Stefan Lorant, *The Presidency: A Pictorial History,* New York, 1951, pp. 54, 61.

Chapter Two: Andrew Jackson

1. Wilfred E. Binkley and Malcolm C. Moos, *A Grammar of American Politics*, New York, 1958, p. 130.

2. For a vivid picture of the campaigning of the period, see Claude G. Bowers, *Party Battles of the Jackson Period*, Boston, 1922, pp. 242–246.

3. Eugene A. Roseboom, *A History of Presidential Elections*, New York, 1938, p. 80.

4. Florence Weston, *The Presidential Campaign of 1828*, Washington, 1938, pp. 168ff.

5. *Ibid.*, p. 171.

6. *Ibid.*

7. Farrand, *Records . . .*, III, 227.

8. W. C. Webster, "A Comparative Study of the State Constitutions of the American Revolution," in *Annals of the American Academy of Political and Social Science*, IX (1897), 380.

9. Weston, *op. cit.*, p. 171.

10. *Ibid.*

11. *Ibid.*

12. Arthur M. Schlesinger, Jr., *The Age of Jackson*, New York, 1945, pp. 352ff.

13. Bureau of the Census, *Historical Statistics of the United States: Colonial Times to 1957;* see "Migration."

14. Leonard Wibberly, *The Coming of the Green*, New York, 1958, p. 18.

15. *Ibid.*, p. 19.

16. *Ibid.*, p. 20.

17. *Ibid.*, p. 23.

18. For a detailed account of the incident see Ray A. Billington, *The Protestant Crusade*, New York, 1938, pp. 68–76.

19. Carlton Mabee, *The American Leonardo*, New York, 1943, pp. 164ff.

20. Louis D. Scisco, "Political Nativism in New York State," in *Studies in History, Economics and Public Law*, Columbia University (New York, 1901), III, No. 2, pp. 20–21.

21. E. L. Morse (ed.), *Samuel F. B. Morse: His Letters and Journals*, Boston and New York, 1914, pp. 36–37.

22. Scisco, *op. cit.*

23. *Ibid.*, pp. 23, 28ff.

24. Oscar Handlin, *Boston's Immigrants*, Cambridge, 1959, pp. 190ff.

25. Gustavus Myers, *History of Tammany Hall*, New York, 1917, p. 46.

26. *Ibid.*, p. 131.

27. *Ibid.*, p. 136.

Chapter Three: James K. Polk: The Emergence of Americanism

1. Schlesinger, *The Age of Jackson*, p. 351.

2. For detailed accounts of the disturbances, see the *Presbyterian*, a contemporary weekly, Philadelphia, May 11 and 18, 1844, and Sister M. St. Henry, "Nativism in Pennsylvania, 1840–1860," *American Catholic Historical Society Record*, XLVII.

3. *Presbyterian*.

4. *Ibid.*

5. Irving Stone, *They Also Ran*, New York, 1954, p. 56.

6. Roseboom, *A History of Presidential Elections*, p. 132.

7. Scisco, "*Political Nativism . . . ,*" pp. 48–51.

8. Myers, *History of Tammany Hall*, pp. 121, 191.

9. Eugene I. McCormac, *James K. Polk: A Political Biography*, Berkeley, 1922, p. 281.

10. Myers, *op. cit.*, p. 137. See also W. Dean Burnham, *Presidential Ballots, 1836–1932*, Baltimore, 1954, pp. 29–30.

11. W. Darrell Overdyke, *The Know-Nothing Party in the South*, Louisiana State University, 1950, p. 13.

12. Ralph Waldo Emerson, *Complete Works*, 1876.

13. *Speech of Peter W. Gray Delivered in the Democratic Convention at Austin Upon the Resolution to Nominate Sam Houston*, Austin, 1852, p. 23.

14. Overdyke, *op. cit.*, p. 90.

15. Wibberly, *The Coming of the Green*, p. 22.

16. S. P. Sherman (ed.), *Essays and Poems of Emerson*, New York, 1921, xxiii.

17. *Congressional Globe*, 33rd Cong., 2nd Sess., Appendix, pp. 94ff.

18. Bureau of the Census, *Historical Statistics*.

19. Aaron Abell, *American Catholicism and Social Action*, Garden City, 1960, p. 18.

20. *Congressional Globe, ibid.*, p. 112.

21. *Ibid.*, p. 94.

22. *Ibid.*, p. 112.

23. Orestes W. Brownson, "Native Americanism," *Essays and Reviews*, New York, 1852, pp. 441ff.

24. *Ibid.*

25. *Ibid.*, pp. 373ff.

Chapter Four: Franklin Pierce and John C. Frémont

1. London *Times*, Sept. 22, 1852.

2. New York *Daily Times*, Oct. 7, 1852.

3. *Ibid.*, Sept. 25, 1852.

4. Roy F. Nichols, *Franklin Pierce*, Philadelphia, 1931, pp. 130–131.

5. *Ibid.*, pp. 193, 209.

6. New York *Daily Times*, Sept. 25, 1852.

7. Nichols, *op. cit.*, p. 210.

8. New York *Daily Times*, Oct. 16, 1852.

9. *Ibid.*

10. *Ibid.*, Oct. 29, 1852.

11. Burnham, *Presidential Ballots*, pp. 42–53.

12. Billington, *The Protestant Crusade*, pp. 300–303. See also James M. King, *Facing the Twentieth Century*, American Union League Society, 1899, p. 192.

13. See Overdyke, *The Know-Nothing Party . . .* ; also Billington, *op. cit.*

14. Billington, *op. cit.*, p. 313.

15. *Ibid.*, p. 388.

16. *Ibid.*, p. 394.

17. *Ibid.*, p. 412.

18. Minor, *The Story of the Democratic Party*, p. 252.

19. *Ibid.*

20. New York *Daily Times*, Oct. 3, 1856.

21. *Ibid.*

22. *Ibid.*

23. Lorant, *The Presidency*, p. 221.

24. New York *Daily Times*, Oct. 6, 1856.

25. *Ibid.*, Oct. 7, 1856.

26. *Ibid.*, Oct. 14, 1856.

27. *Ibid.*, Oct. 28 and Nov. 1, 1856.

28. *Ibid.*, Nov. 3, 1856.

29. *Ibid.*, Nov. 4, 1856.

30. Burnham, *op. cit.*, pp. 58ff.

31. Bureau of the Census, *Historical Statistics.*

32. Burnham, *op. cit.*, pp. 60ff.

33. New York *Herald Tribune*, May, 8, 1860.

34. Burnham, *op. cit.*, pp. 62ff.

Chapter Five: From Hayes to Grover Cleveland

1. Dixon Ryan Fox, "The Negro Vote in Old New York," in *Political Science Quarterly*, XXX, June, 1917, pp. 225ff.

2. Carl Wittke, *The Irish in America*, Baton Rouge, 1950, p. 144.

3. *Ibid.*, pp. 136, 156.

4. Lorant, *The Presidency*, p. 320.

5. *Ibid.*, p. 329.

6. R. G. Caldwell, *James A. Garfield: Party Chieftain*, New York, 1931, p. 251.

7. For accounts of the apprehension expressed by James G. Blaine, James J. Hill, and Carl Schurz, see Allan Nevins, *Grover Cleveland*, New York, 1932, pp. 186, 188, 624.

8. Lorant, *op. cit.*, p. 381.

9. Minor, *The Story of the Democratic Party*, p. 341.

10. New York *Times*, July 5, 1884.

11. H. C. Thomas, *Return of the Democratic Party to Power in 1884*, New York, 1919, p. 179.

12. *Ibid.*, pp. 182, 195.

13. Nevins, *op. cit.*, pp. 170ff.

14. New York *Times*, Oct. 31, 1884.

15. For verbatim reports of the comment, see Nevins, *op. cit.*, and David S. Muzzey, *James G. Blaine*, New York, 1934. Also see, for accounts of Blaine's reaction, David G. Farrelly in *Western Political Quarterly*, VIII, No. 2 (June, 1955), p. 262, and *Facing the Twentieth Century* by James M. King, A.U.L.S., p. 408.

16. King, *op. cit.*, pp. 409ff.

17. Nevins, *op. cit.*, p. 182.

18. King, *op. cit.*, p. 411.

19. *Ibid.*

20. Muzzey, *op. cit.*, p. 317.

21. See New York *Times*, Nov. 3–5, 1884, for accounts.

22. *Ibid.*

23. King, *op. cit.*

24. Nevins, *op. cit.*, p. 184.

25. New York *Times*, Nov. 7, 1884.

26. *Ibid.*

27. *Ibid.*, Nov. 8, 1884.

Chapter Six: Roosevelt, Wilson, and the Shaping of Modern America

1. Wibberly, *The Coming of the Green*, p. 148.

2. Abell, *American Catholicism and Social Action*, pp. 25ff.

3. *Ibid.*, p. 24.

4. Bureau of the Census, *Historical Statistics*, p. 14.

5. James Myers and H. W. Laidler, *What Do You Know About Labor?* New York, 1956, p. 251.

6. Matthew Josephson, *President-Makers*, New York, 1938, p. 387.

7. Edgar Eugene Robinson, *The Presidential Vote 1896–1932*, Stanford, 1934, pp. 19, 57ff.

8. Bernard Smith (ed.), *The Democratic Spirit*, New York, 1941, p. 640.

9. Arthur Schlesinger, *Critical Period in American Religion, 1875–1900*, Boston, 1932, p. 9.

10. *American Facts and Dates*, New York, 1956, p. 355.

11. Samuel E. Morison and Henry S. Commager, *The Growth of the American Republic*, New York, 1956, II, 362.

12. Abell, *op. cit.*, p. 63.

13. *Ibid.*, p. 70.

14. New York *Herald Tribune*, March 3, 1887.

15. Anne Fremantle (ed.), *The*

Papal Encyclicals in Their Historical Context, New York, 1956, pp. 166ff.

16. Myers, *History of Bigotry*, p. 173. (Capricorn Books edition).

17. *Ibid.*, p. 163.

18. *Ibid., passim.*

19. Schlesinger, *ibid.*, p. 24.

20. Myers, *ibid.*, p. 177.

21. Maria Monk, *Awful Disclosures of Maria Monk*, New York, 1836.

22. *Ibid.*, p. 195.

23. *Ibid.*, p. 62.

24. *Ibid.*, p. 113.

25. *Ibid.*, p. 94.

26. *Ibid.*, p. 36.

27. *Ibid.*, p. 225.

28. *Ibid.*, p. 154.

29. Margaret Leech, *In the Days of McKinley*, New York, 1959, p. 77.

30. Samuel P. Orth and Henry Jones Ford, *The Age of Reform*, in *Chronicles of America*, XX, New Haven, 1919, p. 91.

31. *Ibid.*, p. 73.

32. *North American Review*, March, 1909, pp. 323, 327.

33. Stokes, *Church and State*, II, 405, 406.

34. *Ibid.*

35. *Ibid.*

36. *Ibid.*

37. Myers, *ibid.*, p. 229.

38. *Yearbook of American Churches*, p. 272.

39. Sister Mary Patrice Thaman, C.PP.S., *Manners and Morals of the Nineteen Twenties*, New York, 1954, p. 40. The quotation is from Isaiah 1:4, 5, 6.

40. Bureau of the Census, *Historical Statistics*, p. 56.

41. *Ibid.*

Chapter Seven: Alfred E. Smith: A New Kind of Candidate

1. New York *Times*, Nov. 8, 1928.

2. *Ibid.*

3. Oscar Handlin, *Al Smith and His America*, Boston, 1958, p. 120.

4. Myers, *History of Bigotry*, p. 240. (Capricorn Books edition).

5. Handlin, *ibid.*, pp. 123ff.

6. Roseboom, *A History of Presidential Elections*, p. 425.

7. *Christian Index*, July 26, 1928.

8. *Bob Schuler's Magazine*, Los Angeles, 1928, p. 8.

9. *America*, June 9, 1928, p. 197.

10. New York *Times*, Sept, 20, 1928, p. 4; Sept. 23, p. 4.

11. Myers, *ibid.*, pp. 258, 260.

12. *Bob Schuler's Magazine*, loc. cit.

13. *Ibid.*, p. 10.

14. *Ibid.*, p. 31.

15. Myers, *ibid.*, p. 268.

16. *Bob Schuler's Magazine*, pp. 23, 29.

17. *Ibid.*, p. 10.

18. *Ibid.*, p. 94.

19. *Ibid.*, p. 96.

20. Theodore A. Schroeder, *Al Smith, the Pope and the Presidency*, published by the author, 1928.

21. Bruce T. Calvert, *Al Smith and the Presidency*, Mountain View, N.J., 1928.

22. *Ibid.*, p. 16.

23. *Ibid.*, p. 6.

24. *Ibid.*, p. 16.

25. *Longinque Oceani*, Jan. 6, 1895.

26. *Immortale Dei*, Nov. 1, 1895.

27. *Christian Century*, 1928, pp. 847, 1383 (July 5 and Nov. 15).

28. *Catholic World*, .Sept. 7, 1928, p. 103.

29. *Commonweal*, Sept., 1928.

30. *Christian Herald*, Oct. 11, 1928, p. 1217.

31. *Christian Herald*, Nov. 1, 1928, p. 1317.

32. *Atlantic Monthly*, May 27, 1927, pp. 721ff.

33. Schroeder, *op. cit.*, p. 12.

34. *Ibid.*, p. 10.

35. Handlin, *ibid.*, p. 120.

36. *America*, Aug. 25, 1928, p. 457.

37. *Campaign Addresses of Alfred E. Smith*, Washington, D.C., 1929, p. 43.

38. *Ibid.*, p. 53.

39. Handlin, *ibid.*, pp. 85ff.

40. New York *Times*, July 28, 1928, p. 2.

41. Luke Ebersole, *Church Lobbying in the Nation's Capital*, New York, 1951, p. 9.

42. *World Almanac*, 1929.

43. Samuel Lubell, *The Future of American Politics*, New York, 1952, p. 34.

44. William F. Ogburn and Nell Talbot, in *Social Forces*, December, 1929.

Chapter Eight: Franklin D. Roosevelt: The Testing of America's Ideals

1. Arthur M. Schlesinger, Jr., *The Crisis of the Old Order, 1919–1933*, Boston, 1957, p. 311.

2. Oswald Garrison Villard, in *American Mercury*, 34 (1935), pp. 145ff.

3. Schlesinger, *op. cit.*

4. For aspects of the continuity of thought involved, see D. R. Fusfeld, *The Economic Thought of Franklin Delano Roosevelt and the Origins of the New Deal*, New York, 1956, pp. 54ff.

5. James M. Burns, Jr., *Roosevelt: The Lion and the Fox*, New York, 1956, p. 271.

6. Abell, *American Catholicism and Social Action*, p. 242.

7. New York *Times,* Jan. 21, 1937, p. 1.

8. Hadley Cantril and Mildred Strunk (eds.), *Public Opinion 1935–46,* Princeton, 1951, p. 703.

9. *Opinion News,* American Institute of Public Opinion, April, 1937.

10. New York *Times,* Jan. 5, 1939.

11. *Ibid.,* Jan. 7, 1941, p. 1.

12. *Ibid.,* Feb. 11, 1940.

13. *Ibid.,* Jan. 21, 1945, p. 1.

14. *Opinion News,* July, 1943.

15. Cantril and Strunk, *op. cit.,* p. 478.

16. New York *Times,* March 6, 1946, p. 1.

17. *Opinion News,* March 18, 1947.

18. *Ibid.,* Feb. 15, 1948.

19. Stokes, *Church and State,* II, 749.

20. *America,* Sept. 24, 1960.

21. James M. Burns, Jr., *John F. Kennedy: A Political Profile,* New York, 1960, p. 242.

22. Henry P. Van Dusen (ed.), *The Spiritual Legacy of John Foster Dulles,* Philadelphia, 1960, p. 222.

23. "The Catholic in the Modern World," *Commonweal,* Dec. 16, 1959.

24. Paul Simon, in *Commonweal,* July 22, 1960.

25. For a fuller discussion of these events, see *New York Times Magazine,* Feb. 8, 1959, Arnoldo Cortesi, and the London *Observer* of Dec. 4, 1960, for Patrick O'Donovan, "The Archbishop's Quest."

26. "A Talk with Der Alte," *Reporter,* Jan. 5, 1961, p. 17.

27. C. L. Sulzberger, in the New York *Times,* Dec. 5, 1960.

28. Krishnaswami, *Report on Discrimination in Religion,* Human Rights Division of the Economic and Social Council, E/CN.4/sub.2/200.

29. New York *Times,* Jan. 11, 1961, p. 13.

30. *Ibid.,* Jan. 30, 1961, p. 20.

31. *Ibid.*

32. New York *Times,* May 17, 1961.

33. New York *Herald Tribune,* Jan. 5, 1961.

34. New York *Times,* Jan. 8, 1961, p. 76.

35. New York *Herald Tribune,* Jan. 2, 1961.

36. *New Republic,* Nov. 25, 1957, p. 13.

37. H. Richard Niebuhr and D. D. Williams (eds.), *The Ministry in Historical Perspectives,* New York, 1956, p. 152.

38. New York *Times,* Dec. 30, 1960, p. 41.

39. Public Affairs Information Service, May, 1948.

40. New York *Times,* Sept. 2, 1961, p. 8.

41. *Ibid.,* Feb. 15, 1961, p. 35.

42. *Look* magazine, Sept. 30, 1958, p. 102.

Chapter Nine: John F. Kennedy: From New Hampshire to Los Angeles

1. Lubell, *The Future of American Politics*, p. 78.

2. Burns, *John F. Kennedy*, p. 85.

3. *Ibid.*, p. 86.

4. *Ibid.*, p. 103. The term is credited to the late Paul Dever, then governor of Massachusetts.

5. *Congressional Record*, 84th Cong., 2nd Sess., Vol. 102, Part 4; see pp. 5231–33, 5156–65, 5573–74.

6. Lubell, *op. cit.*

7. *U.S. News & World Report*, Aug. 10, 1956, pp. 41ff.

8. *Ibid.*

9. *Ibid.*, Aug. 17, 1956, pp. 1, 6.

10. For fuller treatment of the 1956 convention activity, see Burns, pp. 186ff., and the New York *Times* of Aug. 17–18, 1956.

11. Helen Hill Miller, "A Catholic for President?" *New Republic*, Nov. 18, 1957, p. 12.

12. New York *Times*, Nov. 5, 1958, p. 22; Nov. 6, p. 26.

13. *Ibid.*, Nov. 14, 1958, p. 14.

14. *Ibid.*, Nov. 21, 1958, p. 21.

15. *Look*, March 3, 1959.

16. *America*, March 7, 1959, p. 651.

17. Burns, *ibid.*, p. 249.

18. New York *Times*, April 11, 1959.

19. *Ibid.*, Feb. 10, 1960, p. 16.

20. *Ibid.*, June 25, 1959.

21. *Ibid.*, Nov. 14, 1959, p. 24.

22. *Ibid.*, Feb. 10, 1960, p. 16.

23. *Ibid.*, Feb. 11, 1960, p. 29.

24. *Ibid.*, Feb. 6, 1960, p. 9.

25. *Ibid.*, June 11, 1960, p. 11.

26. *Facts*, Vol. 13, No. 9 (June–July 1960), p. 159, Anti-Defamation League.

27. *Public Opinion Quarterly*, Spring, 1961, p. 129.

28. New York *Times*, March 22, 1960, p. 20.

29. Several versions of the oath were in circulation during the campaign. See *Congressional Record*, 62nd Cong., 2nd Sess., Vol. XLIX, p. 3216, Feb. 15, 1913.

30. For this and subsequent pieces of campaign literature the authors are indebted to the Anti-Defamation League of B'nai B'rith.

31. New York *Times*, March 27, 1960, p. 50.

32. *Common Sense*, June 1, 1960, p. 1.

33. New York *Times*, March 9, 1960.

34. *Ibid.*, April 24, 1960, p. 58.

35. *Ibid.*, May 2, 1960, p. 15.

36. *Ibid.*, April 24, 1960, p. 58.

37. *Ibid.*, April 4, 1960, p. 21.

38. *Ibid.*, April 1, 1960, p. 16.

39. *Ibid.*, April 10, 1960, IV, p. 2.

40. *Ibid.*, p. 10.

41. *Ibid.*

42. *Ibid.*, April 9, 1960, p. 45.

43. *Ibid.*, April 24, 1960, p. 16.

44. *Ibid.*

45. *Ibid.*, p. 54.

46. *Ibid.*, p. 16.

47. *Ibid.*, April 21, 1960, p. 1.

48. Douglas Cater, "A Day In West Virginia," *Reporter*, May 12, 1960, p. 8.

49. New York *Herald Tribune*, April 22, 1960, p. 1.

50. *Ibid.*

51. New York *Times*, April 21, 1960, p. 16.

52. New York *Herald Tribune*, April 28, 1960, p. 1.

53. New York *Times*, April 29, 1960, p. 23.

54. *Ibid.*, May 11, 1960, p. 1.

55. *Look* magazine, May 10, 1960.

56. *Ibid.*

57. New York *Times*, April 21, 1960.

58. Cantrill and Strunk, *Public Opinion*, p. 105.

59. New York *Times*, May 3, 1960, p. 28.

60. New York *Times*, May 1, 1960, p. 57.

61. *Ibid.*, May 3, 1960, p. 1.

62. *Congressional Quarterly Almanac*, Vol. XVI (1960), p. 807.

Chapter Ten: John F. Kennedy: The Washington Manifesto

1. New York *Herald Tribune*, July 3, 1960, p. 4.

2. *Ibid.*

3. New York *Times*, March 6, 1960, p. 29.

4. *Commonweal*, March 18, 1960.

5. New York *Herald Tribune*, July 5, 1960, p. 11.

6. *Ibid.*

7. New York *Times*, July 1, 1960, p. 5.

8. Communication in the files of Anti-Defamation League of B'nai B'rith, New York City.

9. For convention proceedings see New York *Times*, particularly July 10, 1960, p. 46, and *Reporter*, Aug. 4, "A Tide in the Affairs of John F. Kennedy."

10. New York *Times*, July 14, 1960, p. 15.

11. New York *Herald Tribune*, July 14, 1960, p. 1.

12. New York *Times*, July 1, 1960.

13. *Ibid.*, July 16, 1960, p. 1.

14. *Ibid.*

15. "Polls: The People's Primary," New York *Herald Tribune*, Jan. 20, 1960.

16. *Reporter*, Aug. 4, 1960, p. 15.

17. New York *Times*, July 26, 1960, p. 22.

18. New York *Herald Tribune*, Nov. 10, 1960.

19. *Ibid.,* July 5, 1960, p. 11. See also New York *Times,* Sept. 4, 1960, and Chicago (Ill.) *Sun-Times,* Aug. 31, 1960.

20. New York *Times,* Oct. 31, 1960, p. 19.

21. Douglas Cater, "The Protestant Issue," *Reporter,* Oct. 13, 1960, p. 32.

22. New York *Times,* Sept. 4, 1960, p. 48.

23. *Ibid.*

24. *Ibid.,* Aug. 4, 1960, p. 11; Aug. 5, p. 7.

25. *Ibid.,* Aug. 24, 1960, p. 19.

26. *Ibid.,* Aug. 28, 1960, p. 44.

27. *Ibid.,* Sept. 2, 1960, p. 8; Sept. 3, p. 20.

28. *Ibid.,* Sept. 17, p. 23; Sept. 27, p. 40.

29. *Ibid.,* Sept. 6, p. 22.

30. *Ibid.,* Sept. 11, p. 13.

31. *Ibid.,* Sept. 7, p. 34.

32. *Ibid.,* Sept. 4, p. 48.

33. *Ibid.,* p. 1.

34. *Ibid.,* Aug. 25, p. 20.

35. *Ibid.,* Aug. 31, p. 19.

36. *Ibid.,* Sept. 4, p. 49.

37. *Ibid.,* Sept. 8, p. 16.

38. *Ibid.,* p. 25.

39. *Christian Science Monitor,* Sept. 8, p. 1.

40. *Newsday,* Sept. 8, 1960, p. 98.

41. *Ibid.*

42. *Ibid.*

43. New York *Times,* Sept. 8, 1960, p. 25.

44. *Ibid.*

45. *Ibid.*

46. *Ibid.,* Sept. 14, 1960, p. 30.

47. *Ibid.,* Sept. 12, p. 17.

48. *Ibid.,* Sept. 11, p. 69.

49. *Ibid.,* Sept. 12, p. 22.

50. *America,* Sept. 24, 1960, p. 707.

51. *Ibid.,* p. 705.

52. New York *Times,* Sept. 9, 1960.

53. New York *Herald Tribune,* Sept. 11, 1960, p. 16.

54. New York *Times,* Sept. 10, 1960, p. 1.

55. *America, loc. cit.*

56. New York *Times,* Sept. 16, 1960, p. 18.

57. *Christian Science Monitor,* Sept. 19, 1960, p. 5.

Chapter Eleven: John F. Kennedy: Houston and the Public Conscience

1. *Newsweek,* Sept. 19, 1960, p. 36.

2. New York *Herald Tribune,* Sept. 10, 1960, p. 6.

3. New York *Times,* Sept. 12, 1960, p. 1.

4. *Ibid.,* Sept. 2, 1960, p. 19.

5. Houston *Chronicle,* Sept. 13,

1960, p. 8. See also *Christian Science Monitor*, Sept. 9, p. 10.

6. Houston *Chronicle, loc. cit.*

7. Rev. John W. Turnbull, "The Clergy Faces Mr. Kennedy," *Reporter*, Oct. 13, 1960, p. 33.

8. New York *Times*, Sept. 13, 1960.

9. *Ibid.*

10. *Reporter, loc. cit.*

11. New York *Times, loc. cit.*

12. *Reporter, loc. cit.*

13. Houston *Chronicle, loc. cit.*

14. New York *Times, loc. cit.*

15. Houston *Chronicle, loc. cit.*

16. *Christian Science Monitor*, Sept. 14, p. 3.

17. *Ibid.*

18. New York *Times*, May 18, 1960, p. 1.

19. *Ibid.*, May 19, 1960, p. 32.

20. *America*, Sept. 24, 1960, p. 696.

21. New York *Times*, Sept. 28, 1960, p. 1.

22. *Ibid.*

23. Schroeder, *Al Smith, the Pope and the Presidency.*

24. *Look*, May 10, 1960.

25. New York *Times*, Sept. 28, 1960, *loc. cit.*

26. New York *Herald Tribune*, Oct. 20, 1960, p. 1.

27. New York *Journal-American*, Nov. 11, 1960.

28. New York *Times*, Sept. 21, 1960, p. 24.

29. *Ibid.*, Sept. 17, 1960, p. 13.

30. *Ibid.*, Sept. 12, 1960, p. 22.

31. *Ibid.*

32. Robert A. Ashworth, *The Story of the National Conference of Christians and Jews*, March, 1950, pp. 3, 4, 6.

33. National Conference of Christians and Jews, 1960 Report from the President.

34. Ashworth, *op. cit.*, p. 87.

35. New York *Herald Tribune*, Oct. 27, 1960, p. 9.

36. *Congressional Quarterly Almanac*, p. 804.

37. New York *Times*, Sept. 13, 1960, p. 25.

38. United States Code, Title 18, Section 612, p. 3239, United States Government Printing Office, 1959.

39. New York *Times*, Sept. 18, 1960, p. 44.

40. New York *Herald Tribune*, Oct. 21, 1960, p. 10; also, Oct. 22, p. 4, and Nov. 18, 1960.

41. New York *Times*, Oct. 16, 1960, p. 56.

42. *Ibid.*, Oct. 22, 1960, pp. 1, 13; Oct. 28, 1960, p. 12.

43. *Ibid.*

44. *Public Opinion Quarterly*, Summer, 1961.

45. Thomas B. Morgan, "The People-Machine," *Harper's* magazine, January, 1961, p. 54.

46. New York *Times*, Sept. 20, 1960, p. 1.

47. New York *Herald Tribune*, Oct. 20, 1960, p. 1.

Chapter Twelve: John F. Kennedy: The Ultimate Test

1. New York *Times*, Oct. 12, 1960, p. 34.

2. New York *Herald Tribune*, Oct. 13, 1960, p. 12.

3. *Ibid.*

4. New York *Times*, *op. cit.*, p. 32.

5. *Ibid.*, Oct. 13, 1960, p. 25.

6. *Ibid.*, Nov. 3, 1960, p. 30.

7. *Ibid.*, Oct., 14, 1960, pp. 20, 23.

8. *Ibid.*

9. New York *Herald Tribune*, Oct. 21, 1960, p. 10.

10. *Methodist Challenge*, XXVIII, No. 2 (August, 1959), p. 10.

11. Communication in the files of the Anti-Defamation League of B'nai B'rith, New York City.

12. New York *Times*, Sept. 17, 1960, p. 14; see also Oct. 16, pp. 1, 56.

13. *Ibid.*, Sept. 17, 1960.

14. New York *Herald Tribune*, Oct. 16, 1960, pp. 1, 40. See also New York *Times*, Oct. 17, 1960, p. 24.

15. New York *Times*, Oct. 20, 1960, p. 32.

16. New York *Herald Tribune*, Oct. 16, 1960, p. 40.

17. "The Protestant Issue," *Reporter*, Oct. 13, 1960, p. 32.

18. New York *Herald Tribune*, Oct. 20, 1960, p. 1.

19. New York *Times*, Oct. 21, 1960, p. 14.

20. *Christian Science Monitor*, Oct. 24, 1960, p. 12; Oct. 31, p. 2. See also New York *Herald Tribune*, Oct. 22, 1960, pp. 1, 9, and New York *Times*, Oct. 30, 1960, p. 4.

21. *Christian Science Monitor*, Oct. 29, 1960, p. 7.

22. New York *Times*, Oct. 28, 1960, p. 19.

23. *Ibid.*

24. *Ibid.*, Oct. 31, 1960, p. 19.

25. *Ibid.*, Nov. 5, 1960, p. 9.

26. *Ibid.*, Oct. 31, 1960, p. 19.

27. *Ibid.*, Oct. 29, 1960, p. 12.

28. *Ibid.*, Nov. 1, 1960, p. 1.

29. *Ibid.*, April 19, 1960.

30. Tocqueville Alexis de, *Democracy in America*, New York, 1956, p. 300ff.

31. New York *Times*, Oct. 21, 1960, p. 14.

32. *Ibid.*, Nov. 7, 1960, p. 25.

33. *Ibid.*, Oct. 26, 1960, p. 23; Oct. 27, p. 25.

34. *Ibid.*, Oct. 16, 1960, p. 1; Nov. 5, p. 9.

35. *Ibid.*, Nov. 5, 1960, p. 15.

36. *Christian Science Monitor*, Oct. 25, 1960, p. 3.

37. New York *Times*, Sept. 17, 1960, p. 14.

38. New York *World-Telegram and Sun*, Oct. 11, 1960.

39. New York *Times*, Oct. 21, 1960, p. 14.

40. *Congressional Quarterly Almanac*, 86th Cong., 2nd Sess., p. 811. See also New York *Herald Tribune*, Dec. 5, 1960, for David Lawrence's discussion of the Gallup survey referred to.

41. *Public Opinion Quarterly*, Spring, 1961, p. 131.

42. New York *Times*, Nov. 8, 1960, p. 23, and Nov. 3, p. 30.

43. *Ibid.*, Oct. 16, 1960, p. 56.

44. New York *Herald Tribune*, Nov. 8, 1960, p. 21.

45. *Christian Science Monitor*, Oct. 27, 1960, p. 14.

46. New York *Times*, Dec. 16, 1960.

47. Edgar Eugene Robinson, *The New United States*, Stanford, 1946, p. 75.

48. New York *Journal-American*, Nov. 11, 1960.

49. New York *Herald Tribune*, Nov. 10, 1960.

Chapter Thirteen: John F. Kennedy: A Catholic Becomes President

1. All election figures are from the *World Almanac* of 1961, 1957, and 1949, except where otherwise indicated. Figures are also based on Robinson, *The Presidential Vote*, pp. 57ff., and *America Votes* III, Richard D. Scammon (ed.), Pittsburgh, 1959, pp. 224–226, 267, 451–453.

2. *Congressional Quarterly Almanac, op. cit.*, p. 812.

3. Philadelphia *Bulletin*, Dec. 4, 1960, Sec. I, p. 12.

4. New York *Times*, Feb. 26, 1961.

5. *Ibid.*, May 8, 1960, p. 51.

6. New York *Herald Tribune*, Dec. 5, 1960.

7. New York *Times*, May 8, 1960.

8. *The 1960 Elections*, Washington, D.C., April, 1961 (Revised, Second Printing), p. 13.

9. *Ibid.*

10. *Ibid.*, p. 21.

11. New York *Times*, Jan. 12, 1961, p. 1.

12. *Ibid.*

13. Philadelphia *Inquirer*, Jan. 17, 1961.

14. New York *Times*, Feb. 23, 1961.

15. *Ibid.*, Feb. 26, 1961, p. 59.

16. Clinton L. Rossiter, *Seedtime of the Republic*, New York, 1953, p. 432.

17. New York *Times*, Jan. 21, 1961, p. 1.

INDEX

DATE DUE

JUL 29 '64			
NOV 12 '66			
APR 4 '67			
MAY 4 '67			
DEC 10 '68			
NOV 2 '70			
APR 3 '70			
MAY 8 '88			
GAYLORD			PRINTED IN U.S.A.